*BRITISH
SELF-TAUGHT:
WITH COMMENTS IN
AMERICAN*

British

SELF-TAUGHT:
WITH
COMMENTS IN
American

by NORMAN W. SCHUR

THE MACMILLAN COMPANY
NEW YORK, NEW YORK

WITH DRAWINGS BY *Alex Graham*

The Macmillan Company
866 Third Avenue, New York, N.Y. 10022
Collier-Macmillan Canada Ltd., Toronto, Ontario

Library of Congress Catalog Card Number: 70–127941

First Printing

Printed in the United States of America

PE   Schur, Norman W.
1704
.S4   British self-taught: with
1973   comments in American

423.1 Sch86b

Acknowledgments

Help, far beyond the reasonable bounds of hospitality, has come to me from many kind and patient English friends. In addition to much painstaking correspondence over the years there have been sessions in many an English home, garden, and pub: countless words, gallons of tea, barrels of beer. I am indebted to the late Kenneth Fearon, to B. T. Flanagan, John and Sarah Freeland, Philip Harding, Charles and Isobel Kirby (she for her skills not only in stenography but in smoking out misconceptions and weeding out archaisms), Ronald Smith, Peter Tanter, C. E. Thompson, Alan Vaughan, and Donald Walker; not a single philologist in the lot, all of immensely varied backgrounds, with nothing whatever in common—except kindness, intelligence, humor, and taste. On the American side, I owe much to Edmée Busch, who helped put the manuscript into shape. My secretary, Dorothy Neidecker, has been stubbornly loyal and helpful through many difficult and sometimes discouraging moments of self-doubt. My friend Robert Lewis made important suggestions at the outset and urged me on when I faltered. I am deeply indebted to Matthew Macmillan, director of the British Council's English Teaching Information Centre, for his painstaking reading of the entire manuscript and many valuable suggestions.

I must end with a note of gratitude to my wife, Marjorie. There was a time, several years ago right after my return alone from the annual summer in England, when the then still sketchy manuscript (hardly more than a skeleton list, existing only in one small notebook) just plain vanished. I was sure I had brought it back. Letters went back and forth between us, searches on both sides proved fruitless; in great dejection I abandoned the project, but Marjorie persisted. One day her cable arrived: *Glossary Found. On Its Way.* Accidentally left behind, it had been stored in a most unlikely place by our over-enthusiastic daily (q.v.). For my wife's dogged persistence in the search and patient listening thereafter, I give my most loving thanks.

Preface

A few years ago during a sojourn in England, I began to notice how many words and phrases spoken and written by Englishmen were unfamiliar to my American ears and eyes. Occasionally they were unintelligible; often the context made their meaning clear. Most of the time it was only a question of what seemed to me preferred usage. I had never heard of being *lumbered* with a job, for example, but the context left little doubt. On the other hand, I really didn't know what a *lumber room* was. I heard that a young student had *gone up*, and, vaguely wondering up where, asked an English friend whether *going up* by any chance meant *being promoted*. He replied that the boy was too young to be in the army.

I began to note these peculiarities down. The list grew and grew and eventually reached the proportions of a glossary, with occasional reflections on British institutions, customs, and idiosyncrasies in cases where it seemed no simple American equivalent could be found or would suffice. It is still growing. Occasionally I have to eliminate an item because the American term has replaced, or all but replaced, its former equivalent among the English. In this age of jet travel, what with the movies (the cinema), TV (the telly), and radio (the wireless), linguistic parochialism is bound to diminish. Mario Pei (*Words in Sheep's Clothing*, Hawthorn Books, Inc., New York, 1969) goes even further: ". . . In these days of rapid communication and easy interchange," he writes, after referring to the different meanings given to the same word in the two countries, "such differences are less important than you would think." I wonder. True, the latest edition of *The Pocket Oxford Dictionary* included a good many American terms not found previously; *teen-age, paperback, T-shirt, supermarket, sacred cow, sick joke,* and many more. And in their recorded dialogue, published under the title *A Common Language, British and American English* in 1964 by the British Broadcasting Corporation and the Voice of America, Professors Randolph Quirk of University College, London, and Albert H. Marckwardt of Princeton University agree, according to the Foreword, that "the two varieties of English have never been so different as people have imagined, and the dominant tendency, for several decades now, has clearly been that of convergence and even greater similarity." Yet the process is slow and the differences linger. Herbert R. Mayes agrees. In his London Letter in the *Saturday Review* of November 14, 1970, he writes, ". . . There still are . . . enough archaisms here to keep an American off balance. . . . The British are stubborn. . . ." Mr. Mayes is well supported in his opinion by a letter to *The Times* on September 8, 1971, from Brigadier R. B. Rathbone of Gloucestershire, resenting the "gross misuse" of the word *dessert*. "Why, oh why," cries the Brigadier, "do we quietly absorb, instead of resisting, these unnecessary (and in this case misleading) transatlantic importations, which, far from enriching, nearly always degrade our beautiful language?" Equally outraged, in his letter to *The Times* on April 6, 1972 (headed "Foreigners, be careful of English"), Mr. Dixon Harry of Nottinghamshire insists that "the British will always be British and will not accept Americanized versions of perfectly good English words." He too finds the Americanization process "very degrading both to our language and people," referring to the invasion as "such slights." "Our language is for the use of English-speaking people," he proclaims, "it is not for the convenience of foreigners!" And Suzanne Haire (Lady Haire of Whiteabbey, formerly with the BBC, now living in New York), writing in *The New York Times* of January 11, 1972 of her "study of 'American-English' at its source," mentions the "bizarre misunderstandings [which] can result from expressions which have different meanings on the two sides of the Atlantic." The example she selected was the colloquial noun *tube*, meaning *subway* in England and *TV* in the States.

It has been hard to apply criteria of exclusion and inclusion. I have included some slang words and phrases and many colloquialisms but omitted others because they seemed too narrowly regional, or ephemeral. A *roke* is a *ground fog*, but only in Norfolk. In certain parts of Surrey they eat *clod and stickin,* an unattractive-sounding *stew*. Avoid Lancashiremen and Yorkshiremen who are *razat:* they're *sore* at you. Such narrowly restricted dialectal terms, though amusing, have been reluctantly passed by.

The majority of the items included would be mutually intelligible, despite a fixed preference as to usage. For instance, if an English girl and an American girl were out shopping together, the English girl, pointing to a show window, would probably say, "I'd like to go into that shop and look at that frock," while her friend would more likely say, "I'd like to go into that store and look at that dress." The English girl might have said "dress" but would not have said "store." The American girl might have said "shop" but would never have said "frock." And the person who waited on them would be a "saleswoman" to the American girl, and a "shop assistant" to her friend. It is all rather delicate and subtle.

I find that American usage tends to be more literal. We say "baby carriage" and the English say "pram" (an abbreviation of perambulator). Any Englishman would understand *baby carriage* but no recently arrived American (unless steeped in Christie, Sayers, and Allingham) would know what a pram was. The same would apply to *cleaning woman* and *char*, or *ball-point pen* and *biro*. In general it appears that American expressions are easier for Englishmen than the other way around.

Often a word or phrase has a number of meanings which are

the same in both countries, in addition to one or more which are exclusively English. Thus, a *duck* in the ordinary sense is a *duck* in both countries. In England it also means a *goose egg*, in sports scoring. In setting forth such a peculiarity of English usage, I have for brevity's sake often taken the liberty of omitting any mention of shared common meanings.

Language is so much a living, expanding, and contracting thing that there is no point at which any compilation of this sort ends. Even the great Dr. Johnson, in the words of John Moore (*You English Words*, J. B. Lippincott Company, Philadelphia, 1962, p. 54), ". . . knew well that his dictionary began to be outdated even while the proofs were on their way back to the printer. It is the despair and delight of lexicographers, that in language they are dealing with a living thing. . . ." My pastime slowly took on tangible form and somewhat to my own surprise emerged as a serious compilation. I would be grateful if (in addition to my omissions and possible erroneous inclusions and definitions) new items which appeared from time to time were called to my attention. Many of the items included must evoke some controversy and even censure. "A dictionary-maker," says the great H. W. Fowler (*The Concise Oxford Dictionary*, Oxford University Press, 5th ed., 1964), "unless he is a monster of omniscience, must deal with a great many matters of which he has no first-hand knowledge. That he has been guilty of errors and omissions in some of these he will learn soon after publication, sometimes with gratitude to his enlightener, sometimes otherwise." "It is the fate of those who toil at the lower employments of life," wrote Dr. Johnson in the preface to his Dictionary, ". . . to be exposed to censure, without hope of praise; to be disgraced by miscarriage, or punished for neglect. . . . Among these unhappy mortals is the writer of dictionaries. . . ." Again and again when I inquired about the precise meaning of an unfamiliar term, I received as many answers as the number of kind English friends consulted. My final choice of American equivalent sometimes represented a compromise, a solution usually satisfactory to no one.

Are there two languages? Opinions differ. "British and American English undoubtedly are different," writes John W. Clark,

Associate Professor of English, University of Minnesota, in *British and American English Since 1900* (Greenwood Press, New York, 1968), co-authored by the great Eric Partridge. "American English, especially today, might be called, I think, in comparison with British English, a smart-aleck language. Perhaps it would be more accurate as well as more up to date to call it a wise-guy language. . . . Another way of saying it is to say that British English has more *frein* and American English more *élan*. Yet another is to say that British English is stuffy and American English bumptious." *Webster's Seventh New Collegiate Dictionary* defines British English as "English characteristic of England and clearly distinguishable from that used in U.S. . . ." Evelyn Waugh's amusing dedication page in *The Loved One* reads in part: "My thanks are due . . . to Mrs. Reginald Allen who corrected my American; to Mr. Cyril Connolly who corrected my English." The anonymous author of the article entitled "Broadcasting of the Year" in a *Whitaker's Almanac* of the middle twenties talks of the introduction of international broadcasting and characterizes the American emanations as particularly successful "because of the *similarity* of the languages."

American clients of mine whose book was brought out in an English edition found their royalty account debited with a translation fee. A common clause in authors' contracts for the English publication of American books requires the author's consent to "Anglicization" of the text, and it works the other way round as well. When another client's book came out in an English edition, the publisher made seven word changes in the tiny volume: *maybe* became *perhaps; rock* became *stone; do* (dishes) became *wash; package* became *parcel;* etc., etc. (It caused a row; they hadn't been consulted. I was called in as attorney to prevent further printings!) The English edition of Damon Runyon's work included a glossary. (Not a very accurate one: *old tomato* was translated *loose woman!*) In 1926 the producer, Jed Harris got S. N. Behrman, then his press agent, to prepare a glossary, in Behrman's words, "to explain the esoteric Broadway argot [of Philip Dunning's play *Broadway*] to English audiences." In 1939 Oxford brought out Horwill's *Anglo-American Interpreter*. The preface

xi

begins this way: "An American, if taken suddenly ill while on a visit to London, might die in the street through being unable to make himself understood." (No one would know what he meant when he asked for the nearest *drugstore!*) Herbert Mayes, in that same London Letter, says that this is now beginning to change: "It is rare that an American novel is Anglicized. The British edition of *Time* is published exactly as it would be in the States: no substituting of underground for subway, tin for can, or express post for special delivery." Yet in *Time* itself (February 14, 1972), Keith R. Johnson registers the complaint, in his review of the final volume (in translation) of De Gaulle's *Memoirs,* that the American publishers, ". . . neglected to alter Anglicisms that will baffle many U.S. readers—for example 'council flats' for public housing."

In *Memoirs of the Second World War* Churchill tells how an Anglo-American misunderstanding of the meaning of a single word at a high-level military meeting resulted in "long and even acrimonious argument." During that war, Admiral Lord Louis Mountbatten made the statement that he thought he was qualified to act as "Anglo-American interpreter" between the Americans and British in Southeast Asia. And on a more humble level, upon a recent arrival at Heathrow Airport, London, I picked up a copy of *Welcome,* a newspaper available without charge to passengers at that airport, and was gratified to read Sylvia Goldberg's article headed "Perils of the Spoken Word," which begins: "One thing American visitors to Britain are seldom warned about is the 'language problem'" and goes on to point out that the "most mundane negotiation, the simplest attempt at communication with the natives can lead to unutterable confusion." On September 15, 1970, Russell Baker's column in *The New York Times,* bearing a London dateline, began: "One of the hardest languages for an American to learn is English," and the language he was referring to was English English. About a year later, Henry Stanhope's review of *Welcome to Britain* (Whitehall Press, 1971) in the September 3, 1971, London *Times* referred to a glossary in the book as going ". . . some way towards bridging the linguistic gulf, broader than the Atlantic Ocean, which still separates our cultures." Consciously or not, they were echoing Oscar Wilde's epigram: "The English have really everything in common with the Americans, except of course language."

We read in Gen. 11:6–7, "And the Lord said [viewing Babel], Behold, the people is one, and they have all one language. . . .Go to, let us go down, and there confound their language, that they may not understand one another's speech." Bad enough with Chinese and Uzbek: did He have to fragmentize English too?

In *Less Than Kin,* William Clark recalls the Shavian quip that Britain and America are two countries divided by a common tongue. Dylan Thomas, in *A Visit to America,* describes himself as "up against the barrier of a common language." Not all agree: Ronald Mansbridge, manager emeritus of the American branch of the Cambridge University Press, in his foreword to *Longitude 30 West* (a confidential report to the Syndics of the Cambridge University Press by Lord Acton), refers to the two countries as "strongly linked together—let us reject the old joke 'divided'—by the English language." In *Sir Michael & Sir George,* J. B. Priestley presents one character's thoughts on this subject as follows: "Sir George, not for the first time, thought how difficult it was to achieve real communication with some Americans, just because they used the same words but gave them different meanings," and S. Gorley Putt (*View from Atlantis,* subtitled *The Americans and Ourselves*) includes a section entitled *English-Speaking Disunion?* and wonders whether the "happy coincidence of our common tongue . . . always represents an unmixed blessing." Frederick Wood's attempt at consolation in his preface to *Current English Usage* (Macmillan & Co. Ltd., London, 1962) might seem even more offensive: "Certain words and constructions have been described as Americanisms. This does not necessarily mean that they are bad English." In *An Open Letter To The Hon'ble Mrs Peter Rodd (Nancy Mitford) On A Very Serious Subject* Evelyn Waugh, discussing the American influence, writes: ". . . American polite vocabulary is very different from ours. . . . [it] is pulverized between two stones, refinement and overstatement." Cyril Connolly went pretty far in *The Sunday Times* (London) of December 11, 1966: ". . . the American language is in a state of flux based on the survival of the unfittest." On the other hand

xiii

Charles Smithson, the English hero of John Fowles' *The French Lieutenant's Woman*, bored and unhappy on the Continent, runs into two Philadelphians and leaps to the "pleasure of conversing with someone in a not too alien tongue," which brings to mind Putt's reference to visitors between the two lands as being "greeted in (*approximately*) the same language." Robert Knittel, the Editorial Director of Collins Publishing, says that halfway across the ocean our two languages nuzzle up to each other and fraternize enough to become "mid-Atlinguish."

What is the relationship between "English" and "American"? Would it offend my compatriots if their idiom were characterized as a dialect of the mother tongue? Mencken thought the shoe was on the other foot. In his response in *The Times* on April 20, 1972, to Mr. Dixon Harry's testy letter of April 12, Mr. Bernard F. Shinkman of London quoted Fowler quoting Mencken on the subject of what was standard and what was dialect. It was Mencken's theme that England, displaced by the United States as the most populous English-speaking country, was no longer entitled to pose as arbiter of English usage. "When two-thirds of the people who use a certain language decide to call it a *freight* train instead of a *goods* train, they are right; the first is correct usage and the second a dialect." (According to Marcus Cunliffe, in *The Literature of the United States*, a chauvinistic delegate to the Continental Congress actually moved that the new nation drop the use of the English language entirely, while another delegate proposed an amendment that the United States retain the English language and make the English learn Greek!) Or has the relationship been more accurately described by Mario Pei when he refers to "the two major branches of the English language," or the English literary critic who speaks of being "bilingual in the two branches of English?" And, finally, what useful purpose may this book serve?

Well, if it were to give some people a little pleasure, and occasionally a little enlightenment, and especially if it prevented even the tiniest bit of Anglo-American misunderstanding, I should be pleased indeed.

Introductory Notes

[Some explanatory comments on the author's approach, especially in the matter of inclusion and exclusion, together with clarifications of several puzzling peculiarities of English usage.]

1. Many words have multiple meanings. Thus, the noun *note* can mean a *musical note* (do, re, mi, etc.), a *written evidence of debt* (promissory note), a *memorandum* (he made a note of it), a *message* (he passed her a note), and so on. In England it has an additional meaning that it does not have in America: a *piece of paper money*. Thus, a one-pound *note*, a five-pound *note*. The American equivalent, in that sense, is *bill*: a five-dollar *bill*, etc. Correspondingly, the word *bill* has a number of meanings: the *beak* of a bird, the *draft* of a proposed law, etc. It should be obvious that in including the pairing **note—bill**, the author is not overlooking the fact that the British noun *note* has other meanings shared with America or that the American noun *bill* has other meanings shared with England. It would lengthen the discussion of such an item unduly to list or refer to all the shared meanings. It is to be assumed that in the case of words with more than one meaning, those not dealt with are common to both countries.

2. The inclusion of a particular pairing should not be taken to mean that the English do not also use the American word. It

means only that the Americans do not (or do not usually) use the British word. The English say both *wireless* and *radio*, but the Americans never use *wireless* to mean *radio*.

3. When dates are expressed in figures, the English follow the European method of day, month, year: thus, 10/7/69 becomes 7/10/69.

4. Where the only difference is one of spelling the item has generally been omitted, but it might be well to point out that there are certain orthographical differences between the two countries. These fall into two main categories: word formation groups and individual words. Typical word ending peculiarities (sometimes only preferences) occur in the *-our* group (*colour, honour*); the *-re* group (*centre, theatre*); the *-ise* words (*criticise, agonise;* though *-ize* would now appear to be preferred); certain conjugated forms (*travelled, travelling*) or derived forms (*traveller, jeweller*) where the English double the final consonant; *-xion* words (*connexion, inflexion;* but inconsistently, *confection, inspection*); *-ce* words (*defence, pretence, licence* as a noun, but *license* preferred as a verb). Some common individual differences are found in *cheque, gaol* (jail), *kerb, pyjamas, storey* (meaning *floor* of a building), *tyre, aluminium, grey, whisky* (but note *Irish whiskey*), *manoeuvre,* and again in the consonant-doubling department, *waggon, carburettor* (or *carburetter*), and others.

5. No attempt is made to include cant terms, a few still current, peculiar to particular groups. To select a couple of categories: The taxi-drivers of London have their own code: Charing Cross Underground (subway) Station is the *Rats' Hole;* St. Pancras Station, the *Box of Bricks;* the Army and Navy Store in Victoria Street is the *Sugar Box;* the St. Thomas' Hospital cab-rank (taxi stand) is the *Poultice Shop;* the one at London Bridge the *Sand Bin;* Harley Street (where doctors' offices cluster) is *Pill Island;* Bedford Row (where lawyers' offices proliferate) is *Shark's Parade;* and the Tower of London is *Sparrow Corner.* London busmen indulge in a lingo of their own: The last bus is the *Ghost Train;* to slow up (because of exceeding the schedule) is to *scratch about;* passengers on their way to the greyhound races are *dogs;* a busful is a *domino load,* and a *stone-cold* bus is

an empty one; a plainclothes bus inspector is a *spot* and he can *book* (report) a driver; passengers are *rabbits;* a *short one* is an unfinished trip; an accident is a *set;* to arrive late for duty is to *slip up;* a *cushy road* is an easy trip, and a busy one is known as *having a road on.* In the days when trolley cars competed, the English term *tramcar* became the rhyming equivalent *jam jar.* Sports talk is another matter. Any newspaper report or broadcast or telecast on a cricket or rugby match would be as unintelligible to an American reader as an American sportswriter's or announcer's commentary on a baseball game. To understand these categories of terminology, the writer can only refer the reader to technical works on the respective subjects.

6. London slang is almost a language of its own, and to complicate matters, it keeps shifting all the time. George Orwell in *Down and Out in Paris and London* (1933) gives a list of cant words in this category including the following:

gagger	*beggar; street performer*
moocher	*beggar*
clodhopper	*street dancer*
glimmer	*car watcher*
split	*detective*
flattie	*policeman*
clod	*policeman*
toby	*tramp*
drop	*money to a beggar*
slang	*street-peddler's license*
Smoke	*London*
judy	*woman*
spike	*flophouse*
lump	*flophouse*
deaner	*shilling*
hog	*shilling*
tosheroon	*half-crown*
sprowsie	*sixpence*
shackles	*soup*
chat	*louse*

7. It often happens that both countries use both words in a pairing, but each country has a preference. Here is a sample list of such pairings where each pair might well be considered synonyms on both sides of the Atlantic but the preferences are as indicated below:

ENGLAND	AMERICA
snag (describing a troublesome situation)	*trouble, problem, catch, hitch*
position (describing the way things stand)	*situation*
wretched (weather, person, luck, etc.)	*awful, terrible*
engaged (busy)	*tied up*
queer (peculiar)	*funny*
blunt (e.g., of a pencil)	*dull*
sea	*ocean; beach*
crash (automobile, train)	*collision*
tidy	*clean*
trade	*business*
tablet	*pill*
motor-car	*automobile*

8. British and American usages in the matter of prepositions vary frequently. This is especially true of the prepositions *in* and *on*. Englishmen live *in* rather than *on* such and such a street (although they do live *on* a road); in England animals are *on* heat rather than *in* heat; the British say that predictable events are *on* the cards rather than *in* the cards; and athletes in England are *on* form rather than *in* form. Things that are on the way (in a stage of development) are described in England as *on* train as well as *in* train. *Different from* is heard in England but *different to* is more commonly heard, and *other to*, although not frequent, has been used where Americans would of course say *other than*. Nervous *of* (doing something) for nervous *about*, the advantage *of* for the advantage *over*, an increase *on* rather than an increase *over*, frontage *to* instead of frontage *on*, *by* auction for *at* auction,

membership *of* for membership *in,* dry *off* for dry *out,* chat *to* for chat *with,* cater *for* rather than cater *to,* snowed *up* for snowed *in,* are further examples. At times where the usage differs but the meaning is perfectly clear, such a pairing has been omitted, unless the author has felt that the phrase deserves inclusion because the idiom is a matter of unusual interest.

9. Since this volume is an American glossary of Briticisms, there is no listing of *Americanisms* which would need interpretation to Englishmen. It may be well, however, to include a short list of typical Americanisms that might baffle an Englishman: *blanket* as an adjective, meaning *general* or *overall; accommodations* for *facilities; coed; fall* for *autumn;* to *buck,* meaning to *resist; gentile* for *non-Jew; graft* for *bribe; highball* for *whiskey and soda with ice; kill* (a story) for *suppress; machine* for *political party organization; paddle* for *spank; rattle* for *fluster; slash* meaning *reduce; keep tabs on* for *check on; truck garden* for *vegetable garden; shirtwaist* (*blouse*), *lima bean* (*broad bean,* a similar species), *pipe dream,* and so on and so on. The brothers Fowler have some interesting things to say about *fall* and *autumn.* In *Modern English Usage, fall* is described as "either an Americanism, a provincialism or an archaism" which is "out of place in Britain." The brothers refer the reader to their earlier book, *The King's English,* on the very same subject, with prose so good that one must quote it *in extenso:*

> Fall is better on the merits than *autumn,* in every way; it is short, Saxon (like the other three season names), picturesque; it reveals its derivation to everyone who uses it, not to the scholar only, like *autumn;* and we (the English) once had as good a right to it as the Americans; but we have chosen to let the right lapse, and to use the word now is no better than larceny.

10. The English tend to lengthen (they feel that we tend to shorten!) the first word of many compound nouns, particularly by adding the ending *-ing.* Thus, sail*ing* boat, row*ing* boat, dial*ing* tone, bank*ing* account, wash*ing* day, danc*ing* hall, spark*ing* plug. This happens occasionally to single nouns as well: turn*ing* for

turn, and part*ing* for a *part* in your hair as well as the sweet sorrow variety. Other examples are found in department*al* store, cook*ery* book, and high*ly* strung. A similar practice is the adding of -*'s* in such Briticisms as barber*'s* shop, tailor*'s* shop, doll*'s* house (any little girl's, not only the Ibsen variety), etc. *Innings* has an -*s* in the singular as well as the plural. Note also stocking*ed* feet, ice*d* water, wheel*ed* chair, twin-bed*ded* room, two-room*ed* flat. But watch out: sometimes *they* do the shortening, as in *swing* door for *swinging* door, *sunk* garden for *sunken* garden, spring-*clean* for spring *cleaning,* and there are other instances of such English contrariety. A related lengthening process is seen in the English insistence on adding an object to the verb in certain phrases where the American usage is content with the verb alone: to *move house,* to *shower oneself.* Also note *pour with rain.* What else would it pour with?

11. The book is intended to explain Briticisms, not only those in current use, but those which might puzzle an American reader of a book by an English author published some years ago. For example, *wireless,* for *radio,* is very old-fashioned and will undoubtedly be out of current usage within a very short time, but an American reading in an English detective story published ten or twenty years ago that so and so had heard certain news on his *wireless* might be misled to believe that so and so had a Marconi system of his own, when all that happened was that he had turned on the *radio.* Or take the case of *responsions,* which was originally the name for the first of three examinations for a B.A. degree at Oxford and later the name for the Oxford entrance exam. *Responsions* were abolished in 1960 but a novel published before that date, or one published last week but describing events before 1960, might well speak of *responsions* and the fact that the practice has been abolished would not be a reason for excluding that interesting word from the book.

12. Food names are very puzzling and of butchers' terms only a few labels of specific cuts of meat are included. There are a good many that would baffle an American shopper: *rump steak* is *sirloin; sirloin* is *porterhouse;* a *baron* is a *double sirloin; silverside* is *top round.* It seems worse at the fish store (*fishmonger*): here

one can hear of *brill* (similar to a small turbot), *coalfish,* also
called *coley fillet* and *saithe* (black cod), *witch* (resembling but
inferior to lemon sole), *John Dorey* (a flat fish with a big head),
huss, also called *dogfish, rig,* and *robin huss* (similar to a small
conger eel—and the *robin* is thought by fishmongers to be a corruption of *robbin',* i.e., *robbing,* because the *huss* eats other fish
and is thus robbin' the fisherman), and other strange species, to
say nothing of unfamiliar seafoods like *winkles* and *prawns.* At the
bakery one finds all kinds of goodies with alien names. Ignore the
labels and purchase by sight and smell.

13. Rhyming slang is a type of cant which has developed from
the peculiarly cockney game of replacing certain common words
with phrases which end with a word that rhymes with the word
replaced. Thus:

boat race	face
daisy roots	boots
German bands	hands
loaf of bread	head
mince pies	eyes
north and south	mouth
plates of meat	feet
tit for tat	hat
Uncle Ned	head
whistle and flute	suit
Mutt and Jeff	deaf

And many more. One doesn't run into these expressions very
often, but when one does meet them, they can be pretty puzzling, especially when the cant phrase itself becomes truncated
or otherwise corrupted through cockney usage. Thus *loaf of
bread* is shortened to *loaf, mince pies* becomes *minces, tit for tat*
turns into *titfer, whistle and flute* loses the *flute, German bands*
winds up as *Germans,* and so on. The results: *loaf* for *head,*
minces for *eyes, whistle* for *suit,* etc., etc., come out as quite arbitrary substitutes miles removed from the words they stand for.

One often heard outside the cockney world is *loaf,* particularly in the expressions "Use your loaf!" ("Use your bean!") and "Mind your loaf!" (Low bridge!"). In certain cases there is a further hurdle in that the replaced word is itself a Briticism requiring explanation, like the case of *daisy roots* for *boots,* where *daisy roots* becomes *daisies, boots* would be *shoes* in America, and we wind up with *daisies* for *shoes,* an etymological riddle.

14. For the subtleties of variations in the vocabulary of spoken (and to a much smaller extent, written) English English based on class distinctions, the reader is referred to *U and Non-U, an Essay in Sociological Linguistics,* by Prof. Alan S. C. Ross, of Birmingham University (England), which first appeared (1954) in a Finnish (of all things!) philological journal bearing the German name *Neuphilologische Mitteilungen* (which might be hard to find), later, in somewhat condensed form in *Encounter,* and still later in *Noblesse Oblige,* a collection of articles edited by Nancy Mitford (Hamish Hamilton, London, 1956; Penguin Books Ltd., 1959). His article was commented on by Miss Mitford in *Encounter,* in a piece entitled *The English Aristocracy.* (Living in France, she must have come across Ross in French translation, for she refers to the Finnish periodical as the *Bulletin de la Société Néo-Philologique de Helsinki.*) She in turn was answered, still in *Encounter,* by Evelyn Waugh in *An Open Letter to the Hon'ble Mrs Peter Rodd (Nancy Mitford) On a Very Serious Subject.* The Mitford and Waugh articles, too, are included in *Noblesse Oblige.* All these comments gave currency to the concept of U and Non-U as linguistic categories constituting "class-indicators." (The *U,* incidentally, doesn't stand for *You,* as in *While-U-Wait,* but for *upper class.*) It is felt that these distinctions would be lost on most Americans, whose ears are not attuned to English class differences based on accent or vocabulary, and who suffer from a feeling of inferiority equally in the spoken presence of London cabbies and Oxford dons. References to class differences in the text are therefore few and far between.

15. Abbreviations are common in informal English correspondence. Some, but not all, have been included in the alphabetical listing. Some common ones are:

circs.	*circumstances*
hosp.	*hospital*
op.	*operation*
prb.	*probably*
s.a.p.	*soon as possible*
v.	*very*
w.	*with*
w/e	*weekend*

People's names are often abbreviated. An Englishman in a hurry might write you that M. had been down for the w/e w. N. and would prb. return the favour soon, unless the circs. changed because N. had to go to hosp. for a v. minor op. s.a.p.

16. A good many of the entries are far from common and may even be considered extremely rare, but the author, after serious reflection, has felt that the sin of exclusion is graver than the sin of inclusion.

17. It sometimes happens that the English have concocted a colloquialism or a slang word where the Americans have not. Thus, *gongs* is affectionate military slang for *medals*. Invitations to rigorously formal social occasions sometimes request the wearing of decorations in addition to formal evening clothes. Miniature medals are worn on such occasions. They do clink while the wearers are waltzing and that must be the origin of *gongs*. In the few cases where the author has been unable to turn up a slang or colloquial American equivalent, he begs to be forgiven for resulting stylistic imbalance between the two terms in the pairing.

18. Currency. Up to August 1, 1969, English coins in regular use were the halfpenny (pronounced *hay'pny*), penny, threepence (pronounced *thruppence*, sometimes *threppence;* sometimes called *threppenny bit*), sixpence (nicknamed *tanner*, sometimes *bender*), shilling, florin (2 shillings), and half-crown (2½ shillings). Twenty shillings made a pound; 12 pence (plural of *penny*) made a shilling. Thus there were 240 pence in a pound. The farthing (¼ penny) was discontinued years ago; the halfpenny was demonetized on August 1, 1969; the half-crown on

xxiii

January 1, 1970. The *guinea* existed only as a convenient way of denoting 21 shillings, i.e., one pound, one shilling. The symbol for pound is £, placed before the number, like the dollar sign; for shilling (or shillings) it was *s.*, for penny or pence *d.*; but there was also the oblique line and dash meaning *shilling(s)* written after the number, thus: 15/— meant 15 shillings. If there were pence as well, the dash was omitted; thus 15/9, orally *fifteen and nine*, meant 15 shillings and 9 pence. But on February 15, 1971, the English decimalized their currency, eliminating shillings as such, leaving only pounds and pence (now abbreviated to *p*), with 100 new pence to the pound. What used to be a shilling is now 5 new pence, a florin is now 10 new pence, and so on. (The *new* soon began to be dropped.) The old shillings and 2-shilling pieces (the same sizes as the new 5- and 10-pence pieces but different designs) are still in circulation but will gradually become collectors' items. What was one pound two shillings (£1.2.0) is now written £1.10. On decimalization day ("D-Day") the remaining old coins all became a thing of the past . . . or did they? Although the mint thereafter turned out only the new halfpennies, pennies, and 2, 5, 10, and 50 pence pieces, lo! the old pennies, threepences, and sixpences were nevertheless at first allowed to circulate alongside the new coins for a year and a half (the old pennies and threepences were later excommunicated and the sixpences "restyled" 2½ p, as of September 1, 1971), either because they went into the old telephone and vending machine coin slots or out of sentimental attachment to relics of the old regime, or because the English cannot resist the attraction for introducing into almost any situation a bit of amiably maddening confusion or something to grumble about. (Look out for nongriping Englishmen—they're getting ready to mutiny!) With sixpence temporarily worth less than three pence, there was bound to be a fair amount of consternation, indignation, error, high amusement, cries in Parliament of "Resign!," and general hilarity. Despite all this streamlining, however, it is to be doubted that the Polynesian idyll will be re-entitled *The Moon and Two and One-Half Pence;* and for a certainty, things will go on not being worth a farthing and ladies will go on spending a penny, albeit a new one.

19. The book is addressed to the written language. Pronunciation is another matter. The spoken language is often difficult for Americans in London, let alone Devon or Shropshire. There is the matter of intonation generally, and there is a problem with vowels (the broad *a* and the short *o*, which is somewhere between the *o* in *not* and *note*). The *time of day* becomes the *toym of die* in Kent and Sussex; *roundabout* (meaning a traffic circle or merry-go-round) comes out *rayndabayt* in those counties; and so it goes. In an amusing article ("Gaffes in Gilead," *The New York Times*, May 12, 1971), Gertrude M. Miller, a BBC pronunciation specialist, lists some horrendous examples, from which I select:

Place Names

Prinknash	pronounced	*Prinnij*
Culzean		*K'lane*
Caius (a Cambridge college)		*Keez*
Magdalene (a Cambridge college)		*Mawdlin*
Belvoir		*Beever*
Wemyss		*Weems*
Kirkcudbright		*Kirkoobri*
Dalziel		*Dee-ell*

Some conspicuous omissions are:

Wrotham	pronounced	*Root'm*
Lympne		*Limm*
Derby		*Darby*
Hertford		*Hartford*

Family Names

Ruthven	pronounced	*Rivv'n*
Leveson-Gower		*Looss'n-Gor*
Menzies		*Ming-iss*
Cholmondeley		*Chumley*

A spectacular omission is *Featherstonehaugh,* pronounced *Fanshaw.*

A special note on county abbreviations:

Bucks	*Buckinghamshire*
Hants	*Hampshire*
Lancs	*Lancashire*
Wilts	*Wiltshire*

These are **Standard English** (q.v.) if so written (and analogous to abbreviated American state names), but when so pronounced they are colloquial. Bucks, Hants, etc. in the spoken language are as confusing to Americans as Mass. is to an Englishman.

It is not only place and family names that present difficulty. Many common nouns are normally accented or pronounced differently from the usual American way. Here are a few:

Accent only

coro'llary
ga'rage
labo'ratory
cente'nary (and related words)

Pronunciation

clerk	*clark*
herb	sounding the *h*
lieutenant	*leftenant*
missile	second *i* is long
privacy	short *i*
schedule	*shedule*
solder	sounding the *l*
vitamin	first *i* is short

Differences in the pronunciation of Latin are another matter and of insufficient general interest to go into here.

20. It may be of interest to point out a few syntactical differences in English and American usage. *Who* has become an acceptable English colloquialism for *whom.* On the other hand the

objective case is used there, colloquially but almost universally, for predicate nominative pronouns as in "It's *me*," "She's taller than *him*," usages popular in America only in less educated circles. But getting back to *who*, the English often use it as a relative pronoun where Americans would use *which:* "the companies *who* pay well," "the colleges *who* admit women." A singular noun which describes an institution like a university or a political body is followed by a verb in the third person singular in America, third person plural in England. Thus, Harvard *plays* Yale, but Oxford *play* Cambridge; in America Congress *adjourns,* in England the House of Commons *rise*. There are other idiosyncrasies as well, but a thorough study would be the subject of another book.

21. Inherent in many units of measure are figurative connotations, image-creating in the semantic sense, which exist alongside their scientific functions. For years beyond the inevitable adoption of the metric system in the English-speaking countries, to their citizens things will inch, not centimeter, along; a miss will remain as good as a mile, not 1.609 kilometers; a ton of something will create an image which its metric equivalent won't; 90°F will be a sizzler, while 32.2°C won't alarm anyone. Even today a similar British-American image dichotomy exists in the case of some units. No matter how often an American tells himself a stone (applied to human beings) is 14 lbs., 15 stone does not evoke for him the image of a fat person; and even "a few hundred yards yonder" creates only a fuzzy notion compared with "about a quarter of a mile down the road."

22. Briticisms which may be familiar to many Americans have nevertheless been included where in the author's opinion they have not gained sufficient currency in America to be considered naturalized. Undoubtedly in years to come, as jets become bigger and faster and the world continues to shrink, many such items will acquire dual citizenship. In this area too, inclusion was considered the lesser evil.

23. Before decimalization, in money matters percentages were often expressed in terms of so-and-so many *shillings in the pound*. Income-tax rates were always so expressed. Since there were 20

xxvii

shillings to a pound, *40 percent* would be expressed as 8 *shillings in the pound.* Since old shillings are still circulating, despite decimalization, this usage will undoubtedly linger for a time.

24. *Do* and *done* keep popping up in England in situations where they would be omitted in America. If you ask an English friend whether he thinks Charles has mailed your letters and he is not sure, he will answer, "He may have *done.*" An American would have said, "He may have," without the *done.* If you said to an Englishman, "Walking two miles before breakfast makes a fellow feel good," he might reply, "Judging from your rosy cheeks, it must *do.*" An American would have left out the *do.*

25. Usage differs between the two countries in the matter of the definite article. Sometimes they leave it out where we put it in. Thus, in England, you are *in hospital* or go *to hospital;* and if things are against you you are *down at heel.* Sometimes they put it in where we leave it out. Thus, an Englishman will have *the gift of the gab,* or will visit a shop on *the High Street,* which is the equivalent of *Main Street;* and they will call an unidentified person *someone or the other.* Sometimes the English use a definite article when we are content with the indefinite one. Thus, Englishmen go *on the spree* instead of *on a spree.* They use both *a hell of a time* and *the hell of a time,* either of which can mean a *terribly good time* or a *terribly bad time,* depending on the context and the emphasis: *a hell of a time* usually means *a rough time* and *the hell of a time* generally means *a good time.* On occasion the *the* is not omitted but replaced by a possessive pronoun. Thus, *half his time he doesn't know what he is doing.*

26. The English equivalents of automotive terms in common use, such as *boot* (*trunk*) and *bonnet* (*hood*), appear in the alphabetical listing below. For the benefit of car buffs or technicians and other specialists concerned with scientific automotive terminology, this list, kindly supplied by British Leyland Motors, Inc., and only minimally amplified by the author, may be of interest. The usual order followed in this book (English-American) is here reversed, on the theory that in this case the American reader knows the American equivalent and might thus more readily locate the relevant pairing.

USA	ENGLISH
Body parts	
Bumper guard	Overrider
Cowl	Scuttle
Dashboard	Facia panel
Door post	Door pillar
Door stop	Check strap
Door vent	Quarter light
Fender	Wing
Firewall	Bulkhead
Hood	Bonnet
License plate	Number plate
Rear seat back or backrest	Rear seat squab
Rocker panel	Valance
Skirt	Apron
Toe pan	Toe board
Trunk	Boot
Windshield	Windscreen
Wheelhouse or housing	Wheel arch
Brake parts	
Parking brake	Hand brake
Chassis parts	
Muffler	Exhaust silencer
Side rail	Side member
Electrical Equipment	
Back up lamp	Reverse lamp
Dimmer switch	Dip switch
Dome lamp	Roof lamp
Gas pump or fuel pump	Petrol pump
Generator	Dynamo
Ignition set	Ignition harness

USA	ENGLISH
Parking lamp	Side lamp
Rear lamp	Tail lamp
Spark plug	Sparking plug
Voltage regulator	Control box

Motor and clutch parts—	**Engine and clutch parts**
Carburetor	Carburetter
Clutch throwout bearing	Clutch release bearing
Cylinder crankcase	Cylinder block
Hose clamp	Hose clip
Pan	Sump
Piston or wrist pin	Gudgeon pin
Rod (conrod) bearing	Big-end

Rear axle and transmission parts

USA	ENGLISH
Axle shaft	Half shaft
Drive shaft	Propeller shaft
Grease fitting	Grease nipple
Ring gear and pinion	Crown wheel and pinion

Steering parts

USA	ENGLISH
Control arm	Wishbone
King pin	Swivel pin
Pitman arm	Drop arm
Steering idler	Steering relay
Steering knuckle	Stub axle
Steering post	Steering column
Tie bar or track bar	Track rod

Tools and accessories

USA	ENGLISH
Antenna	Aerial
Crank handle	Starting handle
Wheel wrench	Wheel brace
Wrench	Spanner

USA	ENGLISH
Transmission parts—	**Gearbox parts**
Counter shaft	Layshaft
Gear shift lever	Gear lever
Output shaft	Main shaft
Parking lock	Parking brake
Shift bar	Selector rod
Transmission casing	Gearbox housing
Tires	
Tire	Tyre
Tread	Track

27. *Mr* is the title of the common man in both countries. (Note the absence of the period in *Mr, Mrs, Messrs, Dr,* etc.) *Mr,* not *Dr,* is also the title of a surgeon or dentist, although Jones, your family physician, is *Dr* Jones. Correspondence that would be addressed to *Mr.* John Smith in America is usually addressed to John Smith, *Esq.* (with a period) or *Esquire* in England, a quaint practice followed in America only in communications between lawyers.

Abbreviations

adj.	adjective
adv.	adverb
app.	approximate
col.	colloquial
conj.	conjunction
interj.	interjection
n.	noun
n.A.e.	no American equivalent
pl.	plural
prep.	preposition
q.v.	which see
sl.	slang
v.i.	verb, intransitive
v.t.	verb, transitive

lexicographer. A writer of dictionaries; a harmless drudge . . .
—*Johnson's Dictionary*

Though a linguist should pride himself to have all the tongues that Babel cleft the world into, yet if he had not studied the solid things in them as well as the words and lexicons, yet he were nothing so much to be esteemed a learned man as any yeoman competently wise in his mother dialect only.

—*John Milton*

. . . The American language is in a state of flux based on the survival of the unfittest.

—*Cyril Connolly*, in
The Sunday Times (London),
December 11, 1966

When the American people get through with the English language, it will look as if it had been run over by a musical comedy.
—"Mr. Dooley" (Finley Peter Dunne)

Consider the influence of the USA. There are few families without American connexions today and American polite vocabulary is very different from ours. We fight shy of abbreviations and euphemisms. They rejoice in them. The blind and maimed are called "handicapped," the destitute, "underprivileged." "Toilet" is pure American (but remember that our "lavatory" is equally a euphemism). Remember too that the American vocabulary is pulverized between two stones, refinement and overstatement.

—Evelyn Waugh, in *An Open Letter To The Hon'ble Mrs Peter Rodd (Nancy Mitford) On a Very Serious Subject*

. . . Why, oh why, do we quietly absorb, instead of resisting, these unnecessary . . . transatlantic importations which, far from enriching, nearly always degrade our beautiful language?

—Brigadier R. B. Rathbone, in a letter to the (London) *Times* dated September 6, 1971

For Marjorie—Incurable Anglophile

abandonment, n.   **abandon**

In the sense of uninhibited conduct.

about, adv.   **around**

Used as an adverb indicating place, meaning *near,* or *in the vicinity,* as in: "Is your father about?" In the sense of *approximately,* Americans use both terms interchangeably, but the English much prefer *about.*

academicals, n. pl.   **cap and gown**

accept, v.i.   **agree**

For instance, "I cannot *accept* that you have met the conditions of the contract." A common use in England.

accident tout   **ambulance chaser**

accommodation, n.   **accommodations**

In the sense of food and lodgings, the English use the singular. They seem not to use the word at all as the Americans do to in-

ENGLISH   AMERICAN

clude travel facilities, such as train and ship staterooms, plane seats, etc.

account, n.   **(1) bill**
                                 (2) charge account

(1) Notification of an amount owing.

(2) The term *charge account* is not used in England.

accountant, *see* **chartered accountant; commission agent; turf accountant**

accumulator, n.   **battery**

Battery, too, is heard in England.

ack emma   **A.M.**

And *pip emma* is P.M. Both generally outmoded.

act for   **represent**

Lawyers in England *act for,* rather than *represent,* their clients.

action replay   **instant replay**

TV term.

A.D.C.   **time and charges**

These letters stand for *Advice of Duration and Charges,* and are what one says to the long-distance operator in order to learn the cost of the call.

admass, n.   **mass-media public**

The gullible section of the public (*mass*) which is most easily influenced by mass-media advertising (*ads*); especially the TV-proletariat, as it were.

Admiralty, n.   **Navy Department**

A department of government.

adopt, v.t. **nominate**

At the caucuses and conventions Americans *nominate* candidates who *run* for election. The English nominate potential candidates and finally *adopt* the ones who are going to **stand** (q.v.) for election.

advert, n. (col.) **ad**

Abbreviation of advertisement.

aerodrome, n. **airfield**

aeroplane, n. **airplane**

afters, n. pl. (col.) **dessert**

Thus: "What's for *afters?*"

against the collar (col.) **tough going**

One meaning of *collar* is the *roll* around a horse's neck. This meaning gives rise to the colloquial phrases *against the collar* and *collar-work*, both of which indicate *uphill effort*.

agent, *see* **commission agent; estate agent; turf accountant**

A.G.M., *see* **Annual General Meeting**

agree, v.t. **concede**

Agree is never used transitively in America any more. It is always followed by a clause introduced by *that* (*I agree that it is so*) or by *to* (*I agree to your terms; I agree to go away*), or is used intransitively (*You say it's a good painting; I agree* or *You want $100 for that old car; I agree*). In England it is used in all those ways but often transitively as well where Americans would use *concede* or *admit* (*I agree the liability for income taxes; I agree the claim for damages*).

3

agreed verdict   **consent decree**

Legal term.

agricultural labourer   **farmhand**

agricultural show   **state or county fair**

An *agricultural show* represents roughly the same aspect of
English life as an American *state fair* or *county fair*. The Tunbridge Wells Agricultural Show or the Kent (County) Agricultural Show serve about the same cultural and economic purposes
as, for example, the Kansas State Fair, the Great Barrington
Fair in Massachusetts, or the Danbury Fair in Connecticut.

air bed, *see* **li-lo**

airy-fairy, adj. (col.)   **fanciful** (app.)

In its original sense *airy-fairy* meant *light* and *delicate,* like a
fairy. It has now acquired a disparaging use meaning *unsub-
stantial, superficial,* perhaps with connotations of whimsy, arti-
ness, pretentiousness. Example: "This progressive education is
a lot of *airy-fairy* nonsense." There would appear to be no precise American colloquial counterpart.

aisle, n.   **church aisle**

In America *aisle* is used generically. In England the *aisle* in a
shop is a *gangway;* in a train it is a *corridor;* in a theater, either
may be used.

ait, n.   **islet**

Pronounced *eight* but sometimes spelled *eyot* indicating its relationship to *islet.* It is not a common word and most often describes a *little island* in a river or brook.

albert, n.   **watch chain**

Also called an *Albert chain;* if used alone, the A drops to lower
case. Based on the sartorial habits of Victoria's Prince Consort.

ale-house politician	cracker barrel politician

A-levels, n. pl.	college entrance examinations; Scholastic Aptitude Tests (S.A.T.; app.)

The *A* stands for *advanced* just as the *O* in *O-levels* stands for *ordinary*. At the age of fifteen or sixteen, students in England take their *O-levels*, and at seventeen or eighteen, their *A-levels*. Both are known as *G.C.E.* examinations. *G.C.E.* stands for *General Certificate of Education*, which is required for admission to any university. Oxford and Cambridge have additional examinations of their own as do several others, but the practice is waning in favor of a central clearing-house for university applicants. The American definition must be approximate because of the procedural differences in the two educational systems. A Frenchman who had lived in England, after making vain efforts to explain the English school system to a compatriot, finally wound up with: "Ça ne s'explique pas, mais ça marche." ("You can't explain it, but it works.")

all found, *see* **fully found**

all in (col.)   everything thrown in

I.e., *all included*. Thus: The holiday cost us £100 *all in* (i.e., travel, **accommodation** [q.v.], and all other expenses). Nothing to do with the American and English meaning *all tuckered out*. An *all-in* policy is an *all-risk* (insurance) policy. An English insurance company advertisement of the early 1900s spoke of such a policy, enumerating the dozen or so risks covered by the omnibus contract. Included as items 7, 8, and 9 were Riots, Strikes, and Civil Insurrections. These three were bracketed by a connecting brace, on the other side of which, in fine print, occurred the phrase: Except in Ireland.

5

all my eye and Betty Martin! (col.)   **baloney!**

All kinds of derivations proposed. The most likely would seem to be *Mihi beata mater* (which appears to be Latin for something like *Grant to me, blessed Mother*). According to one legend, the imperfectly understood phrase was reported back to England by a sailor who had been abroad and to him it sounded like *all my eye and Betty Martin*. Sounds spurious. The English often shorten the expression to *all my eye!* Cf. American *my eye!*

all over the shop (col.)   **in a mess;
in wild disorder**

allotment, n.   **small rented
farming plot**

all-round, adj.   **all-around**

all the fun of the fair (col.)   **great fun**

More damn fun! Often used ironically to describe a tight situation.

amenities, n. pl.   **conveniences**

Referring to household facilities. *Amenities* in the American sense is *civilities* in England. The American term *conveniences* also is used and is found in the abbreviated phrase, *mod. con.*, which stands for *modern conveniences. Mod. con.* appears in advertisements and is used conversationally in discussing a house or an apartment in the same literal but half-humorous way in which Englishmen conversationally use the abbreviation *two veg.* (pronounced *vej.*), meaning two vegetables accompanying the entrée in a meal.

anglepoise lamp   **adjustable table lamp** (app.)

Originally a trademark, now becoming generic. The term describes a table lamp with a base built of a series of hinged arms with springs and counterweights that adjust the height, beam direction, and so on.

6

ENGLISH   AMERICAN

Annual General Meeting   **Annual Meeting of Shareholders (Stockholders)**

Usually abbreviated to *A.G.M.* What the English call an *Extraordinary General Meeting* is called a *Special Meeting of Shareholders (Stockholders)* in America.

anorak, n.   **parka**

An Eskimo word.

another pair of shoes, *see* **boot**

another place   **n.A.e.**

This is the way the House of Commons refers to the House of Lords, but it doesn't work the other way around. *The other place* (note the definite article) is the way Oxford and Cambridge refer to each other. In this case it's mutual. These circumlocutions are reminiscent of the old days when CBS and NBC referred to each other as *another network.*

answer, v.i. (col.)   **work**

Answer is sometimes used colloquially in phrases indicating inappropriateness, such as, "It won't *answer,*" or "It didn't *answer.*" For example, a person reads an advertisement of the help-wanted or houses-for-rent variety, goes to investigate, finds the situation unsatisfactory, and in answer to a friend's question says, "It didn't *answer.*"

anti-clockwise, adj., adv.   **counterclockwise**

apartment, n.   **room**

The English equivalent of an American *apartment* is a **flat** (q.v.), but they are coming to use *apartment* in the American sense.

appeal, n.   **n.A.e.**

For a special meaning in cricket, *see* **Howzat!**

approach, v. t.   **service**

That which a ram does to an ewe under appropriate conditions.

approved school   **reform school**

argy-bargy, n., v.i. (sl.)   **squabble**

Derived from *argue.*

armchair socialist (col.)   **parlor pink**

arsy-tarsy, adj. (sl.)   **bass-ackwards**

arterial road   **main road**

Synonymous with *major road* and *trunk road.* A common traffic sign used to be: *Halt—Major Road.* This appeared (sometimes still does) on what Americans call *stop signs,* at junctions where secondary roads ran into *main roads. Stop* now generally replaces *Halt* on traffic signs not only in England but in many other countries (cf. СТОП in the U.S.S.R.). *See also* **Halt.**

articulated lorry   **trailer truck**

The verb *articulate* has been used so widely as an intransitive verb meaning to *speak clearly* that most people have forgotten that it is also a transitive verb meaning to *connect by joints.*

as bright as a new penny (col.)   **as bright as a button**

Intelligent and lively.

Asdic, n.   **sonar**

Stands for *Allied Submarine Detection Investigation Committee,* just as *sonar* stands for *Sound Navigation Ranging.* Both are marine depth-measuring devices and are used in ferreting out submarines.

as dim as a Toc H lamp (col.)   **thick-headed**

Toc H (initials of Talbot House, *T* being called *toc* in military

8

signaling) is an organization for social service and fellowship with branches throughout the British Commonwealth, so-called because it originated at Talbot House, a rest center for soldiers at Poperinghe, Belgium. Talbot House, founded by the Rev. T. B. Clayton (usually referred to as "Tubby Clayton"), was named for Gilbert Talbot, who was killed in action in 1915. In front of each Toc H location hangs a lamp (like an Aladdin's lamp) which is always dimly lit. Sometimes a sign with a lamp replaces the lamp itself. The *dim* in this phrase is short for *dim-witted* and is thus a mild pun. The expression, like the institution itself, is on the way out.

as easy as kiss your hand (col.)   **as easy as pie**

the Ashes, n. pl. (col.)   **n.A.e.**

This is a symbolic term meaning *victory* in test cricket with Australia (*see* **test**). Thus we have the expressions *win the Ashes; retain* (or *hold*) *the Ashes; bring back* (or *win back* or *regain*) *the Ashes,* etc., depending upon circumstances. When England and Australia play in a test series for *the Ashes* no physical trophy changes hands. Yet after the term came into use, under the circumstances described below, the abstraction did materialize into a pile of physical ashes which are contained in an urn which is in turn contained in a velvet bag, now resting permanently at Lord's Cricket Ground in London, the Mecca, Vatican, and Canterbury Cathedral of English cricket. The story is told in a brochure put out by the Marylebone Cricket Club (always referred to as the *M.C.C.*) which, with its headquarters at Lord's, is the official body in charge of English cricket. (The author once asked a stranger in a country pub what the initials *M.C.C.* stood for and was informed in the same tone of disdain as those in which a stranger at the counter in a Brooklyn bar and grill, in the old days, might have answered an Englishman asking the name of the sport practised by the Dodgers.) Herewith some excerpts from the brochure:

> When the . . . Australian team . . . met England . . . on August 28, 1882, England was still unbeaten on her own soil. Here follows a tragic account of the disaster of that

date. . . . In an atmosphere of tension and excitement which mounted as the wickets fell, Australia achieved her first victory in a test match in England by 7 runs. It was a glorious finish and Australia's triumph was well deserved. . . .

The *Sporting Times* reflected the sentiments of English cricketing circles by printing a mock obituary notice, which ran as follows:

In affectionate remembrance

of

ENGLISH CRICKET

which died at the Oval on

29th August 1882,

Deeply lamented by a large circle

of sorrowing friends and

acquaintances.

R.I.P.

N.B.—The body will be cremated and

the ashes taken to Australia . . .

The ashes

So was coined the expression "the Ashes," which is used whenever a series of test matches is played between England and Australia.

Almost immediately after the match, an English team under the captaincy of the Hon. Ivo Bligh (afterwards Lord Darnley) left for Australia on tour. . . . It had been commonly said that Ivo Bligh had gone on a pilgrimage to "recover the Ashes," and so, after the second defeat of . . . [the Australian] team, some Melbourne ladies burned and collected the ashes of a bail [one of the parts of a wicket], which they placed in a small pottery urn and presented to him. . . . An additional gift . . . was a red velvet bag to contain the Ashes. . . .

as nice as ninepence (col.)   **as nice as pie**

Unexpectedly pleasant and helpful.

as safe as a bank (col.)   **perfectly O.K.**

as safe as houses (col.)   **perfectly O.K.**

assessment for, *see* **suffer an assessment for**

assessor, n.   **adjuster**

One who investigates an insurance claim.

assistant, n.   **clerk; salesman; saleslady**

Assistant, in this English use, is short for *shop assistant,* which usually means a *sales person* or *salesclerk,* but can also mean in a more general sense a *shop attendant,* who may not be there to sell you anything but to help out generally. In England one hears of a *bootmaker's assistant,* who would be called a *shoe clerk* in America; a *florist's assistant,* who would be described in America as a *salesman* or *saleslady at a florist's,* etc. *Assistant* and *shop assistant* have always seemed to be euphemisms to

11

raise the spirits without raising the wages of the persons involved. *See also* **clerk.**

association football (soccer), *see* **football**

as soon as look at you (col.)	**as quick as a wink**

as soon as say knife (col.)	**as quick as a wink**

Interchangeable with *before you can say knife.*

as under	**as follows**

For instance, at the top of a bill for services, one might see "For professional services *as under*."

at half-cock (col.)	**half-cocked**

In the expression *go off at half-cock.*

athletics, n. pl.	**sports**

Athlete, though used in the broad sense, generally connotes participation in track and field. In an English school one goes *in* for *athletics,* rather than *out* for *sports.*

at the side of (col.)	**beside**

Used in odious comparisons. "She's ugly *at the side of* her cousin Betty."

au pair	**giving services for board and lodging**

This term from French applies generically to service bartering arrangements between two parties, with little or no money changing hands. A doctor and a lawyer might thus make an *au pair* arrangement. The term is heard generally in the expression *au pair girl* (often called just an *au pair*) and refers to the common English custom of a family's giving a home to a girl from abroad who helps mother with the children and the housekeeping. English families also exchange children with foreign families in order to broaden the children's experience, this being another type of *au pair* arrangement. The *pair* in *au pair* has nothing to do with the English use of **pair** (q.v.), meaning *floor* of a building.

aubergine, n. **eggplant**

Aunt Sally (col.) **patsy**

An *Aunt Sally* is a *butt.* The term is derived from the fair game in which one throws balls at a figure known as *Aunt Sally.* It has also come to mean a *stepchild,* someone or something overlooked or bypassed. Thus a certain department of the government which received inadequate appropriation might be called the *Aunt Sally* of the Treasury.

𝕭 | B

backbencher, n. **n.A.e.**

A member of the House of Commons or other body not entitled to a seat on the front benches, which are occupied by ministers (cabinet members) and other members of the government and opposition leaders. *See also* **front bench.**

back-end, n. **late autumn**

Mainly north of England.

back-room boy, *see* **boffin**

back slang   n.A.e.

Slang created by spelling words backwards, an exclusively
English pastime. Example: *ecilop* is *back slang* for *police,* and
the origin of the slang noun *slop,* meaning *policeman.*

backwardation, n.   **delayed delivery
                                              penalty**

A London Stock Exchange term. It consists of a percentage of
the selling price payable by the seller of shares for the privilege
of delaying their delivery. *See also* **contango.**

backwoodsman, n.   n.A.e.

The literal use of this word in English is the same as the American. Figuratively it describes a peer who rarely, if ever, attends
the House of Lords.

bad hat (col.)   **bad egg**

bad patch (col.)   **rough time**

When things are not going well with someone, the English say
that he is in or going through a *bad patch;* in America he would
be described as having a *rough time* of it.

bad show!   **hard luck!**

A *ghastly show* is a *terrible mess.*

bag, n. (sl.)   **POW camp**

bag, v. i.   **drop off course**

Nautical term.

bag a brace, *see* **duck** (1)

bagging-hook, n.   **small scythe**

A rustic term synonymous with **swop** (q.v.).

bagman, n. traveling salesman

In America *bagman* is an abusive term meaning a *graft collector*. While a congressman, the Rev. Adam Clayton Powell called a Harlem lady a *bagwoman* on a television program. She recovered a huge judgment against him for defamation of character. The word has a quite different slang meaning (not actionable at law) in both languages—*bag fox*—describing the poor fox which is cruelly brought to the hunt in a bag and released for the chase.

bags, n. pl. (sl.) slacks

Oxford bags were a 1920s style characterized by the exaggerated width of the trouser legs.

bags I! (sl.) **I dibsy!** (**I claim!**)

This is schoolboy slang. Sometimes "*I bag!* or "*I bags!*" "*Bags, first innings!*" is another variant. *First innings* in this context means a first crack at something (*see* **first innings**).

bags of . . . (sl.) **piles of . . .**

Usually in the phrase *bags of money*.

bait, n. (sl.) (1) **fit (of anger)**
(2) **grub (food)**

When it means a *towering rage* or *fit of anger*, it can be spelled *bate*.

baked potato, *see* **jacket potato**

bakehouse, n. bakery

Where bread is baked, not sold.

baker-legged, adj. (sl.) knock-kneed

15

Balaam, n. (col.)   **fillers; miscellaneous stock items to fill newspaper space**

The prophet Balaam could not meet the requirements of Balak, king of Moab, when commanded to curse the Israelites, and the curse became a blessing instead (Num. 22–24). Balaam thus became the prototype of the disappointing prophet or ineffective ally. It is not easy to see the connection.

Balaclava, n.   **woolen helmet**

Short for *Balaclava helmet,* which is made of wool and pulled over the head, leaving the face exposed. Balaclava was the site of an important battle of the Crimean War. That war made two other contributions to fashion: the sleeve named for Lord Raglan, who occupied the town of Balaclava, and the sweater which was the invention of the seventh Earl of Cardigan, commander of the famous Light Brigade.

ball in your court (col.)   **up to you**

"The ball's in your court" means "It is your next move." A variant is *"The ball's at your foot."*

balls, n. pl. (sl.)   **(1) crap (nonsense)**
                                             (2) mess

(1) This word is used by itself, as a rather inelegant expletive, in America. In England it appears in expressions like "That's a lot of *balls,*" i.e., stuff and nonsense, or balderdash, or in rude terms, *crap.*

(2) To make a *balls* of something is to make a *mess* of it, to *louse it up.* A variant of *balls* in this sense is *balls-up.* The familiar expressions to *ball up* (a situation) and *all balled up* are of course echoes of this usage. Synonymous with *balls* and *balls-up* in this sense are **cock** and **cock-up** (qq.v.). One wonders why the names of these particular closely related portions of the male anatomy are thus pejoratively exploited.

bally, adj., adv. (sl.) **damned**

Expressing disgust, like *bloody*. But it can, by a kind of reverse English, express the exact opposite, i.e., satisfaction, as in: "We bet on three races and won the *bally* lot."

bandit-proof, adj. **bulletproof**

Bulletproof is also used in England.

bandy-legged, adj. **bowlegged**

Referring to persons, and occasionally used also in America. In England, a table or other piece of furniture would be *bow-legged*.

banger, n. (sl.) (1) **sausage**
(2) **jalopy**
(3) **firecracker**

Three distinct meanings:
(1) A *banger* eaten at an agricultural show (state or county fair in America) is a *sausage*. This name is derived from its tendency to burst open in the frying pan with a small bang.
(2) The *banger* which got the visitors to the fair is a *jalopy*.
(3) Schoolboy slang.

bang on (sl.) **on the nose**

Exactly as planned or predicted. Literally, *bang on target*, of World I vintage.

banjo, v.t. (sl.) **beat up**

An underworld term heard in London.

bank holiday, n. **legal holiday**

Also used as an adjective, as in *bank-holiday* Monday. Bank holidays were introduced in 1871 by John Lubbock, for many years a Liberal Member of Parliament. He wrote a number of books: *The Pleasures of Life, Peace and Happiness, The Beau-*

ties of Nature, and *Ants, Bees, and Wasps.* The connection between these subject matters and an extra day off is obvious. For
years the grateful public called bank holidays "St. Lubbock's
Days."

bank note, *see* **note**

bant, v.i.   **diet**

To *bant* is to *diet.* Dr. W. Banting, who died in 1878, originated
a treatment for overweight based on abstinence from sugar,
starch, etc. His name became a common noun: *banting* became
and remained the name of this dieting procedure. The word
ending *-ing* looked like a gerund, so by back-formation the verb
to *bant* came into being. Rare today. *See also* **slim.**

bar, conj.   **but (except)**

Heard more in the country than in the city. After digging holes
in the lawn to repair land drains: "We'll fill them all *bar* the
bottom one." Thus also: "All over *bar* the shouting."

bar, n., *see* **lounge bar; private bar; pub**

bar, v.t. (sl.)   **loathe** (app.)

When you *bar* something, you can't stand it. No equivalent
American slang.

bar billiards, *see* **billiards-saloon**

bargee, n.   **barge operator**

This is mainly a canal-boat term. There is a great deal of canal
slang which would have no equivalent in America because the
English inland waterways system has no real American equivalent. *Lucky bargee* is a colloquialism which, like its American
equivalents *lucky stiff* and *lucky dog,* implies a certain degree
of friendly envy but has no canal connotation.

barge pole (col.)   **ten-foot pole**

That with which an Englishman would refuse to touch certain other Englishmen. Can also be used of an unsavory proposition.

bar man   **bartender**

The English also say *bartender*. The female of the species is a *barmaid*—traditionally bright, breezy, and buxom.

barmy on the crumpet, *see* **biscuit**

barney (barny), n. (sl.)   **squabble**

baron of beef, *see* **sirloin**

barrel, n.   **weight unit** (app.)

A *barrel* is a varying unit of weight (or other quantitative measure). It depends on what it is a *barrel* of. It works this way:

Commodity	Weight in lbs.
soft soap	256
butter	224
beef	200
flour	196
gunpowder	100

But careful: Applied to beer and tar, *barrel* is a unit of volume expressed in gallons and works this way:

Commodity	No. of gals.
beer	36
tar	26½

And remember, a *gallon* is an *Imperial gallon,* equal to approximately 120 percent of an American gallon (120.095 percent is a little closer; *see* **gallon**). And to make things just a bit less certain, a *barrel* of fish is *500 fish!* For other examples of the English determination to keep things charmingly flexible, or doggedly inconsistent (as Mencken put it in *The American Lan-*

guage: Supplement I, Alfred A. Knopf, Inc., New York, 1961, p. 495), *see* **score; stone.**

barrier, n. gate

Railroad term meaning the *gate* through which one passes to and from the platform. A guard standing at the *barrier* punches your ticket (or glances at it again if it is a **season ticket** [q.v.]) as you leave. If you don't have it as you leave, you pay the fare to the guard (who takes you at your word when you tell him where you boarded the train) and get a receipt, or else you throw yourself on his mercy and explain its mysterious disappearance, usually without success. There is no *conductor* (an American term, in railroad idiom; *conductor,* in English transportation, is confined to buses) to take your ticket on the train.

barrister, n. trial lawyer

A *barrister* is also known as *counsel.* Apart from serving as *trial lawyers, barristers* are resorted to by *solicitors* (general practitioners) for written expert opinions in special fields of the law. The **solicitor** (q.v.) is the man the client retains. The *solicitor* retains the *barrister* or *counsel.* The *solicitor* can try cases in certain inferior courts. The *barrister-solicitor* dichotomy is a legal institution in England. It exists in practice in America, where, technically, any attorney may try cases, but most practitioners resort to trial counsel in litigated matters. *See* also **brief; called to the bar; chambers.**

barrow, n. pushcart

This word means *pushcart* when referring to a street vendor. In gardening, it is the equivalent of *wheelbarrow,* which term is also used. *See also* **trolley.** *Pushcart* is sometimes used in England to mean *baby carriage.*

basin, n. sink

Basin is used when referring to any room other than the kitchen. *Sink* must be used in England when referring to a kitchen. In

America *sink* may be used without distinction as to the nature of the room, though *wash basin* is often used to describe a bathroom sink.

bat, *see* **carry one's bat; off his own bat**

bate, *see* **bait**

bath, n.   **bathtub**

In England as in America one can *take a bath,* although in England one usually *has,* rather than *takes,* a *bath.* One sits or soaks in the *bath* in England rather than in the *bathtub,* as in America.

bath, v.t.   **bathe**

In England one *baths* the baby.

bath bun   **sweet bun** (app.)

A type of *sweet bun* which is filled with small seedless raisins called **sultanas** (q.v.) and candied citrus rinds, having a glazed top studded with coarse grains of white sugar. The term has been heard occasionally in unkind slang usage to mean *old bag,* i.e., *crone.*

bath-chair, n.   **wheelchair**

Sometimes the "b" is capitalized, showing derivation from the city of Bath where their use originated as pleasure vehicles. Also called *invalid's chair.*

bath chap   **pig's cheek**

A butcher's term. *Chap* is a variant of *chop.* The *pig's cheek is* usually smoked.

bathe, n.   **swim**

In England one *swims* in the sea, but one also takes a *bathe* in the sea.

bathing costume   **bathing suit**

Sometimes *bathing dress* or *swimming costume. Bathing dress* used to be confined to women's outfits. All these terms are rather old-fashioned: In England today *bathing suit* or simply *costume* is the term generally used and applies indiscriminately to both sexes.

Bath Oliver   **dry cookie** (app.)

A type of *cookie* (the English say **biscuit** [q.v.]) invented by a Dr. W. Oliver (d. 1764) of the city of Bath. The cookie is about a quarter of an inch thick, dry, and sweetish—not quite so sweet as an American graham cracker. Incidentally, graham crackers got their name from graham flour, which is made from whole kernels of wheat, and graham flour got its name from Dr. Sylvester Graham, who was born thirty years after Dr. W. Oliver died, and himself died in 1851. What is this affinity between physicians and cookies?

batman, n.   **officer's servant**

Not to be confused with either the hero of the comic book and television program or the cricket term *batsman,* which has approximately the same relationship to the game of cricket as *batter* to *baseball.*

baton, n.   **billy; nightstick**

Also called a *truncheon.* Carried by policemen.

Battersea box   **n.A.e.**

Little enameled copper cases with decorated hinged tops: cylindrical, bottle-shaped for perfume, bonbonnières, etc. The authentic antique boxes were produced at Battersea, a part of London, for only a few years (1753–56) and are rare and expensive. Good copies are being made today with traditional or new designs.

BBC English   **cultured speech** (app.)

The reference is to the speech of the announcers, considered by many to be the most acceptable pronunciation of English.

beach, n.   gravel

When an Englishman wants to close up a ditch with *fill* or *gravel* he uses *beach*. When he wants to swim in the ocean, he goes to the *sea*, not the *beach*.

beadle, *see* **bumble**

beak, n. (sl.)   (1) **schoolmaster**
                                                      (2) **magistrate**

No precise American slang for either meaning.

beam ends, *see* **on one's beam ends**

bean, n. (sl.)   (1) **cent** (app.)
                                                      (2) **pep** (app.)
                                                      (3) **hell** (app.)
                                                      (4) **chap**

All kinds of slang uses:
(1) "I haven't a *bean*" means "I'm *broke*."
(2) Full of *beans* means full of *pep*.
(3) To give someone *beans* is to give him *hell*.
(4) Now rather outmoded.

bean-feast, n. (sl.)   company picnic

Also called a *beano*. Apparently, pork and beans (in England *beans and bacon*) were considered an indispensable element of the annual company celebration. The meaning has been extended to mean any merry occasion.

bearing-rein, n.   sidecheck

beastly, adj., adv. (col.)   (1) **unpleasant**
                                                      (2) **terribly** (very)

(1) *Beastly* in America means something a good deal stronger than it does in England. In America *beastly* means *disgusting, abominable*. In England it means *unpleasant, undesirable*.
(2) It is never used as an adverb in America. In England it is

23

an intensifying adverb, like *bloody* in *bloody awful,* or *jolly* in *jolly good.* Thus, "He got *beastly* drunk"; "It's snowing *beastly* hard." Like **bally** (q.v.), rather precious.

beat up (col.)   **pick up**

In the sense of picking somebody up, by prearrangement, to go somewhere together. Planning to go out to dinner and the theater one might say, "I'll be around at about 7 P.M. to *beat you up."* This usage faintly recalls the image of African beaters who rouse the beasts of the jungle from their lethargy for the benefit of white hunters.

beck, n.   **brook**

bed-board, n.   **headboard**

The term has a quite different meaning in America—a wide board placed under a mattress for the benefit of sleepers with back trouble.

bedding, n.   **annuals**

A single annual plant is called a *bedder.* Americans are occasionally surprised to see *bedding* advertised for sale in plant nurseries. Also used as an adjective, as in *bedding* plants.

bed-sitter, n. (col.)   **one-room apartment**

Colloquial for *bed-sitting-room,* meaning a *combination bedroom-living room.*

beefeater, n.   **yeoman of the guard;**
                                                              Tower of London guide

A *warder* (*guard; see* **warder**) of the Tower of London. They are dressed in ornately decorated red uniforms and distinctively shaped top hats, dating from the fifteenth century. For a better description (if you can't get to the Tower), see a performance of Gilbert and Sullivan's *Yeomen of the Guard* or the label on a bottle of a popular gin. The Tower of London, originally a royal fortress and palace, became a prison and the *warders* thus became *jailers*. (A related American prison term is *warden*, i.e., the head man at a prison, whose title in England is *governor*.) Nowadays the Tower, a huge collection of buildings housing many objects of historical interest, including the crown jewels, is crawling with tourists, and the *beefeaters* are its official guides, amazingly knowledgeable and literate, who take groups around, dispensing history and wit in large doses. The name is supposed to have developed from the concept of *well-fed* (i.e., *beef-fed*) royal servants.

Beefeater

beer and skittles (col.)   **a bed of roses**

Skittles being, literally, a ninepins game, *beer and skittles* would seem to be an apt phrase for *fun and games, high amusement.* Almost always used negatively: "Life is not all *beer and skittles*," or "This job is not all *beer and skittles*."

25

beetle-crusher, n. (sl.) clodhopper

beetroot, n. beet

Beet, in England, describes a related plant, the root of which is white, not red, used for either the feeding of cattle or the making of sugar, and usually called *sugar beet,* but the table vegetable known in America as *beet* is always called *beetroot* in England. Beetroot does not add an -s in the plural.

before you can say knife, *see* **as soon as say knife**

beggar, n. (col.) guy; son of a gun

The English use *beggar* literally, as we do. They also use it figuratively, in a pejorative sense, to describe an unsavory character, or favorably, to convey admiration, as in the expression, *a plucky little beggar.*

beginners! n. pl. places, please!

Stage manager's cry.

behindhand, adj. behind

As in a maid *behindhand* with her housework.

belt, n. girdle

Belt started out as a shortening of what in America would be known as a *garter belt* and in England as a *suspender belt* (*see* **braces; suspenders**). But then *belt* became generic for anything used by ladies to contain a certain part of the anatomy and the equivalent of the American term *girdle,* which is now also widely heard in England.

belted earl earl

All earls are belted, i.e., theoretically they wear sword belts. *Belted earl* is an affectionately jocular term, like *noble lord* (all lords are noble) and *gracious duke* (all dukes are "Your Grace," but an ungracious duke must happen once in a while).

belt up (sl.)   shut up

The English also say *pack it up* or *put a sock in it.*

bend, n.   curve

Referring to roads and used on road signs. A *double bend* is an
"S" *curve.*

bender, n. (sl.)   sixpence

See also Introductory Note 18.

Bermudian rigged   **Marconi rigged**

Sailing term, describing triangular sails.

bespoke, adj.   made to order;
                                                          custom made

Used in the phrases *bespoke* clothes, *bespoke* tailor.

beyond the next turning   **in the next block**

In England a **block** (q.v.) is a large building. In America a *block*
is the space between two streets. *In the next block,* in England
would mean *in the next apartment house* or *office building.*

big bug, *see* **insect**

big pot, *see* **pot**

bill, n.   (1) **check**
                                                                (2) **pruning knife**

(1) In England one asks the waiter for his *bill,* less frequently
   his *check.* (The Englishman might pay his *bill* by *cheque,*
   however.)
(2) A country term, describing a kind of miniature machete
   with a curve at the end of the blade.

bill broker   discounter

One engaged in the business of discounting notes and other negotiable instruments.

billiards-saloon, n.   poolroom (app.)

The game of *pool* in England has a set of rules quite different from *pool* (or *straight pool*) as the term is understood in America, where there are many variations of the game, each with its own set of rules. *Bar billiards* is an English game, played with balls and cues, on a table much smaller than a standard American table, and a bar-billiards table is a frequent and thoroughly enjoyable adornment of English pubs. The American *poolroom* used to have connotations of shady characters, including bookies and drifters, but like so many other things in America, it has become dolled up and quite respectable, even invading the wholesome precincts of many a YMCA building. *Billiards-saloon* has never had any derogatory connotations.

billion, adj., n.   trillion;
million million;
$1,000,000^2$

One followed by twelve *zeros* (which would be called *naughts, noughts,* or *ciphers* in England). An American *billion* is only *one thousand million* (1,000,000,000), which is called a *thousand million* or a *milliard* in England. There are wholly different nomenclature systems in the two countries for numbers big enough to be stated in powers of a million. While this may not be material in computing your bank balance, it might prove important to mathematicians, astronomers, and astronauts, for whose benefit the following partial table is submitted:

English	American	Number	Formation		
million	million	1,000,000	1 with	6	zeros
milliard	billion	1,000,000,000	1	9	"
billion	trillion	$1,000,000^2$	1	12	"
thousand billion	quadrillion	$1,000 \times 1,000,000^2$	1	15	"

English	American	Number	Formation		
trillion thousand	quintillion	$1,000,000^3$	1	18	"
trillion	sextillion	$1,000 \times 1,000,000^3$	1	21	"
quadrillion thousand	septillion	$1,000,000^4$	1	24	"
quadrillion	octillion	$1,000 \times 1,000,000^4$	1	27	"
quintillion thousand	nonillion	$1,000,000^5$	1	30	"
quintillion	decillion	$1,000 \times 1,000,000^5$	1	33	"
sextillion		$1,000,000^6$			
(sexillion)			1	36	"
septillion		$1,000,000^7$	1	42	"
octillion		$1,000,000^8$	1	48	"
nonillion		$1,000,000^9$	1	54	"
decillion		$1,000,000^{10}$	1	60	"
centillion		$1,000,000^{100}$	1	600	"

bill of quantity   **cost estimate**

Especially in the building contracting business.

billycock, *see* **bowler**

bin, n.   **hop sack**

Made of canvas and used in hop-picking.

bin, n., *see also* **bread bin; orderly bin; waste bin**

bind, v.i. (sl.)   **gripe**

bint, n. (sl.)   **moll**

From the Arabic word for *girl,* adopted by British soldiers in the
Middle East in World War II. It can have the less sinister
meaning of *floozy.*

bird, n. (sl.)   **dame**

Now more commonly used than **bint** (q.v.). For a wholly unrelated use, *see* **give . . . the bird.**

biro, n. (col.)   **ball-point pen**

Birthday Honours   **titles conferred**

A miscellany of titles conferred on the sovereign's birthday, including knight (the female equivalent being *dame*), baron,
O.B.E. (Officer of the Order of the British Empire), M.B.E.
(Member of the Order of the British Empire), C.H. (Companion of Honour), P.C. (Privy Councillor). Titles are also conferred on New Year's Day.

biscuit, n.   **cracker**

In America *biscuit* would be taken to mean *soda biscuit,* which
would be called *scone* in England. The English usage lingers
on in the trademark *Uneeda Biscuit.* The American usage is
seen in the trademark *Ritz Cracker.* To get *cookies* in England,
ask for *sweet biscuits, tea biscuits,* or even *petits fours.* If you
ask for *crackers,* you may get *firecrackers* or even *explosive bon-
bons,* or *snappers,* the kind used at children's parties. But if you
ask for *snappers,* you would probably get *snaps,* the kind used in
dressmaking. *Crackers* also serves in England as a slang adjective (predicate only) whose American equivalent is *cracked*
(i.e., *crazy*) which is sometimes used in England, too, and is
synonymous with *barmy* (a variant of *balmy*), which, however,
means only *flighty* in America. Somehow this all comes together
in the English slang expression *barmy on the crumpet,* meaning *wrong in the head,* or *nutty,* a *crumpet* being a type of
American *sweet biscuit* and also English slang for *head,* like *nut*
in America, and synonymous with *loaf,* which is short for *loaf of
bread* (cockney rhyming slang). (For another English slang use
of *crumpet, see* **crumpet.**) The difference in usage is officially
recognized in the radio jingle (to the tune of *Gallagher &
Sheean*) of the venerable English biscuit firm of Huntley &
Palmer, which ends with the couplet:

> We're not cookies, Mr. Huntley.
> No, we're biscuits, Mr. P.

bite on the bullet (col.)   **grin and bear it**

No doubt derived from the practice, in the days before anesthesia, of giving a wounded soldier a bullet to bite on before amputating an appendage.

bit of a knock (sl.)   **tough break**

bit of fluff, *see* **fluff**

bit of goods (sl.)   **number**

An attractive *bit of goods* in England would be *quite a number* or *dish* in America.

bit of stuff (sl.)   **chick**

bitter, n.   **type of beer**

Bitter is used as a noun to mean *bitter beer* (as opposed to mild beer) and rivals tea as England's national drink. *See also* **pint.**

a bit thick, adj. (sl.)   **going too far**

The expression *a bit thick* appears in America sometimes as *a bit much,* but the more common expression in America is *going too far.*

black, v.t.   (1) **shine**
                                (2) **boycott**

Referring to shoes. *See also* **boot.** Also, current slang to describe the interference, presumably on union instructions, by employees of one company with the industrial activities of another company in order to exert pressure in labor disputes.

black coat   **white collar**

Referring to type of position or worker.

blackleg, n.   **scab; strikebreaker**

Black or white?   Cream in your coffee? (app.)

Black needs no explanation; *white* in England means *mixed with hot milk*. Americans who don't want it *black* add cream or milk (cold in either case) to their coffee. The English hostess or waitress usually holds the pot of coffee in one hand and the pitcher (*jug* in England) of hot milk in the other, and inquires, "*Black or white?*" The English system would appear to be universal outside North America.

black spot   (1) accident spot
                                                       (2) trouble spot

Sometimes spelled *blackspot*. This is, unfortunately, a common road sign now also used metaphorically to mean a danger area or *trouble spot*. Thus in a discussion of the unemployment situation, the reporter referred to a certain industry as a *black spot*.

blanket bath   sponge bath

The kind given by a nurse to one bedridden in the hospital or by a spouse or other good friend at home.

blast! (sl.)   damn it!

blether (blather), v.i.   talk nonsense

Mainly Scottish. With an *-s* added, it becomes a plural noun meaning *nonsense*. The vowel changes to *i* in *blithering idiot*.

blighter, n. (sl.)   character; pain; pest

This word originally meant a person of such low character as to *blight* his surroundings; now not quite so pejorative, it has its approximate equivalent in a number of American slang terms of which the above are only a few. Can be used, like **beggar** (q.v.), in a favorable sense, as in *lucky blighter*.

blighty, n. (sl.)   God's country (app.)

English soldiers used this word to mean *back home*, especially after military service abroad, in the same way that Americans are glad to get back to *God's country* after being abroad. It is derived from *bilati,* a Hindustani word meaning *foreign country* and was brought back to their own *blighty* by English soldiers returning from service in India. It is also used to describe a wound serious enough to warrant a soldier's return home: a *blighty* one.

blimey!, interj. (sl.)   **holy mackerel!**

This rather vulgar interjection is a contraction of *"Cor blimey!"* or *"Gor blimey!"* which are distortions of *"God blind me!"*

blimp, n. (col.)   **stuffed shirt**

A pompous, elderly reactionary, from the David Low cartoon character, Colonel Blimp.

blind, adj. (sl.)   **damned**

In the phrase: "I don't know a *blind* thing about it!"

blind, n.   **shade**

In America *blind* indicates a venetian blind or some type of shutter, usually made of wood.

blind road   **dead-end street**

Synonymous with **cul-de-sac** (q.v.).

blinkers, n. pl.   **blinders**

block, n.   **large building**

A *block of flats* in England is an *apartment house* in America. An *office block* in England is an *office building* in America.

block of ice   **ice cube**

bloke, n. (sl.)   **guy**

See also **chap; guy.**

bloody, adj., adv. (sl.)   **lousy; contemptible** (adj.)
                                      damned; goddamned (adv.)

This word is now commonly used as an adverb modifying a pejorative adjective, as in, "It's *bloody* awful." Used as an adjective, its nearest equivalent in America would be *lousy*, as in the
phrase, "a *bloody* shame." *Bloody* is a contraction of *by Our Lady*
and was formerly avoided, at least in mixed company, as blas-
phemous.

blot one's copybook (col.)   **spoil the record**

To mar an otherwise perfect record by an act of indiscretion.

blower, n. (sl.)   **phone**

One Englishman known to the author still calls it "Bell's folly."
Sometimes referred to in American slang as the *horn*.

blowlamp, n.   **blowtorch**

Sometimes **blowflame.**

blow the gaff, *see* **gaff**

blow . . . up   **blow up at . . .**

To *blow* someone *up* is to *blow up at* someone, to *let him have
it*, and a *blowing-up* is what you let him have!

blue, n.   **letter; letter man**

A man who wins his *letter* and becomes a *letter man* in America
wins his *blue* and becomes a *blue* at Oxford or Cambridge. At
London University he wins his *purple* and becomes a *purple*,
and it appears that other universities award other colors; but
neither *purple* nor any other color compares even faintly with
the distinction of a *blue*. Oxford *blue* is dark blue; Cambridge
blue is light blue. A *double-blue* is a *two-letter man;* a *triple-
blue* is a *three-letter man*. The sport in which the English athlete represents his university (i.e., *makes the team* in America)
determines whether he earns a *full blue* or a *half blue*. Cricket,

crew, and football (soccer) are *full blue* sports. Tennis, lacrosse, and hockey are *half blue* sports. A *blue* can therefore be a *full blue* or a *half blue,* but (sacrificing accuracy to delicacy) the term *blue* would appear generically to include *half blue.* Similarly, in most universities, the American athlete can *letter* (v.i.), that is, *earn his letter,* in a *major sport,* like football, basketball, track, or crew, or a *minor sport,* like tennis or fencing, the distinction between *major* and *minor* being generally equivalent to *full blue* and *half blue.* However, at Columbia and other colleges, the distinction between major and minor sports was abolished years ago. This award for excellence in athletics bestows upon the English athlete the right to wear certain articles of apparel which are blue in color: cap, blazer, necktie, and socks. The cap, awarded in cricket, is worn only during the playing of cricket. Socks are awarded in soccer. The blazer can be worn wherever it is appropriate to wear a blazer generally (for instance, out for a walk on a fine Sunday morning). The necktie can be worn wherever it is appropriate to wear a necktie (for instance, when applying for a job, or a bank loan). The tangible form of the award in America is that of a cloth *letter,* the initial of the college, which is sewn on a sweater of contrasting color. The letter can come in two sizes: in colleges which still maintain the distinction between major and minor sports, the larger letter is bestowed upon members of the team in major sports, the smaller size in minor sports. Where the major-minor distinction has been abolished, the size of the letter depends upon the athlete's degree of participation in the sport in which he qualifies. The delicacy mentioned above seems to operate in America, which uses the one term *letter man* without distinction based upon the size of the letter.

blue, v.t. (sl.)   **blow** (squander)

Past tense is *blued. Blue* came about, undoubtedly, as a result of a misunderstanding of *blew* to be the present instead of the past tense of the slang American verb *blow.*

blue-eyed boy (col.)   **fair-haired boy**

board, n.   **sign**

For instance, a "To Let" *board. See also* **notice board.**

boarder, n.   **resident student**

As opposed to a *day student* who lives at home. *Boarder* in the American sense is *lodger* in England.

boater, n.   **straw hat**

bob, n. (sl.)   **shilling**

See also Introductory Note 18.

bob-a-job?   **any odd job?**

English Boy Scouts come to the door and ask, *"Bob-a-job?"* You are supposed to find (or invent) a household chore which the good young man will perform for a *bob* (slang for *shilling*, now obsolete, and equivalent to 5 new pence or about 13 cents). He then turns the proceeds over to the organization for the doing of good works.

bobby, n. (sl.)   **cop**

Named for Sir Robert ("Bobby") Peel, Home Secretary, who founded the Metropolitan Police Force in 1829. A former slang term in England for *cop,* also named after Sir Robert, was *peeler. Copper* is another less common slang term for *cop,* which is also used in America but seems to have gone out of fashion. *Robert* (from the same Sir Robert) was another colloquial name for an English *cop.*

Bob's your uncle! (col.)   **there you are!**
                                                        that's it! voilà!

An expression used at the end of instructions such as road directions, recipes, and the like. For example: "Go about 100 yards, take the first turning on your right, then straight on through a little gate; go 40 yards to a gate on your left marked Main Entrance, but that's not really the main entrance (they just call it that, I haven't a clue why), but 20 yards farther on there's a small gate on your right that really is the main entrance; go through that, you'll see a dismal brown building on your left and—*Bob's your uncle!*" Or: ". . . add a few cloves, stir for five minutes, turn down the flame, let simmer for an hour or so, and —*Bob's your uncle!*"

bod, n. (sl.) **character**

A slang abbreviation of *body* and somewhat pejorative. Example: "I saw somebody who seemed to be a night watchman or some other type of lowly *bod* about the premises."

bodkin, n. **tape needle**

In England the commonest meaning is that of a thick, unpointed needle having a large eye for drawing tape or riboon through a hem or a loop. Its most common American meaning is *dagger,*

Peeler

but it was used that way by Englishmen, too (*see Hamlet,* act 3, scene 1). An unusual meaning in both countries is that of a *fancy hairpin* of the sort no longer used except in costume plays. An English use almost unknown in America is seen in the phrases *ride bodkin,* or *sit bodkin,* which describes the condition of being squeezed between two other persons, like an unlucky Pierre.

boffin, n. (sl.) **research scientist**

Synonymous with *back-room boy,* meaning a person who during World War II worked as a scientist for the war effort, as for instance, in the development of radar. It has come to mean *research scientist* generally, with no relation to the war effort any longer. A gentleman named Jack Rayner of Muswell Hill, a research scientist in the employ of the General Post Office, is of the opinion that he may be the original *boffin* to whom this bit of RAF World War II slang for *civilian scientist* was applied. The word became generic for *research scientist* about the middle of 1943. Early that year Mr. Rayner worked with a scientist who liked to give his colleagues nicknames out of Dickens, and the future Mrs. Rayner was his assistant. The name-giver called her *Mrs. Boffin,* after the character in *Our Mutual Friend.* By simple association Mr. Rayner became *Mr. Boffin,* and was thus addressed by his colleagues on a technical visit to Fighter and Bomber Command Headquarters soon thereafter.

bog, n. (sl.) **john (toilet)**

Not only slang but vulgar. Used in the plural to refer to a communal latrine, as at school or in the service.

bogey (bogy), n. (sl.) **cop**

This word literally means *bugbear,* which should explain its slang use among the criminal element.

bogie, n. **truck (non-driving locomotive wheels)**

Railroad term. *Truck* is an English railroad term meaning *gon-*

dola car (open freight car). An American *truck* is an English **lorry** (q.v.) in its usual context of freight haulage by road.

bogy, *see* **bogey**

boiled sweets   **hard candy**

Sweets, as a general term, is the English equivalent of the American general term *candy. Boiled sweets* always means the kind of candy that is usually sucked rather than chewed.

boiler, *see* **chicken**

boiler suit   **one-piece overall**

boiling, n. (sl.)   **mob**

The whole *boiling,* referring to a group of people, means the whole *mob* of them.

boko, n. (sl.)   **beak** (nose)

As in the expression *biff on the boko.* Rare.

bollard, n.   **traffic post**

A *bollard* in both countries is a post on a ship or dock around which hawsers are tied. An exclusively English meaning is *traffic post,* i.e., a post on a traffic island, to regulate parking.

bomb, n. (sl.)   **smash hit**

A *dazzling success*—the exact opposite of its meaning in America: a *dismal flop!*

bonce, n. (sl.)   (1) **dodo**
                                                               (2) **noodle**

(1) A large playing marble.
(2) A rare usage, usually in the expression *biff on the bonce.*

bonkers, adj. (sl.)   **nuts** (goofy)

bonnet, n.   **hood**

Automobile term. In automobile terminology, *hood* in England
is *roof* or *top* in America.

bonus issue (**bonus share**)   **stock dividend**

boob, n., v.i. (sl.)   **goof**

Though Americans don't use *boob* as a verb, they commonly
use *booboo* to indicate the result.

book, v.t.   (1) **reserve**
                                                   (2) **charge**

(1) In England one *books* or *reserves* a table, theater seats,
    hotel rooms, rental cars, etc. A *booking* (England) is a *re-
    servation* (America); a *booking office* and a *booking clerk*
    (railroad terms) appear in America as *ticket office* and
    ticket agent.
(2) When something is *booked to an account* in England, the
    equivalent in America would be *charged to an account.*
    See also **put down** (2).

book of words (col.)   **instructions**

America seems to lack a colloquialism for the *instructions* that
come in the package and that often need their own instructions.

bookstall, n.   **newsstand**

boot, n.   (1) **trunk (of an auto-**
                                          mobile)
                                      (2) **shoe**

Boot to an American means a piece of footwear which comes
well above the ankle, anywhere from a few inches to just below
the knee. The English use both *boot* and *shoe; boot* is used generically to include all leather footwear; but *shoe,* as in America, normally excludes that which comes above the ankle. If an
agricultural labourer (farmhand) or a countryman generally

wanted to talk about his *rubber boots,* he would refer to his *Wellingtons,* standard country footwear even in dry weather. An English *boot* reaching barely above the ankle would be called a *shoe* in America. A *shoe* coming below the ankle used to be called a *low cut* in America, but that term has practically died out. A *shoe* reaching over the ankle used to be called a *highlow* in England, but that term is now archaic. Quite incidentally, *another pair of shoes* is English for *a horse of a different color,* and *dead man's shoes* means something which somebody is waiting to inherit or succeed, like his boss's job. An American who would never refer to his *shoes* as his *boots* or to the process of *shining* them as *blacking* them nonetheless usually refers to the person who *shines* his *shoes* as a *bootblack,* although he sometimes calls him a *shoeshine boy.* Conversely, the Englishman would refer to the person who *blacks* his *boots* as a *shoeblack.* The English say both *bootlace* and *shoelace,* while in America *shoelace* is used regardless of the height of the *shoe,* and *shoestring* is relegated to the description of a kind of string necktie worn out West. In both countries companies go broke because they were started on a *shoestring,* not a *bootlace,* but they sometimes succeed as a result of a *bootstrap* operation. A *shoe clerk* in America is a *bootmaker's assistant* in England even if the *boots* are not *made* in that shop.

borstal, n. (col.)   **reformatory**

Borstal is the name of a town in Kent where England's original juvenile prison is located. It used to be called Borstal Prison but is now referred to as Borstal Institution, reflecting the modern trend toward rehabilitation, rather than retribution, in the case of young offenders. The Borstal System introduced the indeterminate sentence in juvenile cases requiring observation and treatment. Colloquially *borstal* (lower case) has come to mean that kind of essentially remedial and educational institution, wherever located.

bos (boss), n., v.t., v.i. (sl.)   **miss; bum guess; bum shot**

Bos-eyed is slang for *cockeyed.*

41

bother, n. (col.)   **trouble; row (dispute)**

A *spot of bother* in England is a *bit of trouble* in America, although serious trouble as well can, with British understatement, be lightly referred to as a *spot of bother.* In context a *bother* can mean a *row* (fight or dispute).

bottom, n.   **foot (end)**

In such phrases as *bottom of the garden; bottom of the street,* etc., in the same way that an English street has a *top* rather than a *head.*

bottom drawer   **hope chest**

boundary, *see* **city boundary; town boundary**

bounder, *see* **cad**

bovver boots   **n.A.e.**

It is at least to be hoped that there is no American equivalent. These are offensive weapons consisting of horrible, heavy, metal-tipped boots for kicking which are worn by **skinheads** (q.v.) who travel in gangs looking for a fight. The usual police remedy is to take away the laces, which makes the boots too loose on the feet for effective kicking. *Bovver* is apparently a corruption of **bother** (q.v.), meaning *trouble* in the sense of *looking for trouble*—that kind of trouble. The *v* sound for *th* is the usual cockney pronunciation that sounds like a speech impediment. *Bovver,* in turn, is sometimes recorrupted to *bovvy.*

Bow Bells   **n.A.e.**

The *bells of Bow Church,* also called St. *Mary-le-Bow,* in the center of London. The church got its name from the *bows* (arches) of its steeple and has nothing to do with Bow Street, famed in English detective stories as the address of the principal London Police Court. *Within the sound of Bow Bells* means *in the City of London (see* **City**). One is said to be a true **cockney** (q.v.) if one is born *within the sound of Bow Bells.*

bowler, n.   (1) **derby (hat)**
                                                  (2) **pitcher (cricket; app.)**

(1) Also called in England a *billycock*. Designed in 1850 by a
Mr. Bowler for (the story goes) Mr. William Coke, who
somehow became Mr. Billy Cock.

(2) *Bowler* has an entirely distinct meaning in cricket. The
bowler (from the verb *bowl*) has approximately the same
relationship to cricket as the *pitcher* to baseball.

bowler-hatted (sl.)   **demobilized**

To be *bowler-hatted* is the same as to *get one's bowler,* a
bowler, of course, being the equivalent of a *derby* and thus a
hallmark of civilian attire. The English also use the expression
be demobbed.

bowls, n. pl.   **outdoor bowling game**

A *bowl* (in the singular) in sports is a wooden ball not exactly
spherical, or eccentrically weighted if spherical, so that it can be
made to curve when rolling. Related to *boccie, boules, pétanca*
(or *pétanque*), etc., but the bowling-greens of England are as
meticulously maintained as the putting greens at the best golf
clubs.

box, n.   **intersection area**

Box, or *junction box,* is an English traffic term meaning the
square or rectangular area of a street intersection (*crossroads*).
One sees traffic signs reading "Do not enter *box* until your exit is
clear"—a very good idea indeed—don't start crossing at an intersection and get stuck in the middle, thus blocking traffic coming at right angles.

box, n. (sl.), *see* **goggle-box**

Boxing Day   **first weekday after
                                                  Christmas**

A legal holiday in England, December 26, unless Christmas falls
on a Saturday, in which event, December 27. This is the day on

which Christmas gifts of money are traditionally given to the family's regular delivery men, such as the milkman, postman (mailman), dustman (garbage man), and if you live in the country, baker's boy, grocer's boy, newspaper boy, and if you still have one, gardener, and other miscellaneous roundsmen (*see* **roundsman**). Christmas gifts of this type are called *Christmas-boxes*, although they are given in money and nowadays have nothing whatever to do with boxes. This type of gift seems to have acquired its misleading name from the practice, in the old days, of the recipients' arrival at the door holding out *boxes*. The Christmas gifts to friends and relations given on or before Christmas Day, usually in boxes, are called *Christmas presents*.

box-room, n.   **storage room**

The room in your house for odds and ends, whether they are packed in boxes or not. *See also* **lumber room.**

box-up, n. (sl.)   **mix-up**

Like landing in the wrong seats at the theater and being made to move.

boy, *see* **head boy; old boy; pot-boy; wide boy**

braces, n.   **suspenders**

The American equivalent, *suspenders,* is used in England as the equivalent of American *garters.*

Bradshaw, n.   **national passenger train timetable** (app.)

Short for *Bradshaw's Railroad Guide,* originally published by George Bradshaw in 1839.

brake-van, n.   **caboose**

Railroad term, more commonly called *guard's van.* The American equivalent (*caboose*) is used in England to mean the *kitchen on the deck of a ship.*

bramble, n., v.i.   **blackberry**

To go *brambling* is to go *blackberry picking.*

brandy-butter, n.   **hard sauce**

brandy snap   **n.A.e.**

A type of cookie made according to a special recipe containing a good deal of **golden syrup** (q.v.). Flat and thin or rolled with a cream filler. Delicious and fattening.

brash, n.   **hedge clippings**

Or dry twigs, or both. A rustic term.

brass, n. (sl.)   **dough (money)**

It also has the slang meaning of *cheek* (effrontery) as in America.

brassed off (sl.)   **teed off**

Synonymous with *browned off; cheesed off.*

brass plate, n.   **shingle**

To *put up* your *brass plate* in England is to *hang out* your *shingle* in America.

brazing lamp   **blowtorch**

bread bin   **bread box**

break, n.   **recess**

School term. *Break* is used in both countries to mean a *temporary suspension of activities* generally. *Recess* usually refers to Parliament in England, and the term is not used to mean the daily pause at school.

break a journey at . . .   **stop off at . . .**

breakdown gang   **wrecking crew**

break one's duck, *see* **duck** (1)

break up, v.i.   **end; be over**

School term. "We *break up* on the 26th July" would be said
in England. "School is *over* on July 26th" would be the American equivalent. The *breaking-up* day is the *last* day of school.

breast-pin, n.   **stickpin**

Synonymous with *tiepin*.

breathalyser, n.   **alcohol detector**

A device used by the police to determine whether a driver has
been drinking. The suspect blows into the device. A positive
chemical reaction causes color changes and the license is suspended.

breve, n.   **double whole note**

In the past the British have shown a fine disregard for symme-
try by turning their backs on the metric system. This trend is being reversed, a development which has not brought unalloyed
joy to Anglophiles jealous of tradition. In musical notation the
British have gone even further and rejected common fractions,
as will be seen in the following table of equivalent terms in
everyday use in the respective countries:

English	*American*
breve	double whole note
semibreve	whole note
minim	half note
crotchet	quarter note
quaver	eighth note
semiquaver	sixteenth note
demi-semiquaver	thirty-second note
hemi-demi-semiquaver	sixty-fourth note

The *semibreve* is the longest note in common use. How a *half note*, which is a pretty long note, got the name of *minim* is a great mystery to many people, especially since another (non-musical) English meaning of *minim* is *creature of minimum size or significance,* and its non-musical American meanings have to do with aspects of minuteness. The answer is that at one time it was the shortest note in use. *Crotchet* is another funny one: its everyday meaning outside of musical circles is *whimsy* or *ca-price,* and *crochety* is used in both countries for *cranky* or *grumpy.* There is nothing particularly whimsical, capricious, cranky, crochety, or grumpy about a *quarter note. Quaver* is used in music in both countries to indicate a *trill,* and one can see a connection between *trilling* and *eighth notes.* The greatest mystery of all, to which no solution is herewith submitted, is the connection between *breve,* which is, of course, derived from *brevis* (Latin for *brief*) and a *double whole note,* a note no longer used in musical notation, which is the equivalent in length of *two whole notes,* which makes it anything in the world but brief.

brew-up, n. (col.)   **cup of tea**

No equivalent American colloquialism.

brick wall (col.)   **stone wall**

That up against which it is frustrating to be.

bridewell, n.   **jail**

From St. Bride's Well, in London, an early prison.

bridge coat   **velvet jacket** (app.)

An old-fashioned garment no longer in common use. A long-sleeved velvet jacket, usually black, donned by women for bridge in the evening. Nowadays they play bridge in anything they happen to be wearing, including bikinis. Perhaps the feminine equivalent of another vanishing garment—the *smoking jacket* (also of velvet, most often maroon).

47

brief, n.   **instructions to trial lawyer**

In America a *brief* is a written outline submitted to the court in the course of litigation. In England it is the *solicitor's instructions to the* **barrister** (q.v.). A *briefless* barrister is an *unemployed* one. *See also* **solicitor.**

bright, adj. (col.)   (1) **well**
                                                          (2) **nice**

(1) When asked how he feels, an Englishman might say, "I'm not too *bright*," where an American would use the expressions "not too *well*," or "not *up to snuff*."
(2) When an Englishman says, "It's not very *bright*, is it?" looking up at the sky, he means that it isn't very *nice out*.

bright periods   **fair with occasional showers**

Synonymous with *sunny intervals*. A more literal translation might be *rain with brief intermissions*. There is no real equivalent for English weather report terminology because there is no real equivalent for English weather, which is so often of several sorts within minutes (see *Macbeth*, act 1, scene 3). Although English conversation about the weather is voluminous and almost always gloomy, English weather reports literally and figuratively look on the bright side of things.

brill, *see* Introductory Note 12.

brimstone, n.   **sulphur**

Brimstone and treacle has its repellent equivalent in *sulphur and molasses*.

bring off a touch (sl.)   **make a touch**

Bristols, n. pl. (sl.)   **titties**

A truncation of Bristol Cities—London rhyming slang (*see* Introductory Note 13).

broad, n. **river-widening**

Specifically, a lakelike body of water, especially in East Anglia, formed by the widening of a river and then narrowing down again into a river. The most famous group is known as the *Norfolk Broads.*

broadcloth, n. **black woolen cloth**

In America, *broadcloth* is the equivalent of the English term *poplin.* This is the kind of suiting material used for one's Sunday best.

broadsheet, n. **handbill**

Also called *throwaway* in America.

brolly, n. (col.) **bumbershoot**

The English term is used quite seriously; the American word is faintly humorous.

brothel-creepers, n. pl. (sl.) **crepe-soled suede shoes**

brown, n. (sl., col.) (1) **penny**
(2) **covey of game birds**

(1) *Brown* is an old English slang equivalent of *copper,* old American slang for *penny.*
(2) *The brown* is a colloquialism meaning a *flying covey of game birds,* and firing into *the brown* means, literally, aiming at the *covey* instead of choosing a particular bird, and by extension, firing into a *crowd* (any crowd, not just a group of birds).

browned off **teed off**

Synonyms: *brassed off; cheesed off.*

B.S.T. **British Standard Time**

Five hours later than E.S.T. (Eastern Standard Time) most of the year; six hours later between March 19, when the English move into **summer time** (q.v.) and April 30, when the Americans catch up. They move back together in the fall.

bubble and squeak	**leftover greens and potatoes, mixed together and fried**

Recommended.

bubbly, n. (sl.)	champagne

Synonymous with **champers** (q.v.).

buck, n.	**eel trap**

A basket used to trap eels.

bucket, v.i.	**row hard**

A rowing term. In America the same word means to *ride* (a horse) *hard,* or generally to *drive ahead fast* in any conveyance, and in this connection it is usually used in the expression *bucket along.*

buckshee, adj., adv. (sl.)	**for free** (gratis)

A corruption of *baksheesh,* used in the Near East to mean *alms* or *tip.*

budgerigar, n.	**love bird**

Usually abbreviated to *budgie.*

budget, n.	**budget message**

The annual statement of projected national income and expenditures, made by the Chancellor of the Exchequer (counterpart of the Secretary of the Treasury) in the House of Commons. A *mini-budget* is an interim partial statement of the same sort.

buffer, n.   **bumper**

Railroad term; but an automobile *bumper* is a *fender* in England.

buffer, n. (sl.)   **fogy**

Usually *old buffer*.

buffet, n.   **snack bar**

Both countries use *buffet* to mean *sideboard* or *cupboard,* and the Americans use the terms *buffet supper* and *buffet dinner* to describe meals where the guests serve themselves from a buffet. In all these senses Americans approximate the French pronunciation: *boo-fay*. When it means a piece of furniture, the English pronounce it the way it is spelled (in the way it is pronounced in both countries when it means a *blow*). It is the common English name for a *lunch counter* or *snack bar* at railroad stations, and in that case the English use a quasi–Frenchified pronunciation, educated people saying *boo'-fay;* the others *buffy*. In some cases, as at Charing Cross Station in London, the buffet is more than just a counter and is what Americans would call a *cafeteria*. When you are still lucky enough to find a dining car with the word BUFFET painted in large letters on its side, it's always the *buffy-car*.

bug, n.   **bedbug**

Bug is generic in America and is the equivalent of the generic English word **insect** (q.v.).

bugger, v.t. (sl.)   **screw**

Although the two words, in their clinical sense, refer to different sides of the coin, as it were, they are often identical in their figurative applications.

bugger all (sl.)   **not a goddamned thing**

A coarse intensification of **damn all** (q.v.). Joke: A judge asks the convicted murderer whether he has anything to say before sentence is passed. The unfortunate prisoner mumbles *"Bugger all."* Judge turns to the prosecutor and asks, "What did he say?" Prosecutor answers, *"Bugger all,* my lord." Judge says, "That's funny, I was sure he had said something."

bugger off (sl.)   **get the hell out**

Not only slang—extremely coarse. Delicacy prevents the giving of a closer American equivalent.

builder's merchant   **building supply firm**

building society   **savings and loan association**

buller, n. (sl.)   **proctor's assistant**

Buller is short for *bulldog,* which is slang for a *proctor's assistant.* A **proctor** (q.v.) at Oxford or Cambridge is attended by two *bulldogs,* or *bullers,* who do the dirty work.

bum, n. (sl.)   **behind (rear end); derrière**

bumble, n. (col.)   **bureaucrat**

A *bumble* is a minor official puffed up with his own importance. The English use the word pejoratively, as Americans often use *bureaucrat,* to describe pompous officials (often lowly clerks) in love with red tape who delight in obstructing the expedition of what should be simple procedures. Another English name for such a one is *jack-in-office.* Literally, a *bumble* is a mace-bearing ceremonial official at English universities or churches (also known as a *beadle*), who gets all decked out but really serves little purpose. It is not difficult to see how the word has been extended to mean a puffed-up minor official who gets in the way of progress.

bumf (bumph), n. (sl.)   (1) **paperwork**
                                                   (2) **toilet paper**

An abbreviation of *bum-fodder,* which is slang for *toilet paper,* and pejoratively extended to mean dreary paperwork of the kind associated with bureaucracy and red tape.

bum freezer (sl.)   short jacket

bumping-race, *see* **May Week**

bump of direction   sense of direction

bump-start, v.t.   jump-start

I.e., to start a car by getting it to roll and suddenly throwing it into gear.

bump-supper, *see* **May Week**

bun n. (col.)   squirrel

bunches, n. pl.   clearance items

In periodic sales at clothing shops.

bun-fight, n. (col.)   **tea party** (app.)

Sometimes *bun-feast*. There is no equivalent American colloquialism.

bung, *see under* **pimp**

bungalow, n.   one-story house

An American *bungalow* is the equivalent of an English *cottage*.

bungfull (**bung full;** col.)   chock-full

bung-ho!, interj. (col.)   (1) so long!
                                               (2) cheers!

(1) Synonymous with *Cheerio!*
(2) Synonymous with lots of nice words, like *Santé, Salut, Skol, Prosit,* etc., etc., etc.

53

bunk, n., v.i. (sl.)   **take it on the lam; light out**

Alone, as a verb; or as a noun in *do a bunk. Bunk,* in America as
in England, also means a *place to sleep.* In America this use has
the connotation of cramped space, or makeshift sleeping accommodations, and this is the word always used to designate sleeping space on a boat, cramped or not. It is a verb in America, too.
One *bunks* with a buddy as a temporary sleeping accommodation. Another American meaning not shared with England is
that of *humbug,* and an American slang synonym for *bunk* in
this use is *hokum.* In this sense, *bunk* is short for *bunkum,*
which is occasionally seen in England, sometimes spelled *buncombe* after the congressman (said to be one Felix Walker)
from the district including Buncombe County (N. Car.), from
1817 to 1823. There were those who say he was a dull speaker
and when a speech of his caused a heavy exodus from the floor
of the House of Representatives, he told the few who stayed on
that they could go too, because he intended to go on talking for
quite a while, "but he was talking only for Buncombe." He may
have impressed the folks back home, but his main accomplish-
ment seems to have been the creation of a dramatically descriptive synonym for *hot air.*

bunker, v.i.   **refuel**

bunkered, adj. (sl.)   **messed up**

In England one gets *bunkered* in troublesome situations in
which Americans would describe themselves as *messed up* (en-
tangled). This word is derived from the originally Scottish golf
term for *sand trap.*

bureau, n.   **secretary (writing
desk with drawers)**

Piece of furniture. An American *bureau* is the equivalent of an
English *chest of drawers.*

burk, n. (sl.)   **jerk**

burk, v.t. (col.)   **refuse to admit**

An honest man does not *burk* a fact merely to support a thesis.

burn one's boats (col.)   **burn one's bridges**

bursar, n.   **scholarship student**

A *bursar,* as all readers of C. P. Snow would know, is a *college treasurer,* in England as well as in America. It has an additional meaning in England: *scholarship student,* which is synonymous with another English word unfamiliar to Americans, *exhibitioner.* The grant awarded to the *bursar* is called a *bursary;* the one awarded to the *exhibitioner* is called an *exhibition.* A distinction between the two types of grant is that the *exhibition is* awarded for a term of years.

busby, n.   **bearskin** (hat)

busies, n. pl. (sl.)   **cops** (policemen)

busker, n.   **street entertainer**

buttered eggs   **scrambled eggs**

butter-muslin, n.   **cheesecloth**

Also called *muslin.* The references to different dairy products indicate that the material in question originated in both countries in dairy farm use. However, in each country the name is used for this useful product without any conscious reference to happy days at the farm. What the Americans call *muslin* would be called *calico* in England; but *calico* in America means what the English would call a *cheap cotton print.*

buttons, n. pl. (col.)   **bellhop**

by-law (bye-law), n.   **ordinance**

Used in municipal government. *By-laws* in America usually mean corporate by-laws, i.e., the procedural rules and regulations governing a corporation.

byre, n.   **cowshed**

Scottish.

by the way   **incidental**

By the way is used in both countries adverbially as the equivalent of *incidentally*. It's use as a predicate adjectival phrase in England is fairly common; in America very rare.

𝕮 | C

C Three (C 3), adj. (col.)   **unfit; 4F** (app.)

A term of population classification, designating the class composed of the mentally or physically deficient. The technical term has developed the colloquial connotation of *unfit* or even *worthless*. Perhaps the closest equivalent is the current American Selective Service (draft) classification *4F,* which someday may become (col.) or (sl.) in America.

caboose, n.   **kitchen on the deck of a ship**

An American *caboose* is an English *brake-van* or *guard's van*.

cab-rank, n.   **taxi stand**

cad, n.   **boor**

This word really means a *person of low manners*. It is more or less synonymous with *bounder* which implies a person, seemingly prosperous, who is inherently vulgar and has noisy manners. Both these words are thought by Americans to connote low moral character, especially in relations with women. The emphasis in England, however, is on manners rather than morals. The word is as outdated as the social mores a *cad* contravenes.

cad, n. (sl.) — **grind**

Schoolboys' slang.

Caesar, n. (col.) — **Caesarean**

In both countries *operation* or *section* is understood; but the English sometimes use the name of the author of the *Gallic Wars* while the Americans always use the adjective derived from his name. Noun or adjective, it has always seemed a strained device to have the witches' prophecy, on which Macbeth counted so heavily, come true in the case of MacDuff, because this type of operation is by no means untimely in the usual case.

calendar, n. — **catalogue**

In the sense of a *list of courses* offered by a university, together with appropriate regulations and descriptions of the courses, terms, and examination dates.

calendar, station, *see* **station calendar**

calico, n. — **white cotton cloth; muslin**

Calico as used in America would be called a *cheap cotton print* in England. *Muslin* (or *butter-muslin*) in England would be called *cheesecloth* in America.

call, n., v.t., v.i. — **bid**

Bridge term.

call, v.i.   **be in heat**

Of cats; very descriptive.

call after   **name for**

The English *call* their babies *after* favored relatives and national heroes.

call at   **stop at**

Both countries speak of vessels as *calling at* ports. The English occasionally apply the same term to trains. Thus one sees signs in the Charing Cross Railway Station at the gate (barrier) describing a particular train as "Not *calling at* London Bridge."

call-box, n.   **telephone booth**

Also called a *kiosk.*

called to the bar   **admitted to practice**

This phrase applies only to **barristers** (q.v.) and refers to persons who have received a license to practice as barristers. *See also* **Inns of Court.**

caller, n.   **calling party**

A person making a telephone call is referred to as *caller* and is addressed by the operator as *caller.* In America the *caller* would be referred to as the *calling party* and would be addressed by the operator as *sir* or *madam.*

call to order   **rebuke**

When a person violates the rules of parliamentary procedure or otherwise offends decorum at any meeting, the presiding officer *calls him to order.* In America it is the meeting that is *called to order,* and the phrase refers simply to the formal opening of the meeting.

call up   **draft**

Military service term. A *call-up* card is a *draft* card.

C

cami-knickers, n. pl.   **all-in-one ladies' under-
                                   garment with bodice and
                                   wide legs**

Cami is an abbreviation of *camisole.* American informants advise
that this form of undergarment is obsolete. English informants
say the opposite.

camp bed   **cot**

The English also use the word *cot,* but to them it means what
the Americans call a *crib.*

candidature, n.   **candidacy**

cane, n., v.t.   **whip; switch**

When an American uses a *cane,* as a gentleman's accessory, he
is referring to what the English prefer to call a *walking stick.*

cannon, n.   **carom**

Term in billiards.

canterbury, n.   **magazine rack**

Properly speaking, this word means a low stand with light par-
titions, built to hold music portfolios. This original meaning is
borne out by the fact that the genuine old ones are usually decorated with woodwork carved in the form of a lyre. People use
them, lyre or no lyre, most often to hold magazines, newspapers,
and the like; also unpaid bills.

cap, n.   **letter (in athletics)**

Sports term, usually in the expression *win one's cap.* It generally
indicates that one has played for one's county or one's country.
See also **blue** (n.); **international.**

caravan, n.   **trailer**

As an automobile term. It is also used in the more original
romantic sense.

59

cardan shaft   drive shaft

Automobile term.

cardigan, *see* Balaclava

care a ninepin (sl.)   give a damn

Almost always used negatively, like its American equivalent.

caretaker, n.   janitor

Americans use *caretaker* to mean one who looks after property
in the owner's absence. The rare Englishman who still has one
would more generally refer to his *gardener.*

in Carey Street (col.)   flat broke

The High Court of Justice in Bankruptcy (commonly known as
the Bankruptcy Court) used to be located on Carey Street in
London (it is now located around the corner at Victory House,
Kingsway). That is the origin of the peculiar phrase *to be in
Carey Street,* which is usually used to describe the condition of
being flat broke rather than in technical bankruptcy. Might it
be said that one gets to Carey Street via **Queer Street** (q.v.)?
Incidentally, note the preposition *in.* Americans would say *on*
such and such a street rather than *in* it. Whether *in* or *on,*
Carey Street is a bad place to be.

carny, v.t. (col.)   con (wheedle)

The author has no faith in a supposed derivation from *carnival,*
with its attendant atmosphere of barkers and shills wheedling
and conning the poor innocents.

carousel, n.   merry-go-round

This term is also used by Americans, but the English use *merry-
go-round* less often. A rare English synonym is *giddy-go-round;*
the common English one is *roundabout.*

car park   parking lot

carpet, n.   **rug (carpet) of forty sq. ft. or over**

The English distinguish between *carpet* and *rug* on the basis of size: forty sq. ft. or over is a *carpet;* under that size is a *rug.* The American distinction is based on type of manufacture: a *carpet* is machine made; a *rug* handmade (but the distinction gets a little fuzzy in the case of a good machine-made, imitation Persian "rug").

carpet area   **floor space**

carriage, n.   **(1) car; coach**
       (2) freight

(1) In England a railroad *car* or *coach* is called a *carriage; car* means *automobile* and *coach* means *bus.*
(2) *Carriage* means *freight* in the sense of the *cost of shipping.*

carriage forward   **freight extra**

carriage paid   **freight prepaid**

carriage rug   **lap robe**

carriage, dual, *see* **dual carriageway**

carrier, n.   **express company**

Carrier, in America, can mean any company engaged in the business of carrying freight. It appears in the American expression *common carrier,* meaning such a company whose services are available to the public. The Americans also use it to mean an *insurance company,* by itself or in the expression *insurance carrier. Carrier* is a business term generally in America, where the layman who simply wants to send something somewhere other than by parcel post would get in touch with an *express company* rather than a *carrier.*

carry-cot, n.   **portable bassinet**

carry on   (1) **keep going**
                                                (2) **flirt**
                                                (3) **fuss**

(1) In the giving of road directions, *carry on* seems to mean
keep going straight ahead. Carry on at times means little
more than *O.K.* and once in a while seems to mean nothing
more or less than *so long.*
(2) A rather old-fashioned use.
(3) Can be used as a noun meaning a *fuss.*

carry one's bat (col.)   **stick it out**

To *carry, carry out* or *bring out one's bat* is to outlast the others,
to *stick it out* and finally *put it over* or *bring it off.* Literally, referring to cricket, it describes the batsman who is not put out
and leaves at the end of his innings carrying his bat out with him
instead of leaving it for the next batsman, as apparently used
to occur in the old days. In this affluent society, each player has
his own bat, so that a batsman would walk off the pitch today
carrying his own bat whether or not he was out; but the symbolism of this colloquial phrase lingers on.

carry the can (sl.)   (1) **do the dirty work**
                                                (2) **be the fall guy**

In both meanings the phrase is often lengthened to *carry the can
back.* The *can* in the phrase is said to be the one containing the
dynamite used in blasting operations.

carve-up, n. (col.)   **melon** (**bonanza**)

The English have made a noun of the verb that expresses that
which is usually done to a figurative *melon.*

case, n.   **set**

For example, an English shop advertises a *case* of dessert
spoons, where an American store would speak of a *set,* even
though they came in a case.

cashier, n.   **teller**

Banking term. The English do not use *teller* to mean the man or woman behind the bank counter who handles your money.

casket, n.   **small box**

A *casket* in America means a *coffin.* It never has this meaning in England (*see The Merchant of Venice,* act 2, scene 7).

cast, v.t.   **discard**

Special military term applied to superannuated cavalry horses. Unhappily they are usually slaughtered for horsemeat at a **knacker's yard** (q.v.) rather than sent to pasture.

castor sugar   **finely granulated sugar**

Castor sugar is more finely grained than American *granulated sugar* but not powdery like American powdered or confectioner's sugar, which is called *icing sugar* in England. The equivalent in America is called "Verifine," which is manufactured primarily for iced drinks, cereals, and fruit desserts. Also spelled *caster.*

casual labourer   **transient or occasional laborer**

This term refers to workers like stevedores who show up for work but may or may not get any that day. A rather awkward recent term in this connection is the word *decasualization,* which means the putting of such workers on a permanent footing, with a guaranteed weekly wage. Occasionally, one sees *casual* used by itself as a substantive, meaning *casual labourer.*

casual ward   **flop house**

Synonymous with **doss house** (q.v.).

cat, n. (col.) **whipping**

Undoubtedly a reference to *cat-o'-nine-tails;* rarer as a practice than as a word, but there are still those who advocate "bring back the *cat*," i.e., reintroduce corporal punishment.

catapult, n. **slingshot**

The English also use this word as the Americans do, as both noun and verb.

cat burglar (col.) **second-story man**

catch a packet, *see* **packet**

catch hold of the wrong end of the stick (col.) **miss the point**

Sometimes *get* instead of *catch.*

catch out, v.t. **catch (in a mistake);
detect**

An Englishman will *catch you out* if you commit a solecism. He will also *catch out* a solecism. The Americans omit the *out.*

catch up, v.t. **catch up with**

The Englishman *catches you up* while an American *catches up with you.*

caterer, n. **restaurateur**

The *catering trade* is the *restaurant business.* In America, the term *catering* is confined to the preparation and bringing of food to a home and serving it there, for instance at a wedding, or at some public place for a special occasion. The term *caterer* is broader in England, including the more restricted American sense, and would normally be understood as *restaurateur.*

cat-lap, n. (sl.) **dishwater**

Dull people, novels, or movies would never be likened to *cat-lap.* The term is reserved for weak tea and similar outrages.

catmint, n.   **catnip**

cat's-eyes, n. pl. (col.)   **surface road reflectors**

Reflector studs, set at close intervals into road surfaces along the white lines marking the lanes. Enormously helpful on foggy nights! They are mounted in depressible rubber frames so that they can be driven over without harm to car or them. Strongly recommended for adoption on American country roads. A *cat's-eye,* literally, is an *opalescent gem* in both countries, but in addition it is American children's slang for certain types of multicolored playing marbles.

cat's-meat, n.   **cat food**

cattleman, n.   **cowherd**

A *cattleman* in America is a *rancher* or *cattle owner.* In England, he works for somebody else.

caucus, n.   **political party committee**

A standing political organization, usually elected in England, which formulates party policy, election strategy, and the like. A *caucus* in America is an *ad hoc* political meeting of party regulars.

cause-list, n.   **trial calendar**

Legal term.

cave!, interj. (sl.)   **cheezit!**

Schoolboy slang. Pronounced as though spelled *cavey.* This is the second person singular imperative of the Latin verb *caveo.* This imperative form may be familiar from reproductions of the well-preserved Pompeian floor mosaic showing the picture of a dog and bearing the legend *Cave canem* (*Beware of the dog*). To *keep cave* is to *keep watch, act as lookout.*

cease-line, n.   **disconnected number**

A telephone term.

centenary, n.   **centennial**

Both terms are used in both countries, the above being the preferred usages. Both pronounce *centennial* the same way; but
centenary is accented on the first syllable and has a short *e* in
the second syllable in America; whereas it is accented on the
second syllable, which has a long *e,* in England.

centillion, *see under* **billion**

centre strip   **median divider**

Also called *centre reservation* or *central reservation,* appella-
tions which are as pompous as *median divider. See also* **dual
carriageway.**

century, n. (col.)   **100 runs**

In a cricket game, the batsman who makes 100 runs scores a
century.

cert, n. (sl.)   **sure thing**

Short for *certainty.*

certified, adj. (col.)   **insane**

A past participle used as an adjective, both literally and hyper-
bolically like its American equivalent. An echo is heard in the
American phrase *certifiable lunatic.*

C.H., *see* **Birthday Honours**

chair, n.   **track spike**

Railroad term.

chairman (of a company), n.   **president** (of a corporation)

This usage reflects differences in forms of business organization in the two countries. The Americans do not speak of the *Chairman* of a company or corporation. They speak of the *Chairman of the Board*, meaning the Chairman of the Board of Directors. Such a *Chairman* is not, strictly speaking, a corporate officer. He runs meetings of the Board of Directors but has only one vote on the Board, and often the term implies more honor than power. Thus, an American corporate *President* is often said to have been kicked upstairs when he becomes *Chairman of the Board.* In an English company, the *Chairman* is the equivalent of the *President* of an American corporation. *See also* **managing director.**

chambermaid, n.   **hotel maid**

Not a domestic, as in America.

chambers, n. pl.   **lawyer's office**

The solicitor will invite you to his *office;* a barrister more often to his *chambers.* An American lawyer would never speak of his *chambers,* but that term is applied to a judge's private office (usually adjoining his courtroom).

champers, n. (sl.)   **champagne**

Americans may be more familiar with the other English slang for this patrician beverage: *bubbly.*

champion, adj. (col.)   **fine**

Champion is used adjectivally in America in sports terminology, as for instance, *champion* boxer, *champion* golfer. In England it is occasionally used as the equivalent of *fine* or *great* in the American sense. Thus: "Alf is a *champion* lad!" In the north country *champion!* is used as an exclamation of approval or agreement.

chance-child, n.   **love child**

The English term seems harsh beside the romantic American term. Both countries use the unfeeling term *illegitimate child.*

chancellor, n.   **honorary university head**

University term. *See also* **vice-chancellor.**

Chancellor of the Exchequer   **Secretary of the Treasury**

change, n. (col.)   **rise**

"You won't get much change out of somebody" means "You won't get much of a *response*" (or *reaction*) out of him."

change down   **down-shift**

An automobile term. The English also use the term *change up,* where the Americans would say *shift,* a term which in America is always understood to mean *shifting up,* i.e., shifting into higher gear.

chant, v.t. (sl.)   **tout**

To *sing the praises of,* with a strong implication of fraudulent misrepresentation, and usually seen in the phrase *to chant a horse,* i.e., to push the sale of a defective one, concealing bad points like foul temper or poor vision.

chap, n.   **guy; fellow**

The use of the word *chap* seems affected to most Americans. Its commonest equivalent in America is *guy,* which is slang and seems even a little vulgar. In England a *guy,* literally, is a *person of grotesque appearance,* a *fright,* a word derived from Guy Fawkes, an English traitor whose unsuccessful attempt to blow up the king and Parliament on November 5, 1605, is celebrated by the English on that date each year with bonfires and includes the burning of a grotesque effigy of Fawkes. **Guy** (q.v.) has other English meanings as well. Americans also use *fellow,* a colloquialism, which is less inelegant than *guy* (as opposed to *per-*

son, for instance), but still seems to come off as somewhat deprecatory.

chapel, adj. (col.)   **non-Anglican**

Chapel is a colloquial adjective (usually in the predicate and sometimes mildly pejorative, or at least snobbish) to describe a person adhering to a Protestant sect other than the established Church, i.e., the Church of England (also known as the Anglican Church). It is a shortening of *chapel-folk* or *chapelgoer,* both of which are colloquial labels for members of such sects. The standard English nouns for such a person are *dissenter* and *nonconformist,* which are interchangeable and sometimes capitalized.

chap-fallen, adj.   **dejected**

Chap is here a variant of *chop,* meaning *jaw* (as in, e.g., *lick* one's *chops*). *Chap-fallen* describes a person whose jaws are hanging, i.e., who is in low spirits. Rare.

chapman, n.   **peddler**

Like the itinerant merchant it describes, the word is rarely met with nowadays. Synonymous with *peddler,* which the English spell *pedlar.* They hawked chapbooks, little pamphlets containing street cries, short tales, tracts, and ballads, many of which are now common nursery rhymes (such as the ones about the old woman who lived in a shoe and the baby on the treetop).

char, n. (col.)   **cleaning woman**

This word is displeasing to the ladies whom it describes. It is also used in the combinations *charwoman* and *charlady.* The latter is minimally acceptable to these ladies, who generally prefer to be called *daily help,* **daily woman** (q.v.), or just *daily,* No precise colloquial equivalent in America.

char, n. (sl.)   **tea**

Englishmen love their tea and even the most cultured of them will affectionately offer it to you in the mildly humorous phrase *a cuppa char*. Sometimes the *char* is omitted in this connection and *cuppa* is used alone. No slang American counterpart.

char-a-banc, n.   **excursion bus**

A term rarely heard today but occasionally seen in old travel books. When used, it is pronounced *sharabang*. Now referred to as a **coach** (q.v.).

chargehand, n.   **foreman**

charge-sheet, n.   **police blotter**

To take a person *in charge* is to *arrest* him.

Charles's Wain   **Big Dipper**

Other English names for the Big Dipper: *the Plough; the Great Bear.*

charley, n. (sl.)   **mess; botch job**

charlie, n. (sl.)   **damned fool**

A derogatory term. For instance, "Some *charlie* has broken my vase!" Or, "I felt a proper *charlie* (i.e., a *real idiot*)!" On occasion, *charlie* can take on the connotation of *patsy* (a scapegoat).

chartered accountant   **certified public accountant**

Almost always referred to in America as *CPA.*

chartered surveyor   **licensed architect**

chat show   **talk show**

Television term.

chat up (sl.)   **hand . . . a line**

In England you *chat up* a person in the attempt to *win him over. Sweet-talk* is another American equivalent.

chaw-bacon, n. (sl.)   **hayseed**

Jaw-bacon is a variant.

cheap, adj.   **reduced (in price)**

In America a lady would express pride in her successful shopping expedition by saying, "The dress was *cheap*," or "I bought it *cheap*." However, she would not want to refer to the object of her shopping triumph as a *cheap* dress. If she wanted a new dress when the sales were on, she would never ask the saleslady to show her a *cheap* dress. She would ask for a *reduced* dress. Thus it can be said that, except as a predicate adjective, *cheap* would be avoided in America as a synonym for *inexpensive* because of a reduction. As an attributive adjective, *cheap* in America connotes *tawdriness* in referring to things and persons and has a special slang connotation of *stinginess* when referring to persons, especially in the expression *cheapskate*. These meanings are secondary in the English usage of *cheap*. Thus *cheap* tickets, as advertised on railroad posters, are *excursion fares,* and a *cheap* frock may be a very nice dress indeed, though inexpensive.

cheap Jack (col.)   **peddler**

cheddar, hard, *see* **hard cheese**

cheek, v.t. (sl.)   **to be cheeky to**

To *cheek* someone is to be impudent or rude to him. Not used as a verb in America.

cheerio!, interj. (sl.)   **so long!**

Perfectly intelligible to Americans but never used by them.

cheese it! (sl.)   **pipe down!**

Rather than *"Look out!, Somebody's coming!"* which Americans mean when they holler *"Cheezit!"*

cheesed off (sl.)   **teed off**

Synonymous with *browned off* and *brassed off.*

cheese off! (sl.)   **get lost!**

cheese-paring, adj., n.   **penny-pinching**

A *cheese-paring* sort of chap is a *stingy one,* and the noun *cheese-paring* describes this sorry attitude toward life. As a plural noun *cheese-parings* means *junk,* odds and ends that ought to be thrown away.

cheesy, adj. (sl.)   **swanky**

Cheesy, which means *stylish* or *chic* in England, means quite the opposite in America—*shoddy* or *shabby.*

Chelsea, adj. (col.)   **Villagey** (app.)

One says of a person, "He's very *Chelsea.*" This connotes *Bohemianism.* An approximation would be *Villagey* in America, referring to Greenwich Village in New York City, which is roughly equivalent in tone to the *Chelsea* district of London.

chemist, dispensing, *see* **dispenser**

chemist's shop   **drugstore** (app.)

The *shop* can be omitted.

cheque, n.   **check**

A matter of spelling. But isn't it peculiar that a *check* (or *cheque*) is a form of *draft,* that *draft* is sometimes spelled *draught,* and that *draughts* is the English form of *checkers?* *See also* **crossed cheque.**

chesterfield, n.   **sofa**

In America a *chesterfield* is a dark overcoat, usually with a velvet collar.

chest of drawers   **bureau; dresser**

In England a *bureau* is a writing desk with drawers of the sort Americans refer to as a *secretary,* and a *dresser* is a *kitchen sideboard with shelves.*

chevy (chivy), v.t.   **keep after**

Also *chivvy.* To *put pressure* on someone; to *hurry* him *up*—in the sense of to *chase* him. Probably there is some connection with *Chevy Chase,* an old ballad, and a place in Maryland.

chewing gum   **gum**

In England *gum* by itself would be taken to mean *mucilage.*

chi-ack, v.t. (sl.)   **give a yell at**

To *chi-ack* is to *hail*—whether the object of the hailing is a friend you know who might be plowing in the next field or a girl you don't know but would like to. Many variant spellings: *chy-ack, chi-ike,* etc.

chicken, n.   **young chicken**

Chicken in America covers any size or age. An old one in England would be called a *fowl* (or a *boiler*), and *chicken yard* in America would be *fowl-run* in England.

chicken-flesh, n.   **goose pimples**

Also *goose-flesh.*

chicory, n.   **endive**

In an English vegetable store (*greengrocer*) if you want endive ask for *chicory* and vice versa!

child-minder, n.   **daytime babysitter**

The connotation is that both parents are working. The term *babysitter,* in England, refers to the evening.

73

ENGLISH	AMERICAN

chip, n.   (1) **wood sliver**
                                             (2) **fruit basket**

(1) The material from which fruit and vegetable baskets are made. *See* **punnet.**
(2) The basket itself.

chip in (col.)   **break in**

In the sense of interrupting somebody else's conversation, a meaning not used in America, where it means to *contribute,* in the way children make up a fund to buy teacher a gift. The English use it that way, too, and also have another phrase for that: to *pay one's whack.*

chippings, loose, *see* **loose chippings**

chips, n. pl.   **French fried potatoes**

One sees *French fried potatoes* on some English menus nowadays, especially in the better places. *See also* **crisps.**

chit, n.   **memo**

The English use it as well in its American meaning of an *I.O.U.,* usually for drink or food at a bar or pub.

chivy, chivvy, *see* **chevy**

choky (**chokey**), n. (sl.)   **poky**

choose how (col.)   **like it or not**

A north of England term.

chop, n., v.t., v.i.   **change** (app.)

A special use of *chop* in the expression *chop and change,* which, used transitively, means to *keep changing* (e.g., to keep trading in your car for a new one). To *chop and change,* used intransitively, means to *shilly-shally. Chops and changes* are *variations.* To *chop about* or *chop round* means to *veer,* like a suddenly

74

shifting wind. To *chop in* is to *break into a conversation* (cf.
chip in), to *put in your two cents' worth,* as it were. To *chop
logic* is to argue for argument's sake. The phrase *chop and
change* appears to have originated from Henry VIII's matrimonial variations, in certain instances of which he had to *chop* before he could *change.*

chops of the Channel (col.)   **passage from the Atlantic
                                               Ocean into the English
                                               Channel**

Christian name   **first name**

Americans also say *Christian name* and *given name* but *first
name* is much more common. *See also* **middle name.**

Christmas-box, *see* **Boxing Day**

Christmas club   **n.A.e.**

Different from the American scheme of the same name; a sort
of special layaway plan. In England one can join a Christmas
club usually during the summer, at a neighborhood butcher
shop or grocery store, accumulating modest periodic deposits
there to lessen the impact of the holiday bills for the turkey and
its trappings.

chucker-out, n. (sl.)   **bouncer**

chuffed, adj. (sl.)   (1) **tickled (delighted)**
                                               (2) **sore (disgruntled)**

This curious bit of army slang has two diametrically opposite
meanings, depending on the context. In case of ambiguity, one
can say *chuffed pink* (*tickled pink*) to mean *pleased,* or *dead
chuffed* to mean *displeased.*

chump, n. (sl.)   **nut**

Chump, like *loaf, nod,* and other words, is a colloquialism for
head, like *bean* in America. "Use your *chump*" is commonly

heard, inviting the party addressed to stop being a fool. To be off one's *chump* is to be off one's *nut*.

chump chop   type of lamb chop

Chump is thought to be a portmanteau word made up of *chunk* and *lump* and literally means a *small lump of wood*. In the food department it designates the thick end of a loin of mutton, hence *chump chop,* meaning a mutton or lamp chop which (as opposed to a loin chop) is mostly meat surrounding a little bit of bone in the middle.

chunnel, n. (col.)   Channel tunnel

A portmanteau word. The Channel in question is, of course, the English one.

cine-camera, n.   movie camera

cinema, n.   movies

This word is giving way to *movies* but is still used in England. In America it has a technical rather than popular connotation.

Cinque Ports   n.A.e.

Pronounced *sink ports,* literally (from Old French via Middle English) *Five Ports* on the southeast coast of England, granted various special privileges as of old. Characteristically, there are seven of them (two were added but the *Cinque* stuck): Dover, Sandwich, Romney, Hythe, Rye, Winchelsea, and Hastings.

cipher, *see* nought

circular road   belt highway

See arterial road; ring road.

circular saw   buzz saw

Circus, n.   **Circle**

Used in cities where Americans would normally use *Circle;* thus
Piccadilly *Circus,* Oxford *Circus,* etc., as opposed to Columbus
Circle in New York.

the City, n.   **financial district;
                                          Wall Street**

The *City* of London is a precise geographical section of London
and is one of several "Cities" (e.g., the *City* of Westmin-
ster) included in the make-up of London. The *City* of London
includes the financial district, and *the City,* as an abbreviation
of the *City of London,* is used in England exactly as *Wall Street*
is used in America. Geographically the *City* is larger than the
London financial district which it includes, whereas *Wall Street*
is only a part of the New York financial district in which it is included. The *City* of London measures one square mile and has
5,000 residents; and the sovereign of Great Britain and Northern Ireland cannot enter it without the lord mayor's permission.
The *City editor* of a London newspaper is what would be called
the financial editor in America; but *city editor,* in America,
means the person in charge of local news. For the general
meaning of *city* apart from this specialized use, *see* **village.**

city boundary   **city limits**

City editor   **financial editor**

See **City.**

civilities, *see* **amenities**

civil servant   **government employee**

The *civil service* is a term familiar to Americans, but in the
author's experience, Americans in the civil service have rather
uncivilly expressed resentment at being quite civilly referred
to as civil servants and prefer to be known as government employees.

clap eyes on   **set eyes on**

class, n.   **grade**

University term. In America, one's *college class* is the *year of graduation.* In England, one's *class at university* is the *place in the honours examinations,* e.g., a *first,* an *upper second* or *lower second* (sometimes called a 2.1 or 2.2.), or a *third. Class* is understood.

clean, v.t.   **shine**

Referring to shoes.

clearing bank   **commercial bank**

clear majority   **majority**

In English voting terminology, *majority* means what in America is called a *plurality.* To indicate an arithmetical majority, i.e., more than 50 percent, the English use the term *clear majority.*

clearway, n.   **freeway**

cleg, n.   **horsefly**

Mainly Scottish.

clerk, n.   (1) **lawyer's assistant**
                                                      (2) **church officer**
                                                      (3) **town officer**
                                                      (4) **office or store**
                                                          worker

Pronounced *clark* in England. This word originally meant *clergyman* in England, but that meaning is now archaic.

(1) It is commonly used by English solicitors (lawyers) to describe their *assistants,* and *law clerk* is a term not unknown in America.

(2) It signifies the job of a lay person who renders miscellaneous services to a parish church.

(3) An official, usually a lawyer, in charge of town records who acts generally as the business representative of a town.

(4) *Bank clerks, shop clerks,* and the like, are *general office workers* who keep books, do filing, and take care of miscellaneous office functions. A *clerkess* (rarely used) is a *female clerk,* just as a *manageress* (e.g., of a restaurant or a pet shop) is a *female manager.* Americans often denote the sex of such disparate groups as actors, sculptors, Negroes, and Jews with *-ess,* a practice much decried by feminists, but they stop short of *clerkess* and *manageress. Clerk* in America is also an intransitive verb, meaning *work as a clerk. See also* **assistant.**

clerk of the works   supply man; maintenance man

This title describes a person who acts as overseer of supplies and building materials for a contractor; it also covers the position of one in charge of repairs and maintenance, such as outside painting and sidewalk repair, for instance, of a municipal housing unit (*council house estate*).

clinking, adj. (sl.)   damned good

Thus, a *clinking* game, a *clinking* race, etc. But it can also be used adverbially modifying *good:* a *clinking* good game, a *clinking* good race.

clippie, n. (col.)   bus conductress

In England there are bus conductors of both sexes. A male conductor is simply a *conductor;* a female *conductor* is a *clippie.* Both male and female bus conductors used to *clip* your ticket, i.e., *punch* your ticket, but only the lady conductors are called *clippies.* The word came into being during wartime when they replaced the men.

cloakroom, n.   washroom

Both terms are euphemisms for *toilet,* but beware: Following a *cloakroom* sign in a public place in England may lead you to another destination, because it is also used literally in that country. The English term *cloakroom ticket* has nothing to do with

79

permission to leave the room. All it means is *baggage* or *hat check*.

clobber, n. (sl.)   get-up

This word means *attire* and is generally used when there is something peculiar about the attire, as for example, "He appeared in the strangest *clobber*," or "He had borrowed somebody else's *clobber*."

close, adj.   closed

The English speak of the *close season* in game shooting rather than the *closed season*.

close, n.   dead-end residential area

The English are very fond of addresses involving the words *crescent, gardens, terrace, mews, close, pavement, parade, vale, grove,* and the like. They stick more or less to the facts in things like *crescent,* but streets miles removed from the humblest buttercup ruthlessly cling to epithets like *gardens.* Sometimes they really go to town and name streets "The Garth," "The Dell," and "The (almost anything else)." *Avenue* is common in America, and once in a while the Americans indulge in *square, circle,* or *drive,* more rarely *boulevard,* very rarely *mews,* and there is a street in Hartford, Conn., known as *American Row,* but on the whole they are more prosaic in their designations—to say nothing of their soulless practice of assigning numbers and letters, rather than names, to their streets and avenues. A *close* is a kind of *cul-de-sac* broadened out at its end.

close-crop, n.   crew cut

Despite the prevailing trend, some English young men still fancy the *close-crop.*

closet, n.   toilet bowl

A euphemism. *Water closet* is old-fashioned English for *lavatory.* *Closet* (*see* **pedestal**) is the polite term seen in house-furnishing catalogues for the bowl itself. Never tell a guest in England to hang his clothes in the *closet*. The correct term would be *cupboard*.

clot, n. (sl.)   **jerk**

A strong pejorative. "She is suffering from marital thrombosis," quipped the doctor. "She's got a *clot* for a husband." Mild British humor.

cloth, washing-up, *see* **tea towel; washing-up cloth**

clothes-peg, n.   **clothespin**

clothes-prop, n.   **clothespole**

clotted cream, *see* **Devonshire cream**

club together, v.i.   **join up; pool**

Englishmen *club together* to buy a going-away gift for a friend or a memento for a retiring colleague.

clue, n.   **notion**

"I haven't a *clue*" is a very common colloquial expression in England, meaning "I haven't the *slightest idea.*" Americans sometimes omit the word *idea,* in the same repulsive way in which they omit the *day* or *time* in the expression *Have a happy!*

clueless, adj. (col.)   **hopeless**

Describing someone who doesn't know what it's all about or which end is up.

clutch, n. (col.)   **bunch**

Clutch, in addition to its other uses as noun and verb, means a *set of eggs,* or a *brood of chickens.* Reflecting the usual untidiness and noisiness of the latter and the disagreeable social institution known as the *pecking order, clutch* is used in the term a *clutch of friends* to indicate the type of swarm of followers that might surround a movie star or other celebrity.

clutter, n. **junk**

Clutter literally means *litter* or any untidy miscellany in both countries. But whereas an American might say, "Our weekend guests arrived with an awful lot of *junk*," an Englishman would probably describe them as having brought along a great deal of *clutter*.

coach, n. **bus**

See also **carriage** (1); **motor coach.**

coalfish, n. **black cod**

Also called *coley fillet* and *saithe*.

coarse, adj. **common**

A special meaning applied to fish: *coarse* fish would exclude salmon and trout and other sporting fish caught with a fly. *Coarse* fish are run-of-the-mill items like cod, flounder, and such.

cob, n. **wall material**

A mixture of clay, gravel, and straw.

cock, n. (sl.) **bull**

I.e., stuff and nonsense. We've all heard of *cock and bull* stories. The English have chosen the *cock*, the Americans the *bull*.

cock-a-hoop, adj. (sl.) **on top of the world**

cock a snook (sl.) **thumb one's nose**

Sometimes *cock snooks*.

cockerel, n. (1) **young rooster**
(2) **young tough**

(1) Americans, too, use this word occasionally to mean a *young rooster*.
(2) It has the colloquial English meaning of a *young tough*.

cockney, n., adj. (col.)   **native of London**

Also used adjectivally meaning, literally, *characteristic of a born Londoner.* A cockney accent is not considered to be one of the more socially acceptable ways to pronounce English. But those possessing such an accent are often very proud of it. *See also* **Bow Bells.** Understandably, no American colloquial equivalent.

cock-up, n. (sl.)   **mess; muddle**

"You've never seen such a *cock-up* in your life!" (The bank robbers got away and the police arrested the bank manager by mistake.) *See also* discussion under **balls** (2).

codswallop, n. (sl.)   **baloney**

I.e., hot air.

coffee-stall, n.   **street coffee stand**

Similar to the genus hot dog wagon, or chestnut stand, as seen on the streets of America.

coiner, n. (col.)   **counterfeiter**

coley fillet, *see* **coalfish**

collar stud   **collar button**

collar-work, *see* **against the collar**

collections, n. pl.   **mid-years**

Mid-year examinations at Oxford, Cambridge, and Durham universities.

college, n.   **school; house (dormitory)**

This word, which in American educational terminology always denotes an institution of higher learning and is roughly synonymous with *university,* does not necessarily mean the same thing in England. Thus, King's College and Lansing College are what the English call *public schools,* roughly equivalent to what

Americans call *prep schools,* and City of London College is a secretarial school. On the other hand, Balliol and Corpus Christi, for example, which are Oxford *colleges,* are more or less autonomous institutions forming part of Oxford University, specializing in certain departments, each with its own *house* in the American *college dormitory* sense. The *college* in this sense is residence, foster parent, and spiritual home rather than teacher, which is the function of the faculty. For an excellent discussion of Oxford Colleges, their historical origin and present constitution, see Muriel Beadle, *These Ruins Are Inhabited* (Doubleday & Co., Inc., New York, 1961, p. 77 *ff.*). The phrase *college graduate* would not be used in England. The person would be called a *university man* or *woman.* If the word *graduate* were used as a noun, it would mean *college graduate* in the American sense (*see* **graduate**).

college grounds   campus

An American might speak of *college grounds,* but an Englishman would not understand *campus* in this sense. A Harvard man never speaks of his *campus*—it is always the *Harvard Yard. Yard,* in this context, would be incomprehensible to an Englishman.

college of further education   extension school (app.)

For persons who have left school and wish to continue their general education or learn a trade.

colleger, n.   campus Etonian (app.)

One of the 70 (out of 1,100) Eton students who live *in college* (i.e., *on the campus; see* **college**). The others are **oppidans** (q.v.).

Collins, n. (col.)   bread-and-butter letter

Synonymous with *roofer.* See *Pride and Prejudice,* chap. 23.

ENGLISH   AMERICAN

colt, n. (col.)   (1) **rookie**
                                             (2) **junior varsity
                                                 player** (app.)

(1) In professional cricket, a player in his first season.
(2) At school it can refer to a boy who is a member of any jun-
    ior team, not necessarily cricket.

coloured, adj.   **non-white** (app.)

Colored in America signifies Negro, whether of African or West
Indian origin. In England the term includes Indians, Pakistanis,
and persons of mixed parentage.

combe, *see* **coomb**

combinations, n. pl.   **union suit**

Referring to underwear. *Union suits* are on the way out in
America. *Combinations* are dying out more slowly in England.
Combs (short *o*; the *b* is pronounced) is a colloquial abbrevia-
tion.

comb-out, n.   **intensive search**

Sometimes the Americans use the term *comb* or *combing*.

combs, *see* **combinations**

come, v.t. (sl.)   **act**

To *come* the hero or the bereaved spouse is to *act* the part, to
put it on.

come a heavy over (sl.)   **high-hat**

Also *come the heavy over*.

come a mucker, *see* **mucker**

come a purler (sl.)   **fall on one's face**

Like the American equivalent, used both literally and figuratively. Thus it might apply not only to the physical act of stumbling but also to a business or theatrical fiasco or the messing up of plans for a picnic.

comeback, n. (col.)   **oomph**

A person who does not have much *comeback* is one who does not have much *on the ball,* i.e., is dull and not very good company.

come-day-go-day, adj. (col.)   **shiftless**

Too easygoing, apathetic; a drifter. It sometimes has the additional connotation of carelessness about money—*easy come, easy go.*

come down (col.)   **graduate**

This is a university term. To *come down* is to *graduate;* unless it is used in the expression *come down for the summer vacation.* A vacation from work, generally, is called a *holiday* in England; but in university life, holidays at Christmas, Easter, and Whitsun, and the summer hiatus are known as *vacations,* and the same is true of the Law Court calendar. The long university summer vacation is known as the *long vac.* (Incidentally, *Whitsun,* itself a shortening of *Whit Sunday,* is usually shortened to *Whit* and means the seventh Sunday after Easter, and *Whit Monday* means the Monday after that and is itself a regular holiday in England.) *Come down* means the same thing as *go down* and the choice of phrase depends on the vantage point of the speaker: if you are at the university you talk of *going down;* the student's parents, however, would talk to their friends and relations about John's *coming down.* It depends on the position of the speaker in relation to the university. *Come down* and *go down* are not to be confused with *send down,* also a university term, meaning *expel.* No colloquial American counterpart.

come expensive (col.)

come to a lot of money

To *cost too much*.

come over, v.i. (col.)

go (**become**)

Used in expressions like "I was so astounded I *came over* numb."

comether on, *see* **put the comether on . . .**

come to the horses (sl.)

get down to brass tacks

come to the wrong shop, *see* **shop**

comforter, n.

(1) **baby nipple; pacifier**
(2) **woolen scarf**

Two distinct meanings, as opposed to the American meaning of *comforter,* which is *quilt*. The English usually call a quilt an *eiderdown,* even though the filling is not always made of the soft feathers of the female eider.

coming, adv.

going on

Used adverbially in expressions of age: "Mary is *coming* seventeen."

commem, n. (col.)

n.A.e.

Abbreviation of *commemoration,* an annual celebration at universities in commemoration of founders. Seen in the expression *commem ball,* a dance celebrating the event.

commercial traveller

traveling salesman

In the proper context *traveller* by itself is understood in this sense. Incidental intelligence: The 16,000 members of the United Kingdom Commercial Travellers Benefit Society recently voted to change their name to the British Benefit Society for Representatives and Agents, after a moving valedictory by the retiring chairman. He justified the change on the alleged popular belief that a "commercial traveller" was a dirty old man.

commission agent   **bookmaker**

A lofty euphemism. *See also* **turf accountant.**

commissionaire, n.   **doorman**

Commissionaire is rarely used in America and is a rather old-fashioned word meaning *doorman* or other type of attendant in a hotel or other public place. In England, *commissionaires,* usually doormen but sometimes also messengers and other types of clerk, are normally pensioned military men.

commissioner for Oaths   **notary public**

commode, n.   **chamber pot holder**

This noun, in America, usually means a *chest of drawers.* It has the secondary meaning there, rarely used, of a chest or box holding the chamber pot. In England, it signifies the container of this homely commodity, usually in the form of a chest or chair.

Common Entrance Examinations   **prep school entrance exams**

Prep school in the American definition is what the English call **public school** (q.v.). *Common Entrance Examinations,* though national in scope, are not prepared by a government agency but rather by a private body organized by the *public schools* (in the English sense) of England. The same entrance examinations are given to all candidates for the schools, but each public school has its own requirements as to the grades achieved in these examinations.

company, n.   **corporation**

Business term. **Corporation** (q.v.) in England is used in the sense of a municipality, i.e., a *municipal corporation.* Sometimes called *limited liability company* or **limited company** (q.v.). An American *company* need not be incorporated; it can be a partnership or even a sole proprietorship.

compensation, n.   **damages**

In America, *compensation* includes not only the meaning of *damages* but also more generally, that of *emolument* or *payment,* whether salary or fee. In England *compensation* is not used except to indicate *restitution* or *damages,* i.e., being made whole after suffering physical injury or any other kind of loss.

compère, n.   **master of ceremonies; emcee**

completion, n.   **title closing**

Term used in real-estate transactions.

compositor, n.   **typesetter**

comprehensive school, *see* **eleven plus.**

compulsory purchase   **condemnation**

A legal term, meaning the forcible sale to a public authority of property for public use, pursuant to the right of eminent domain.

conchy, n. (sl.)   **conscientious objector**

confectioner, n.   **candy store**

Synonymous with *sweet shop.*

confidence trick   **confidence game**

conjuror, n.   **magician**

conker, n. (sl.)   **rubber**

No American slang equivalent. A term applying exclusively to the game of darts, which is standard equipment at every proper English pub. When the game score is one-all, if there's time (and there always is) somebody says, "Let's play the *conker,*" meaning the *rubber.*

conkers, n. pl. game with horse chestnuts

Each boy has a string of horse chestnuts and tries to break the other boy's chestnuts. Scoring rules appear to vary regionally.

conservancy, n. river or port commission

For example, the Thames Conservancy.

conservatoire, n. conservatory (music school)

Conservatory, in England, would usually mean a *greenhouse,* but it can also be used to mean a *music school.*

consignment note bill of lading

Railroad term.

consols, n. pl. n.A.e.

Abbreviation of *consolidated annuities,* government securities of Great Britain which were consolidated in 1751 into a 3 percent stock. There are now both 2½ percent and 4 percent *consols* which sell at heavy discounts that vary with fluctuations in prevailing interest rates.

constable, n. patrolman

A *chief constable* would be known in America as a *chief of police.* A *constable* is also a *policeman* and is the usual form of address to a policeman below the rank of sergeant. Constables addressed by Americans as *officer* find that practice quaint.

constituency, n. district

A *Parliamentary constituency* is roughly equivalent in English politics to a *Congressional district* in America.

construe, n. construction

Used as a noun, it means an exercise in syntactical analysis, as in the teacher's warning: "Next Tuesday, we'll have a *construe* of an *unseen* (a passage for sight translation)."

consultant, n.   **specialist (medical)**

contango, n.   **delayed acceptance penalty**

A London Stock Exchange term. It consists of a percentage of the selling price payable by the purchaser of shares for the privilege of postponing acceptance of their delivery. *See* **backwardation.**

convenience, n.   **rest room**

A masterpiece of understatement for one of life's prime necessities! A *public convenience* is a *comfort station*—a battle of euphemisms.

coo!, interj. (sl.)   **gee!**

cook, v.t. (sl.)   **juggle**

To *cook* records or accounts is to *tamper* or *fiddle* with them. In England naughty people *cook the books*. In America this reprehensible practice is known as *juggling the books*.

cooked, adj. (sl.)   **baked**

Especially after sitting in the sun.

cooker, n.   **stove**

Cooker is the normal English word for *stove*. An Englishman would hardly ever say *electric stove*, but *gas stove* is heard. The generic term for this kitchen appliance in England is, however, *cooker*.

cookery book   **cook book**

coomb (combe), n.   **hillside valley**

A *coomb* is a valley on the side of a hill, usually a short one, running up from the sea on a coastline.

cop, *see* **not much cop**

coper, n.   **horse trader**

Also seen in the form *horse-coper*.

copper, *see* **bobby; brown**

copperplate printing   **engraving**

As on stationery, calling cards, and so on.

copse, n., v.t.   **wood (wooded area)**

This is a shortening of *coppice*, a noun shared with America. As a verb it means to *cover* (an area) *with woods*.

cor!, interj. (sl.)   **gee!**

corf, n.   **creel**

After you catch a fish in England, you keep it alive in a *corf* submerged in water.

corn, n.   **grain**

The American term *corn* has its equivalent in the English word *maize,* but more and more the English use the term *sweet corn,* though it is hard to grow in England and is usually found in cans. The English term *corn* is as generic as the American term *grain,* and an English *corn factor* is an American *grain broker;* but *corn-flour* in England is *cornstarch* in America.

corn, n. (sl.)   **dough (money)**

corned beef   **canned pressed beef**

What the Americans call *corned beef* is known as **salt beef** (q.v.) in England.

Corner, n. (sl.)   **Tattersall's betting
                                        rooms**

The Corner is slang for the betting establishment, known as Tattersall's, which was originally located near Hyde Park Corner.

corner-boy, n. (sl.)   **tough**

cornet, n.   **cone**

Special meaning in conjunction with ice cream.

corn factor, *see* **corn,** n.

corn-flour, *see* **corn,** n.   **cornstarch**

---

corporation, n.   **municipality**

The American *corporation* has its equivalent in the English **company** (q.v.). The English *corporation* is understood to be a *municipal corporation.* Thus, a *corporation swimming-bath* would be a *municipal* or *public swimming pool* in America, a *corporation car park* would be a *municipal parking lot,* etc. A sign reading *Corporation of Greenock Cleansing Department* means *Greenock Sanitation Department.*

corridor, n.   **aisle**

Referring to railroad cars. *See also* **aisle.**

corrie, n.   **mountainside hollow**

Scottish.

cos, n.   **romaine**

A type of lettuce.

cosh, n., v.t. (sl.)   **blackjack**

A *cosh* is a *blackjack.* To be *coshed* is to be *hit on the head,* whether with a blackjack or some other unpleasant weapon. *Coshed* would find its American equivalent in *beaned.*

coster, n.   **fruit and vegetable**
        pushcart vendor

Short for *costermonger.* His cart is known in England as a *trolley* or a *barrow. See also* **pearlies.**

costings, n. pl.   **costs**

A business term used in arriving at the price to be charged for a product.

cost the earth, *see* **pay the earth**

costume, n.   **lady's suit**

This is somewhat old-fashioned but still frequently heard, especially in dry cleaning establishments. With most Englishmen, *suits* applies to both sexes. Unisex?

costume, bathing, *see* **bathing costume; swimming costume**

cot, n.   **crib**

cotton, n.   **thread**

In the sense of *sewing thread.* And cotton is not wound on *spools* in England but on *reels.*

cotton wool   **absorbent cotton**

For a metaphorical use, *see* **live in cotton wool.**

coul, *see* **cowl**

council, n. (col.)   **town**

Literally, a local administrative body of a village, town, rural district, city, county, etc. But it is used, particularly in the country, exactly as Americans use *town,* in the sense that it is the *council* to which you apply when there is a problem about schools, sewage, roads, and that sort of thing.

council house   **municipal or public housing unit**

So-called because the government agency regulating housing is known as a *council,* whether *parish council, county council,* or other. The rent in *council houses* is extremely low. In America, municipal housing is often referred to as *low-income hous-ing* or *middle-income housing*. A multi-family unit of this sort in America is called, generically, a *public housing project*. The equivalent in England would be a *council house estate* or *council housing estate*.

councillor, n.   **councilman**

A member of a *council* (e.g., a parish council, rural district council, county council, the Greater London Council—local administrative bodies) is a *councillor*. A member of the New York City *Council* is a *councilman*.

council school   **public school**

The *council school* in England is the government-operated facility which Americans call *public school*. *Public schools* in England are what Americans call *prep schools* or *private schools*.

counsel, *see* **barrister**

counterfoil, n.   **stub**

Referring to checks and checkbooks.

counter-jumper, n. (sl.)   **sales person**

No American slang for this.

country round   **day's route**

Referring to a delivery route (*see* **roundsman**) or round of professional visits.

county, adj., n. (col.)   **quality** (app.)

This word has no exact equivalent in America. It has the connotation of good breeding and activity in local affairs like riding to hounds and opening flower shows. Such a person is *county,* and it is hard to say whether *county* in such case is an adjective or a noun.

courgettes, n. pl.   **zucchini**

Courge is French for gourd or squash. *Courgettes* is the diminutive.

court card   **picture card; face card**

Referring to playing cards.

court of inquiry   **fact-finding board**

court shoes   **pumps**

cove, n. (sl.)   **guy; fellow**

cover, n.   **coverage**

An insurance term, indicating the aggregate risks covered by a particular policy.

covered goods-waggon   **boxcar**

Railroad term.

cowl (coul), n.   **water tub**

This type of water tub usually has two handles and is carried by two men on a heavy stick called a *cowl-staff*.

cracker, n.   **snapper**

The kind served at children's parties.

crackers, adj. (sl.)   **cracked; nuts**

Predicate adjective only.

cracking, adj. (sl.)   **full of pep**

Also expanded to *in cracking form,* but now considered rather old-fashioned.

ENGLISH   AMERICAN

crash repairs   **body work**

Sign on establishments where one gets one's car repaired after the accident which was of course the other fellow's fault.

crawl, v.i. (col.)   **cruise**

Of taxis.

crazy pavement, *see* **pavement**

cream, clotted, *see* **Devonshire cream**

creamed potatoes   **mashed potatoes**

cream tea   **afternoon tea**

The cream is **Devonshire cream** (q.v.), which is rich, sweet, delicious, thicker than American whipped cream, and is meant to be piled on top of the jam on top of the scones, creating in all likelihood a dish with more calories than any other substance known to man.

crease, n.   **foul line** (app.)

As a sports term, the crease is the line behind which a player must stand in the game of **bowls** (q.v.), as well as the line which defines the position of both bowler and batsman in cricket.

creased, adj. (sl.)   **tuckered out**

create, v.i. (sl.)   **explode**

Describing the antics of a testy individual who is provoked in the extreme. It would seem to be short for *create a scene*.

crèche, n.   **nursery**

Used occasionally in America to describe the traditional nativity scene.

credit slip   **deposit slip**

A banking term.

creek, n.   **inlet**

Same word, different meanings: In England a *creek* usually means an *inlet* on a seacoast, or a *small harbor*. Its secondary English meaning is the same as its principal American meaning: a *small stream,* or *minor river tributary.*

crib, n. (sl.)   **pony; trot**

A translation used by students in violation of school rules. This word is sometimes used in America. *Pony* and *trot* do not appear in this connotation in England. *Crib,* the American word for a child's bed, is *cot* in England, except in connection with the Infant Jesus.

cricket, n.   **n.A.e.**

England's national sport, with vital social overtones and symbolism. Thus, *not cricket* means *unfair* or *ungentlemanly,* and "*It isn't cricket*" must be familiar to millions outside England who haven't the slightest acquaintance with the game, so that the very word *cricket* has built into it the strongest implication of fair play.

crickey!, interj. (sl.)   **good heavens!**

crinkle-crankle, adj. (col.)   **winding**

A precious, or at least rare, adjective used to describe serpentine red brick garden walls, full of twists and turns. If this sounds Miltonian, you are probably thinking of quips and cranks and possibly even of wanton wiles. There are fifty-eight *crinkle-crankle* walls in the County of Suffolk and only twenty-eight in all the rest of England. *Crinkle-crankle* is a colloquial variant of *crinkum-crankum,* which describes anything (not only walls) full of twists and turns and is sometimes used by itself as a substantive.

crisps, n. pl.   **potato chips**

Crisps (short for *potato crisps*) are called *potato chips* in America. The English shorten *potato crisps* to *crisps;* Americans never shorten *potato chips* to *chips.* The English term **chips** (q.v.) means *French fried potatoes* in America. The Americans often shorten *French fried potatoes* to *French fries.*

crock, n. (col.)   **wreck**

Often used in the expression a *bit of a crock,* meaning a *chronically ailing person,* not necessarily a hypochondriac. To *crock up* is English slang for *break down* and *crocked* means *broken down,* i.e., *disabled,* rather than *drunk,* which is its special American slang meaning. The Old Crocks' Race from London to Brighton is for vintage cars.

crocodile, n. (col.)   **line of schoolchildren**

Always led or followed (or both) by a teacher or teachers.

croft, n.   **small landholding**

A *crofter* is one who rents a *croft.* Mostly Scottish.

cross bench   **n.A.e.**

The *bench,* in the House of Lords, occupied by independent members who vote with neither the government nor the opposition.

crossed cheque   **n.A.e.**

Cheque means bank check. A *crossed cheque* is so-called because the check is *crossed* by two vertical or oblique lines in the middle of the check, forming a column, or slanted space, within which the mysterious, nay meaningless words *& Co.* are printed at the top, and within which the drawer of the check may write additional instructions, such as the name of the bank through which the check must be paid (i.e., the name of the payee's bank if he knows it—this as a safety measure only, and rarely resorted to). Such a check cannot be cashed; it must either be deposited in the payee's bank or endorsed to a third party and deposited in the endorsee's bank. On English checks the line for the payee's name reads "Pay . . . or order," not "Pay to the order of. . . ." *See also* **cheque.**

crossroads, n.   **intersection**

This word is used in America to mean the *intersection* of roads, but is more apt to be used figuratively in the sense of a dilemma urgently requiring decision. It would not be used in America referring to a street *intersection* in a city, and in the country Americans would use *intersection,* or, in deep rural areas, *four corners.*

cross-talk comedians   **comedy team**

crotchet, n.   **quarter note**

Musical term. *See under* **breve.**

Crocodile

crown, n.   **five shillings**

But there was no crown coin or bill in general circulation even before the recent decimalization of the currency, which also eliminated shillings. From time to time the British mint did strike off commemorative crowns (e.g., the recent Churchill crown) which though legal tender were cherished rather than rendered. *See* Introductory Note 18.

crow to pick (col.)   **bone to pick**

I.e., a disagreeable subject to bring up. The English pick bones as well.

crumpet, n. (sl.)   (1) **toasted English
                                                       muffin** (app.)
                                                  (2) **nut** (**head**)
                                                  (3) **dish** (**babe**)

(1) There are no *English muffins* in England, toasted or otherwise. In England the *muffin* is a light, flat, round, spongy cake which is toasted and buttered. In America a *muffin* is a quick bread made of batter, baked in a cup-shaped pan, which does not have to be toasted. The nearest thing to an English *crumpet* is what Americans call an *English muffin*. It is a small individual flat soft yeast mixture cake which is toasted on a griddle. *Crumpet* is an American noun which technically means the same thing, but anyone seeking crumpets in an American restaurant or bakery must go hungry indefinitely.

(2) As English slang, a *crumpet* means a *head*, for which American slang affords us *nut, bean, noodle,* and goodness knows what else. It is used in England especially in *barmy on the crumpet,* meaning *crazy in the head.*

(3) A *nice bit of crumpet* is English slang for *quite a dish,* i.e., a dazzling woman (at least in the beholder's eye).

cubby, n.   **glove compartment**

An automobile term usually expanded to *cubbyhole. Cubby-*

hole in America is a general term, not confined to automobiles, and means any little nook where one stuffs things.

Crumpet

cuckoo pint (col.)   **jack-in-the-pulpit**

cuffuffle, n. (sl.)   **dither**

Another English slang word for the same state of agitation is *flap. See also* **gefuffle.**

cul-de-sac, n.   **dead-end street**

Cul-de-sac and *blind road* are English terms for what in America would be called a *dead-end street,* at the entrance of which there is often (but by no means always) considerately placed a sign saying *Dead-End Street* or *No Through Road.*

cully, n. (sl.)   **dope (fool)**

This word sometimes appears to have the alternative meaning *pal.*

cupboard, n.   **closet**

cupboard love (col.)   **sucking up**

Describes the activity of a person trying to curry favor, with the strong implication of insincerity and self gain.

cuppa, n. (sl.)   `cup of tea`

See **char** (n.[sl.]). No American slang equivalent.

curate's assistant (col.)   **cake stand**

Having three tiers and very useful at teatime.

curate's egg (col.)   **something both good and bad**

This curious phrase originated from a *Punch* cartoon that appeared in 1895. A humble curate is breakfasting with his bishop, overawed by the very presence of that dignitary, and the caption reads:
> "I'm afraid you've got a bad egg, Mr. Jones."
> "Oh, no, my Lord, I assure you! Parts of it are excellent!"

And so, although the original egg was all bad, and it was only the poor curate's brilliant feat of diplomacy that imparted any virtue at all to it, a *curate's egg* came into the language to mean something *good in parts* (but defective in others); anything with its good points and its bad.

curlies, n. pl. (sl.)   **short hairs**

To have someone by the *short and curlies* is to have him at a considerable disadvantage.

103

curly, adj. (sl.) **gruesome**

A brutal murder might be spoken of as *curly*. A faint reflection of this use may be found in the following American usage: "It would make your hair *curl*."

custom, n. **business**

Commonly used in England where Americans would say *business* or *customers,* as in: "A good-looking store front will attract *custom*."

cut along (col.) **run along**

cut away! (sl.) **beat it!**

cutlet, n. **chop**

Butcher's term.

cut one's lucky (sl.) **take a powder**

cutting, n. **clipping**

Meaning *newspaper clipping*. One resorts to a *cutting service* in England, in America to a *clipping bureau*. Sometimes the sense is clarified by amplifying the term to *press cutting*, and *press cutting agency* is synonymous with *cutting service*.

𝔇 D

dab, n. (col.) **whiz**

Seen in the expression *to be a dab at,* meaning to be especially versed in something. Sometimes lengthened to *dab hand*.

dabbly, adj. (sl.)   wet

A *dabbly* summer is one with frequent rain. Most people think that *dabble* is used only in the expression *to dabble in,* i.e., *engage in superficially,* as to *dabble* in the market or in a hobby. But its primary meaning is to *moisten intermittently*—hence a *dabbly* summer.

daily woman (col.)   cleaning woman

Often shortened to just *daily.* Sometimes *daily help. See also* **char** (n. [col.]).

dame, n.   n.A.e.

A woman who is knighted becomes a *dame.* Judith Anderson is now *Dame Judith,* just as Robert Helpmann is now *Sir Robert. Dame* is a title conferred, not inherited, and is never coupled with the surname, like *Lady,* which may be. *Lady Jane* would be the daughter of a duke or marquess; *Lady Smith* would be the wife of the knighted Mr. Smith.

damn all (sl.)   not a damned thing

This expression is in fairly wide use and would not be considered improper in normal company, even mixed. In the same circumstances Americans might hesitate to say *not a damned thing.* The English expression would be used, for example, by a person looking for a coin to buy a ticket for the underground and finding his pocket empty. He would look at his companion and say, "I've got *damn all.*"

damp course   insulating layer

A *damp course* or *damp-proof course* is a layer of tarred felt, slate, etc., placed above the house foundation to prevent deterioration in the walls of a building by reason of rising moisture, a troublesome phenomenon usually called *rising damp* in England.

dampers, n. pl.　　　　　　　　　　　　　**flat cakes**

Made of flour and water, usually by Boy Scouts, and not recommended for gourmets. *Damper* is used as well in the various senses in which it is used in America in connection with fireplaces, pianos, etc., and figuratively in the sense of a *wet blanket*.

damp squib (col.)　　　　　　　　　　　　　**dud**

Something that fizzles, like a joke or a plan.

Darby and Joan　　　　　　　　　**devoted old couple**

This sentimental nickname for any loving couple of advanced years is supposed to have originated from an allusion in a poem which appeared in 1735 in a publication called *Gentleman's Magazine*. Membership in Darby and Joan Clubs all over England is open to those whom Americans so tactfully call *Senior Citizens* and *Golden Agers*.

darning mushroom　　　　　　　　　　**darning ball**

dashed, adv. (sl.)　　　　　　　　　　　　**damned**

Somewhat milder than *damned* in expressions like *dashed good, dashed bad,* and the like. Also heard in: "Well, I'm *dashed!*" where Americans would say, "Well, I'll be *damned!*"

dataller, n.　　　　　　　　　　　　　**day worker**

Also spelled, and always pronounced, *day-taler.*

daughter concern　　　　　　　　　　　**subsidiary**

A company owned by another company. The family relationship of the subsidiary is recognized in the American expression *parent company,* but the Americans keep the sex of the subsidiary a secret.

davenport, n.　　　　　　　　　　　　**writing table; escritoire**

In America this word means a *sofa.*

daylight robbery (col.)   **highway robbery**

Figure of speech, like *holdup,* meaning an exorbitant price or fee.

day return, *see* **return**

day sister, *see* **sister**

day tripper, *see* **tripper**

dead-alive, adj. (col.)   **dead (more dead than alive)**

Sometimes *dead-and-alive.*

dead keen on, *see* **mad on**

dead set at, *see* **make a dead set at**

dead stock   **farm equipment and machinery**

The term *dead stock* is occasionally used to mean *unemployed capital* or *unsaleable merchandise.* However, it has a special use in connection with the sale of country property. One sees signs advertising an auction of such and such a farm property some-times with *livestock* (which means the same thing in both coun-tries) and sometimes including *dead stock.* After suffering con-siderable depression from the image of deceased cows, sheep, and pigs, the writer inquired of professional auctioneers and was advised that *dead stock* meant *farm equipment.* In its usual sense the word *dead* implies that the subject has previously been alive; as used in this expression *dead* means merely *in-animate.* Undoubtedly, the phrase came about as an echo of the common term *livestock.*

dead to the wide, *see* **to the wide**

deals, n. pl.   **lumber**

Lumber, in England, means *discarded furniture,* not pieces of wood for building. The English call those *timber. Deals* is now

ENGLISH   AMERICAN

used usually to designate fir planks of up to three inches in thickness.

debag, v.t. (sl.)   **cut down to size**

Literally, *debag* means to pull somebody's pants off, *bag* being slang for *pants,* or as the English say, *trousers.* Figuratively, it means to *deflate* him.

decasualization, *see* **casual labourer**

decillion, *see under* **billion**

decoke, v.t.   **decarbonize**

To *do a carbon job* on your car.

decorate, v.t.   **paint**

In context, *decorating* a room or a house means *painting* it, and *house painters* are sometimes referred to as *decorators.* In this sense, the word has nothing to do with *decoration* in its general sense, or with interior decorating. If the occupant prefers wallpaper, *decorate* could include *papering.*

deed-poll, n.   **unilateral deed**

A legal term describing a document signed by a single party. *Poll* is an old verb meaning to *cut evenly,* as for instance, the edge of a sheet. A *deed-poll* is written on a *polled* sheet, one that is cut evenly and not indented. The common use of a *deed-poll* nowadays is as a document by virtue of which one changes one's name. It has to be advertised in the *London Gazette.* Thus, a lady who wants to live as the wife of a man who happens to be married to another lady who won't give him a divorce can execute a *deed-poll,* by virtue of which she changes her last name to his: a very convenient arrangement especially when it comes to registering the birth of a child born to such a union, since both parents would now bear the same surname and the registration would cause no fluttering of eyelids.

degree day   commencement

This is a university term and has nothing to do with weather measurements, as in America. A *degree day*, in America, is a unit of variation from a given point in average outdoor temperature for one day, used in computing heating fuel requirements.

degree of frost   degrees below 32°F.

In America, *20°F* is *20° above zero,* or simply *20 above,* or even more simply, *20.* In England, 20°F is announced as *12° of frost.* Formula: $X°$ of frost in England $= (32 - X)°$ above 0 in America. To the consternation of most Englishmen, in the current drive to Europeanize and therefore decimalize all units of measurement, weather reports on TV and radio and in the newspapers usually state temperatures in centigrade alone, or along with Fahrenheit, and the *degree of frost* idiom will one day disappear.

dekko, n. (sl.)   gander (glance)

demanding money with menaces   extortion

A criminal offense.

demarcation dispute   jurisdictional dispute

Between unions, or between different departments in a company.

demi-semiquaver, n.   thirty-second note

Musical term. *See under* breve.

demob, v.t. (col.)   discharge

A military term. *See* bowler-hatted.

demonstrator, n.   laboratory assistant

dene, n.   sandy stretch by the sea

denominational school	parochial school

departmental store	department store

An example of the English tendency to lengthen (or is it the American tendency to shorten?) the first of the two words in a compound noun. *See* Introductory Note 10.

derby duck (col.)	dead duck

An old-fashioned colloquialism.

de-restricted road	road without speed limit

Until recently there were no speed limits on English country roads. Now the government has imposed an overall speed limit of 70 m.p.h. However, as one approaches a city, town, or village there are signs reading "30" or "40" restricting the driver to those limits while passing through those areas. Once beyond the geographical limits, you find another sign to the effect that all bets are off and a road becomes *de-restricted,* which means that you are now at liberty to kill yourself, your passengers and anyone else who gets in your way.

dessert, n.	fruit course at end of meal

In England *dessert* is a fresh fruit course (sometimes also nuts and/or trifling sweetmeats) served at the end of a meal either after, or in place of, what the English call a **sweet** (q.v.). English *dessert* can be any fresh fruit. *Dessert* in America is a generic term meaning the last course of the meal whether it consists of fruit, pudding, ice cream, or anything of that ilk. (It is well to bear in mind that the plural form *sweets* is the English term for *candy*.) In spite of the aforementioned restricted use of *dessert* in England, the English use *dessert plates, dessert knives, dessert forks,* and *dessert spoons* to designate the implements involved in the eating of a *sweet*. Very confusing. To make matters just a little bit worse, *dessert spoon* has, in addition, the special technical meaning of a certain unit of measure in recipes, whatever they involve, whether dessert, sweet, or a stew!

detached house, *see* semi-detached; terrace

detain, v.t.   keep

Used commonly about people *kept* in the hospital after an accident, as opposed to those whose injuries were superficial. In America you would be *kept in the hospital;* in England you would be *detained in hospital* (no article).

developer, n.   real-estate developer

This term, by itself, would normally mean a *photographic developer* in America. Used by itself, in England, it describes a person engaged in the purchase of land and the erection of buildings on it. It sometimes appears in the phrase *property developer.*

development area   area suffering from temporary or intermittent severe unemployment

devil, n., v.i.   (1) law apprentice (2) literary hack

Americans may be familiar with the old-fashioned term *printer's devil* meaning *printer's errand boy* or *junior apprentice.* In England *devil* has the additional meanings of (1) *assistant to junior legal counsel* in the **chambers** (q.v.) of a **leader** (q.v.) and (2) *hack,* or *ghostwriter. To devil* is to act in either of these lowly capacities, often underpaid in the literary field, and not only unpaid, but a privilege usually paid for, in the legal.

devil on horseback   prune wrapped in bacon

One of many different types of **savoury** (q.v.), served on a small piece of toast.

devilry, n.   deviltry

Devonshire cream   **clotted cream**

Clotted cream is made by scalding milk and skimming off what rises to the top. For one of its delicious applications, *see* **cream tea**.

dhobied, adj. (col.)   **washed**

From *dhobi,* meaning an Indian laundry man.

dibs, n. (sl.)   **dough (money)**

dicey, adj. (sl.)   **touch and go**

A term based on the figurative aspect of the throw of the dice. Applied to the weather in the perennial English problem of whether or not to plan a picnic, and similar games of chance. A somewhat less common English slang equivalent is **dodgy** (q.v.).

dickey, n. (col., sl.)   **rumble seat**

This was the familiar name in the old days for the servant's seat in the rear of a carriage. Sometimes spelled *dickie*.

dicky, adj. (sl.)   **shaky (queasy)**

diddle, v.t. (sl.)   **do**

In the sense of *fleece* or *gouge,* i.e., to *do* somebody out of something.

digs, n. pl. (col.)   **place (rooms; lodging)**

Short for *diggings*. An Englishman speaks of his *digs* in the way an American speaks of his *place,* or, these days, his *pad*.

dim, adj. (col.)   **thick; thickheaded**

Short for *dim-witted*. *See* **as dim as a Toc H lamp.**

dingle, n.   **dell**

Sometimes combined as *dingle-dell.* Usually a deep hollow, shaded with trees.

dinky, adj. (col.)   **cute; cunning**

This word is the equivalent of the American term *cute* or *cunning* in the sense of *sweet* or *adorable,* not in the sense of *sly.* The word *dinky* in America has the pejorative meaning of *ramshackle* and is more or less synonymous with the American slang term *cheesy* which, however, in England means *swanky!* See how careful one must be?

dinner jacket   **tuxedo**

Americans say *dinner jacket* too, but *tuxedo* is unknown in England.

diplomatist, n.   **diplomat**

Both forms are found in both countries, but preferred usages are as indicated.

director, n.   **executive** (app.)

To the Englishman-in-the-street, *director* means about the same thing (in the context of business epithets) as *executive* would mean to an American layman. Directorships in English companies and American corporations (*see* **chairman; company; managing director**) amount roughly to the same thing, although their duties and prerogatives (as a matter of law) and their day to day functions (as a matter of practice) differ in some respects in the two systems. In both countries important personages are frequently elected to membership on boards of directors as window-dressing and don't participate actively in the affairs of the company. But the general connotation of *director* in England is that of an *operating executive* whose American opposite would be the company's vice-president-in-charge-of-something-or-other. Thus, it is common practice for smaller

English companies to list their directors, by name, on their stationery. This is unheard of in America.

directory enquiries, *see* **enquiries**

dish, n.   **serving dish; platter**

Although both countries use *dishes* generically, *dish* in England
usually has the narrower meaning of *serving dish,* and *platter*
is considered archaic. *Dish-clout* (sometimes *dishcloth*) is the
English equivalent of *dish rag* or *dish mop.*

dish, v.t. (col.)   **stump**

This verb is used, especially in politics, to mean *outmaneuver.*
Dished would have its equivalent in the American word
stumped, a word derived from the verb *to stump,* a technical
term in cricket describing one of the ways a batsman is put out.
But *stump up* is English slang for *pay up,* or *come across,* and has
nothing to do with cricket.

dish-clout   **dish rag; dish mop**

dish-washer, *see* **wash up**

dishy, adj. (sl.)   **sexy**

Like its American counterpart, usually applied to women, but
also to inanimate objects like sports cars.

dismal Jimmy (sl.)   **gloomy Gus; calamity
                                                          howler**

dismissal with disgrace   **dishonorable
                                                          discharge**

A term applied to noncommissioned soldiers and sailors alike. A
naval officer would be *dismissed with ignominy,* an army officer
cashiered.

dispenser, n.   pharmacist

In America a *dispenser* usually means a container which feeds out some substance in convenient units, or a *vending machine.* The English use the word *dispenser* that way, too, but primarily it means in England what Americans would call a *pharmacist,* a person in the profession of making up medical prescriptions. *Dispensing Chemist* is a sign commonly seen on the store front of an English drugstore (*chemist's shop*).

dissenter, n.   non-Church of England

A member of a Protestant sect which has split off from the established Church, i.e., the Church of England. *See also* **chapel.**

distemper, n., v.t.   paint with a size base

In both countries, this word has the totally unrelated meaning of a common and fatal disease of cats and dogs. In America as well as England it can also be used to mean *painting with a size base* (rather than an oil base); but this is a most uncommon American use, while it is its most common meaning in England.

divan, n.   sofa; couch

Divan is not nearly so frequent in America as in England, whereas it is preferred to *sofa* in England, and *couch* is rarely used in this connection by the English.

diversion, n.   detour

A traffic term. All too frequently one sees a road sign reading *Diversion* leading one away from the main road and only sometimes back onto it. Much more of a nuisance than a diversion in the usual sense.

divi (divvy), n. (sl.)   dividend

Short for *dividend,* especially that distributed periodically by cooperative societies.

division, n.

(1) **area represented by a Member of Parliament**
(2) **degree of severity of punishment**
(3) **voting line-up**

(1) Corresponds to *Congressional District* (*see* **constituency; member**).
(2) A term used in sentencing convicted criminals. Preceded by *first, second,* or *third,* it means *lenient, medium,* or *severe* treatment in prison, as prescribed by the sentencing judge.
(3) The *division* of the Members of Parliament into two sides for vote-counting. Hence, *division bell,* the *warning bell* in the home or office of a Member of Parliament which rings to let him know that his vote is required in the House of Commons.

division bell, *see* **division** (3)

divvy, *see* **divi**

D-Notice **press publication restriction** (app.)

Notice given by the *"D-Notices Committee"* (made up of representatives of government and press) to newspapers requiring them to omit mention of material that might endanger national defense. The *D* stands for *defense.*

do, n. (sl.) **fast one** (swindle)

do, v.t. **handle**

In America a shop does or doesn't *have, sell, keep* or (sometimes) *make* a particular item. The English often substitute *do* in those cases. A stationer may *do* daily newspapers but not the Sunday edition. An upholsterer may *do* hangings but not slipcovers (which he would call *loose covers*). A certain restaurant will be recommended because, though their soups are indifferent, they *do* a good mixed grill.

do . . . brown (sl.)   **take . . . in**

I.e., to *fool* someone, to *pull the wool over his eyes.*

dock, n.   **basin**

The English use *dock* to mean the water between what Americans call *docks* and the English call *wharves.* But note the expression *dry dock* which means the same thing in both countries.

docker, n.   **longshoreman**

docket, n.   **judgment roll**

In English legal parlance a *docket* is a register in which judgments are entered, but the term can be narrowed in meaning to an *entry* in such a register. In American legal idiom *docket,* sometimes called *court docket,* means *the list of cases* ready for trial.

dock yard, n.   **navy yard**

doctor, v.t.   **castrate**

Applied to animals of both sexes. The English also use the verb *neuter.* The Americans prefer *spay* when applied to female pets and *fix* in the case of male pets.

dodge the column (sl.)   **goof off**

To *shirk one's duty.* The English expression, taken from the military, has a somewhat more elegant sound. It is an extension from the original concept of draft-dodging.

dodgy, adj. (sl.)   **touch and go**

Risky; doubtful; uncertain. See **dicey.**

do . . . down (sl.)   **do . . . dirt**

do for (col.)   be (somebody's) house-
                                              keeper or maid

No precise American colloquial equivalent. When an English
housewife tells you that Mrs. Harris *does for* her, she means
that Mrs. Harris is *acting as her housekeeper,* or is what the
English call her *daily help* (*see* **char; daily woman**). Can be
applied also to outside helpers, like gardeners, handymen, and
others performing similar functions.

doggo, *see* **lie doggo**

dog's body n. (sl.)   **prat boy**

This quaint term is English nautical slang. *Dog's body,* in that
idiom, means a *dish of dried peas boiled in a cloth.* For reasons
apparently lost in history, it also means a *junior naval officer.* As
a matter of obvious practical extension, it came to mean *drudge,*
hence an *errand boy* (in the slang sense) or in an even slangier
sense a *prat boy.*

dog's dinner, *see* **like a dog's dinner**

do . . . in the eye, v.t. (sl.)   **do . . . dirt**

To *do somebody in the eye* is to *play him a dirty trick.*

domestic science   **home economics**

The arts of cooking and sewing are dignified by the educational
terminology of both countries.

don, n.   **college teacher** (app.)

A *don* (contraction of *dominus,* Latin for *lord*) is a *teacher,*
whether the *head* (*dean*), a *fellow* (*assistant*), or *tutor* (*advi-
ser*) at a **college** (q.v.), primarily at Oxford and Cambridge,
but also at other old universities like Edinburgh and Durham.
The derivation from *dominus* is clearly seen in *dominie,* which
is Scottish for *schoolmaster* (*dominie* is a corruption of *domine,*
which is the vocative case of *dominus*).

done to the wide, *see* **to the wide**

donkey's years (col.)   **a dog's age**

Both expressions means the same thing, although donkeys live longer than dogs.

donnybrook, n. (col.)   **free-for-all**

See under **Kilkenny cats.**

doom, n.   **painting of the Last Judgment**

A *doom* may also be a sculptural group depicting the Final Day.

DORA, n.   **n.A.e.**

Acronym for *Defence of the Realm Act,* passed in August 1914, giving the government very wide powers during wartime.

dormitory, n.   **(1) multiple bedroom**
     (2) commuting town

In America *dormitory* (usually shortened to *dorm*) designates what the English call a *hall of residence,* i.e., a house in which students live at college. In England, used by itself, but more commonly in the phrase *dormitory town,* it has acquired the special meaning of *commuting town.* Of late, the term *bedroom community,* meaning the same thing, has come into usage in America.

dorothy bag   **tote bag**

doss, have a, *see* **have a doss**

doss house   **flop house**

But a *doss* is not a *flop. Doss* is English slang for a *bed* in what Americans call a *flop house. Doss house* is common to both languages, but it is hardly ever used in America. In English slang, *doss* is also a verb meaning to *sleep in a flop house*, but, less specifically, to *doss down* is to *go to bed*, usually in rough, make-shift circumstances. *See also* **casual ward.**

dot and carry one (col.)   **gimpy**

A lame person who walks with a limp or drags a leg. Seems rather an unfeeling expression, based on the supposed rhythm of one walking with a wooden leg.

dot, off his, *see* **off his dot**

dotty, adj. (sl.)   **loony**

double, adj., n.   (1) **a telephone term**
                                             (2) **double portion**
                                             (3) **heavy, thick**

(1) *Double* and *treble* are used in giving telephone numbers in England. Thus, Belgravia 2211 was Belgravia *double two double one;* Grosvenor 3111 was Grosvenor *three one double one* or *three treble one.* As in America, the telephone companies are terminating named exchanges. Farewell to Belgravia, London Wall, etc., as well as to Butterfield and Murray Hill! At least the English have not yet begun to change Piccadilly and Regent Street to First Avenue, etc.

(2) A wholly different use of *double* is heard in the pub. If you ask for a whiskey (usually spelled without the *e* in England) you get what Americans would consider a smal-lish quantity and the proof is less as well. One English friend who ordered a whiskey at the Savoy was politely asked by the waiter whether he wanted a single or *double.* "Good God, man!" was the reply, "Drinking a single is like talking to yourself!" When you want a decent drink of whiskey (or gin or any other hard liquor—*spirits* in England) you ask for a *double.* Even the thirstiest English-man, however, would never ask for a treble.

(3) And then there's *double* (heavy) and *single* (light) cream.

double-bedded, adj.   **with a double bed**

When you reserve (*book*) a hotel room for two in England the clerk usually asks you whether you want a *double-bedded room* or a *twin-bedded room. Single-bedded room* is used to describe what would be called a *single room* in America.

double bend, *see* **bend**

double blue, *see* **blue** (n.)

double cream   **heavy cream**

Very heavy cream, much thicker and richer than American heavy cream, which is called just plain *cream* in England.

double-glazed, adj.   **equipped with storm windows**

double saucepan   **double boiler**

do . . . up (col.)   **do . . . in**

To *exhaust, wear out:* "The long walk *did us up.*"

do . . . well, v.t. (col.)   **treat . . . right**

In the English phrase "they *do* you *well*" (referring, for example, to one's experience at a little hotel), the *do* is equivalent to *treat* in America, but an American would be more likely to say "they *treat* you *right,*" or "they *do all right by* you," or "they *take good care of* you." To do yourself well means to *look out for* yourself, i.e., to take good care of your own interests.

dowlas, n.   **heavy linen or muslin**

down, adv. (col.)   **from London**

Conversely, *up* means *to London* (*see* **down train**). A person living outside of London might ask his friend, "How often do you *go up?*" and the meaning would be quite clear: "How often do you *go to London?*" *Come up* would be used if they were talking in London. *Go down* and *come down* would be used, depending on the vantage point of the speaker, to mean *go* or *come to the country*, i.e., a point outside of London. *See also* the university use of **come down**. But people living in Scotland or in the north of England may talk of *going down* (i.e., south) to London—to the confusion of southerners and the despair of geographers.

down, n. (col.)   **gripe**

To *have a down on* someone is to *have a gripe against* him, and to nurse your grudge.

down at heel (col.)   **down at the heels**

But the *the* appears in the variant *down in the mouth*. Note singular of *heel*. See Introductory Note 25.

downs, n. pl.   **uplands**

An American asked an Englishman what the *downs* were and the Englishman answered: "The *downs* are the *ups*." They are, and the South Downs are the open rolling hills of southern England, which are usually dotted with cattle and sheep. *Downs* can be *ups* because the word is etymologically related to *dune* and has nothing to do with the direction *down*.

down train (and **up train**)   **train from London**
                                                          (to London)

A train in England goes *up* to London even if it has to travel south (or east or west) to get there; and it goes *down* from London no matter what direction it has to take to leave that fine city. Most people would think that *up* implied northwards and *down* southwards, but Americans confused by English train terminology should remember how confused Englishmen are when they hear Yankees say "Down East," which really means *up north in Maine*. The *up* end of something seems somehow or other to be more important than the *down* end. Since there can be no more important end to an English railway trip than arrival in London (cf. *All roads lead to Rome*), London must be the *up* end, and one therefore takes the *up train* to London no matter where one starts the journey. *Up* and *down* are not mere oral colloquialisms, but appear in printed timetables and are standard terms on station bulletin boards. However, it so happens that civic spirit has sought to apply the same rule to other large cities. Starting out from London, one would take the *down train* to Manchester, and even a Mancunean in London would not think of the train from London as the *up train;* but a patriotic denizen of Manchester might talk of any train leaving Manchester as a *down train.* When far enough away from London, be careful. In the time of Thomas Hardy it was still safe to use these terms in relation to London exclusively. Thus, in *Jude the Obscure,* in discussing a meeting between Jude and Sue on a mythical road in a mythical town in the mythical County of Wessex, arrangements were made for him to meet her "at the Alfredston Road . . . on his way back from Christminster, if she should come by the up-train which crossed his down-train at that station."

downy, adj. (sl.)   **sharp**

A *downy card* is a *smart cookie.*

doyen, n.   **dean**

Indicating the senior member of the group, like the *doyen* of the diplomatic corps, the *doyen* of the London Bar. *Doyen* is rarely used in America; *dean* is sometimes used in England.

dozy (dozey), adj. (sl.)   **dopey**

Indicating slow-wittedness.

drabbit, n.   **a tan, woven linen material**

This material, a type of drab light brown woven or twilled coarse linen, was used in the old-fashioned English field-laborer's smock, a garment seen in old paintings and engravings, which has gone out of style and was known as a *smock-frock.*

drag from the burning (col.)   save by a hair

The way the United States Cavalry does it again, in movies about the old West.

drain, n. (sl.)   nip

Meaning an undersized drink of something.

drain, laugh like a, *see* laugh like a drain

drains, n. pl   plumbing; sewerage system

The *drains* of the house are its *drain pipes,* or *plumbing and sewerage system.* When a real estate advertisement in England uses the term *main drainage,* it means that the house is connected to a public sewer system so that you needn't worry about septic tanks and that sort of thing.

draper's shop   dry goods store

The *shop* can be omitted, and the *draper's* can also mean a *haberdashery,* in the American sense of *men's shop.* But an English **haberdashery** (q.v.) would be called a *notions store* in America.

draughts, n. pl.   checkers

drawing office   drafting room

drawing-pin, n.   thumbtack

drawing-room, n.   living room

Living room is not commonly used in England. *Lounge* is a rather provincial synonym.

draw the long bow (col.)   exaggerate (app.)

There is no exact American equivalent. Usually found in the expression "I'm not *drawing the long bow,*" where Americans might say, "I'm not *kidding*" (*kidding* in the sense of *exaggerating*).

dressed to the nines (col.)   all dolled up

Sometimes *dressed up to the nines*. *To the nines* is an English colloquialism meaning *to perfection*.

dresser, n.   kitchen sideboard with shelves

Americans use *dresser* principally to mean a *bureau* or *dressing table*, usually with a mirror; i.e., an article of furniture that helps you *dress*.

dressing gown   bathrobe; wrapper

In America *dressing gown* means something a little fancier than *bathrobe*. *Bathrobe* is not used in England. There, both men and women wear *dressing gowns*. In America men usually wear *bathrobes*, women *wrappers* or *robes*.

dress show   fashion show

drill, *see* what's the drill?

driver, n.   motorman

English trams (*tramways*) and American trolleys (*trolley cars*) are both practically obsolete, but when they were in common use the man who operated them was known as a *driver* in England and a *motorman* in America. The same distinction exists today with respect to the *underground* or *tube* (English for *subway*). On a bus, however, he is the *driver* in either country. On an English train, he is the *engine driver;* on an American train, the *engineer*.

drive ... up the wall (col.)   drive ... crazy

"He (she) drives me *up the wall*" is commonly used in England to describe neighbors, bosses, teachers, and other annoying specimens.

driving license   driver's license

drop a brick (col.)   make a booboo

    In the special sense of committing a gross indiscretion.

drop a clanger (sl.)   make a gaffe

drop-head, adj., n.   convertible

    Referring to automobiles.

drop off the hooks (sl.)   kick the bucket

dross, n.   scrap coal

    A mining term. A Scottish housewife will buy *dross* to use with
    household coal as an economy measure.

drug, v.i.   take drugs

    The intransitive use is not known in America.

drum, n. (sl.)   pad

    I.e., living quarters. Hippie equivalent of **digs** (q.v.).

drunk in charge   driving while drunk

    The official charge for the offense of *drunken driving*.

dry martini, *see* **martini**

dual carriageway   divided highway

    See also **centre strip.**

dubbin, n.   saddle soap

duck, n. (col.)   (1) **goose egg** (app.)
                         (2) **honey** (app.)

    (1) As a cricket term, to *get a duck* is to *be bowled* (*put out;*
        app.) without scoring a single run. If this happens on the

first ball bowled (*first pitch;* app.), you get a *golden duck.* This type of *duck* is short for *duck's egg. Love* as a term in tennis scoring used in both countries, meaning *nothing* in America (*nil* in England), is a corruption of *l'oeuf,* French for *the egg,* but what kind of egg—goose or duck—is an open question. To be *out for a duck* is the same thing as *getting a duck.* If the match consists of two innings and you fail to score in either inning, i.e., *get a duck* or are *out for a duck* in both innings, you *bag a brace* or *take a brace* or *get* or *make a pair of spectacles.* The moment you make a run in cricket, you *break your duck.* These terms are, of course, technical cricket talk, but they are used figuratively in all kinds of ways, just as Americans borrow expressions like *make a hit* or *couldn't get to first base* from baseball. Thus, to *break your duck* is to *break the ice,* i.e., to make a start.

(2) *Duck* is used as a form of address traditionally by barmaids and frequently by purveyors of other types of merchandise, especially the older ladies of that group. It is used by females to persons of both sexes, but by males only to females. In this respect it is like kissing but, of course, not to be taken so seriously as all that. It is a term of extremely casual endearment, and in this use is synonymous with *love* and *lovey* as forms of address. *Duck* (or *ducks*), in this use, sometimes becomes *ducky* or even *ducky diamond,* but the latter, fortunately, is comparatively rare.

dues, n. pl.   **commissions**

A percentage payable to an agent.

duff, v.t. (sl.)   **fake**

To *duff* merchandise is to make old stuff look new in order to fool the customer.

duffer, n. (sl.)   **peddler of faked merchandise**

A *duffer* in England is a con man specialist who, selling shoddy goods, claims them to be of great value because they were stolen or smuggled. It is sometimes used in England generically, to mean any *pedlar* (spelled that way in England, *peddler* in America). *Duffer* is used in America as a slang noun meaning *dolt*, but in both countries it more commonly means a person inept at games, e.g., golf. It is commonly used in America in the phrase *old duffer*. However, the expression *old duffer* is not really pejorative, and implies at least affectionate toleration of the ancient character involved.

dug-out, n. (sl.)   **old duffer**

More specifically, a superannuated officer reluctantly taken back into military service.

dull, adj.   **overcast**

A term used all too frequently in describing the weather.

Duck

dumb-waiter, n.   **lazy Susan**

An American *dumbwaiter* is an English *service lift.*

dummy, n.   **baby pacifier**

dumpling, n. (sl.)   **yokel**

Used in the phrases *Norfolk dumpling* and *Devon dumpling,* Norfolk and Devon being counties in England. The seemingly libelous implication is that of a rather slow and cumbersome person or hayseed. The coupling of *dumpling* with the name of other English counties may exist but if so, has escaped the writer's notice. In any event, one must not confuse a *Norfolk dumpling* with a **Norfolk capon** (q.v.).

during hours (col.)   **while the pubs are open**

Pubs (q.v.) used to be open more or less at all hours, but during World War I (usually spoken of as the *Great War* in England), they were forced to close during certain hours. This provision was included in **DORA** (q.v.). DORA also included a provision, still unrepealed, like many New England blue laws, making it illegal to treat another to a drink in a pub. The establishment of pub closing hours was deemed necessary to prevent workers from stopping at a pub for a quick one in the morning on the way to the munitions factory and somehow never getting there. Nowadays, pubs are generally open from 10 A.M. to 2 P.M. and from 6 P.M. to 10:30 P.M., except Saturday nights when they close at 11 P.M. The *hours* in *during hours* refers to those happy ones when the pubs are open. *"Time!"* in the *publican's* or *landlord's* (*saloon keeper's*) announcement (which always has to be repeated several times and eventually becomes an imprecation: "Time, gentlemen, please!") means that the legal closing hour is at hand (or, more often, past).

dust, n.   **household refuse**

In addition to its more usual meaning in both languages.

dustbin, n.   **garbage can**

ENGLISH	AMERICAN
dustcart, n.	**garbage truck**
dustman, n.	**garbage man**
dust road, *see* **metalled road**	
dust-up, n. (sl.)	**brawl**

Kick-up and *punch-up* are synonyms.

dutch, n. (sl.)	**n.A.e.**

Perhaps an abbreviation of *duchess. See* **my old dutch.**

D.V.W.P.   **God willing** (app.)

These initials stand for *Deo volente, weather permitting.* This
is an old-fashioned English joke and reflects the Englishman's
firm belief that English weather is so uncertain that, when plans
are being discussed not only should appeal be made to the Almighty in general but a reference should also be made to the ele-
ments. (Apparently the Englishman feels that the weather is so
bad that even the Almighty does not control it. Otherwise, why
should He be so prejudiced against Englishmen?) *Deo volente*
is Latin and is an example of the ablative absolute use of a
noun and a present participle.

dynamo, n.   **generator**

early closing   **1 P.M. weekday closing**

Every English town has an *early closing day.* This custom is ob-
served in some parts of America, but even in those towns where

it happens there are often nonconforming individual holdouts. In the smaller English towns, all the shops close for lunch, usually from 1 P.M. to 2 P.M. every day, but on *early closing day* they shut at 1 P.M. for good, and many are the frustrations experienced by the unwary visitor or absentminded native. The *A.A. Book*, the familiar useful handbook issued to every member of the English Automobile Association (A.A.), which is about as ubiquitous as the Bible and is to be found in the **cubby** (q.v.) of practically every car in the British Isles, gives the *E C* (*early closing day*) of each town in its exhaustive list. Watch out for Wednesday particularly; Thursday is a fairly close second. Look out for places like Sturminster Newton, with two early closing days a week.

early days   **jumping the gun**

This phrase connotes *prematureness*. Thus: "It's *early days* to reach that conclusion."

earth, n., v.t.
       (1) **ground**
       (2) **cover with soil**
       (3) **run to earth**

(1) Term used in electricity. The Americans *ground* a wire; the English *earth* it. The same distinction occurs in the noun use of this electrical term. As a verb it also has other uses in England with gardening and fox-hunting connotations:

(2) To *earth* the roots of a plant is to *cover* them *with soil*.

(3) To *earth* a fox is to *run* it *to earth*.

earth floor   **dirt floor**

earthly, n. (col.)   **hope** (app.)

Practically always in a negative phrase, like "never had an *earthly*," meaning "never had a hope," i.e., *a chance in the world;* describing someone in a hopeless situation; no future; all pretty grim. The word *chance* is understood.

East, n. **Orient**

The English do not speak of the *East* as the *Orient* except poetically.

East End **East Side** (app.)

The eastern part of London is called the *East End.* The eastern part of New York City is called the *East Side.*

east end of a westbound cow **south end of a northbound horse**

A euphemism.

easy about it, *see* **I'm easy about it**

easy as kiss your hand, *see* **as easy as kiss your hand**

eat one's dinners **study for the bar**

To *study for the bar* is a less general term in England than in America. It refers only to preparation to become a **barrister** (q.v.). An aspiring barrister *eats his dinners* (three dinners in the Hall of his Inn of Court each of four Terms per year) in order to *keep his terms* in compliance with English bar admission requirements. This phrase is a pleasant survival from the days when the **Inns of Court** (q.v.) more or less constituted residential universities where, naturally, the students took their meals.

edge-to-edge, adj. **wall-to-wall**

Used of carpeting. A synonymous term in England would be *fitted carpeting.*

effects not cleared **uncollected funds**

Banking term; *see* **refer to drawer.**

eiderdown, n. **quilt; comforter**

But **comforter** (q.v.) in England has nothing to do with sleeping.

Elastoplast, n.   **Band-Aid**

electric fire   **electric heater**

elevator, n.   **lift**

An *elevator* in England is not a device for vertical conveyance of people. Its generic meaning is *anything that lifts,* but its common meaning is *shoe lift.* (This use is seen in America, too, in the term *elevator shoes.*) Conversely, an English *lift* is an American *elevator.*

eleven, n. (col.)   **cricket team**
                                          soccer team

In American sports terminology, an *eleven* would mean a *football team* (using *football* in the American sense; *see* **football**). An *eleven* in England refers to cricket or soccer and means a *side.* Roman numerals are often used: first XI (the first choice team), second XI (the reserve team). Similarly a rugby team is a XV, but note that a rowing crew is an *eight,* not a VIII.

eleven plus   **n.A.e.**

In theory an examination taken at the end of primary school to decide what type of state secondary education is most suitable for a child. The most academically gifted children go to grammar schools, those with a practical bent go to technical schools, and the remainder, the majority, go to secondary modern schools. In practice the examination is looked upon by parents as a pass/fail examination to the prestigious grammar schools. In many parts of the country this tri-partite system of secondary schools has been replaced by non-selective comprehensive schools which provide for all aptitudes and abilities. State education is free. Parents may opt out of the state system by sending their children to fee-paying private schools. Those private schools catering to children aged 8–12 are called **prep schools** (q.v.); those catering to 13–18 year olds are called **public schools** (q.v.). The entrance examination for public schools is called the **Common Entrance Examination** (q.v.).

Eleven Plus

elevenses, n. pl. (col.)   **morning coffee break** (app.)

Also called *elevens* and *elevensies*. The light refreshments consumed in this widespread English morning exercise consist usually of a cup of coffee and a **biscuit** (q.v.) or two. The coffee is usually very tasty and is made with hot milk instead of cream as in America (*see* **black or white?**). *Morning coffee* is another term used by the English to describe this social practice, which takes place at home, in hotels, or in tearooms. To get a cup of tea for *elevenses* at most tearooms is almost impossible.

Employment Secretary   **Secretary of Labor** (app.)

encash, v.t.   **cash**

end, n.   **butt**

London theatres and other public places are usually provided with wall receptacles, partially filled with sand, bearing the legend "Cigarette *Ends.*" *See also* **stump.**

endive, n.   **chicory**

In an English vegetable store (*greengrocer*) if you want chicory ask for *endive,* and vice versa!

engage, v.t.   **employ**

An Englishman *engages* a chauffeur and *hires* a car; an American *hires* a chauffeur and *rents* a car. In America, one *rents* a house to or from another. In England, you *rent* a house *from* the owner and *let* your own *to* a tenant.

engaged, adj.   **busy**

It is just as annoying to be told by an English telephone operator that the line is *engaged* or to hear the *engaged tone* as it is to hear the word *busy* or the *busy signal* in America. "He's *engaged,*" used by an English *telephonist* (*switchboard operator;* and the word is accented on the second syllable) is just as irritating in England as 'the dreary American equivalents, "he's *busy talking,*" or, "*he's on the wire.*" This maddening word *engaged* is also the English equivalent of the exasperating American term *in conference.*

engine driver   **engineer**

Railroad term.

enough on one's plate (col.)   **plenty to do**

One also sees *a lot on one's plate* (*a lot to do*).

enquiries, n. pl.   **information**

This is the term you use in England when you want *information* to look up a telephone number for you. It also appears on signs in offices, railway stations, etc., where the American sign would read *information.* *Trunk enquiry* means *long-distance in-*

formation. Sometimes the term *enquiries* in telephone context is expanded to *directory enquiries.* When you dial *information* in America now the operator answers *"directory assistance,"* which somehow sounds English rather than American. As the English tend to adopt freer and easier American phraseology and customs, in certain instances the Americans are becoming almost stuffy.

enquiry, n.   investigation

This word is often used where *investigation* would be used in America, e.g., in discussing an attempt to ferret out wrongdoing in a government department. A similar sense is found in the English term *enquiry agent,* which would be *private investigator* or *private detective* in America. It is also used as the equivalent of the American term *hearing,* in a phrase like *planning enquiry,* which is the English equivalent of *zoning hearing.* An *enquiry office* is an *information bureau.*

ENSA, n.   USO (app.)

Stands for *Entertainments National Service Association. USO* stands for *United Service Organizations.* Both supply entertainment to the armed forces. ENSA gave its final show on August 18, 1946, the last of two and a half million performances.

entrance fee   initiation fee

This is the term which the English use to describe the initial fee paid on joining a club.

the Establishment   n.A.e.

The Establishment describes those British institutions (and their representatives) which symbolize tradition and conformity: the upper classes, the Church of England, *The Times,* **Whitehall** (q.v.), and the Marylebone Cricket Club (*see* **Ashes**). *The Establishment* is used roughly the same way in America, but its components are quite different.

estate, n.   **real-estate development**

In addition to its other meanings, some of which are shared with America, *estate* is used in England where *development* would be used in America to signify a more or less uniformly built group of residential buildings. *Estate* is also occasionally used as the flattering description of a house and lot, particularly in real-estate advertisements. An *industrial estate* is a development of workers' housing created by a company, usually a factory, for its personnel.

estate agent   **real-estate broker**

Synonymous with *land agent.*

estate car   **station wagon**

Also called an *estate waggon* or *shooting-brake.*

evens, n. pl. (col.)   **even money**

Evens on . . . means "I will lay you *even money* on. . . ."

everything in the garden's lovely (col.)   **everything's hunky-dory**

An old-fashioned catch phrase from the Roaring Twenties; now practically obsolete.

exchange, n.   **central**

Telephone term.

Exchequer, n.   **Treasury Department**

The *Chancellor of the Exchequer* is the English equivalent of the *Secretary of the Treasury.* The term is used facetiously to refer to the family budget.

exclamation mark   **exclamation point**

exclusive line   **private line**

Telephone term. Sometimes the telephone company in its literature uses the quaint phrase *exclusive working* to describe this
luxury.

ex-directory, adj.   **unlisted**

Referring to telephone numbers.

exeat, n.   **temporary school leave**

Term used in schools and colleges. The connotation is that of a
short holiday. Like the more familiar word *exit,* it is a form of
the Latin verb *exire,* "to go forth"; in this case the third person
singular present subjunctive used in Latin as a third person imperative—literally, *let him go forth.*

exercise book   **notebook**

Sometimes referred to as a *jotter.*

exhibition; exhibitioner, *see* **bursar**

export carriage   **overseas shipping**

Seen as an extra charge item on bills for goods sent overseas,
like tea bought at Fortnum & Mason and shipped to America.
(The cost comes to less, even including the *export carriage.*)

express, adj., adv.   **special delivery**

Post office term.

external painting   **outdoor painting**

Builders' and contractors' term.

extractor fan   **exhaust fan**

extra-mural studies   **extension courses**

Extraordinary General Meeting, *see under*
    Annual General Meeting

$$\mathfrak{F} \mid \text{F}$$

fab, adj. (sl.)   **cool**

A teenage truncation of *fabulous* and synonymous with *gear* and *kinky.* **Kinky** (q.v.) has another grown-up meaning.

face-glove, n.   **face cloth mitt**

A very convenient type of *washrag* or *facecloth,* consisting of a square terrycloth mitt. The English call an ordinary washrag or facecloth a **flannel** (q.v.).

facer, n. (col.)   **poser**

Facer is rarely heard in either country in its literal meaning of *blow in the face.* In England it has the special meaning of *poser,* i.e., a difficulty that you suddenly come up against.

facia, *see under* **fascia**

faculty, n.   **college department**

In America, the *faculty* of a college is its entire teaching body. This would be called *staff* in England, where *faculty* always refers to a group of academically related subject departments, e.g., the Faculty of Medicine, the Faculty of Law, and so on.

faddy, adj. (col.)   **picky**

Often used to describe persons who are fussy about their food and difficult to please.

fag, n., v.t., v.i.   (1) **to toil**
                                                          (2) **to exhaust**
                                                          (3) **various school
                                                              slang meanings**
                                                          (4) **cigarette**

(1) An intransitive verb, meaning to *toil painfully.*

   (2) A transitive verb, meaning *tire* (someone) *out* or *wear*
       (someone) *out*.
   (3) In English school slang, when seniors *fag* it means that
       they *use the services of juniors,* and when juniors *fag* it
       means that they are *rendering services to seniors* and the
       junior so serving is known as a *fag*. The latter usage goes
       back quite far—see Mr. Fag in Sheridan's *The Rivals*.
       Another English slang use is to describe a *boring job,*
       drudgery, and the expression "what a fag!" would be a nor-
       mal reaction to the news of a particularly unwelcome assign-
       ment, e.g., homework, which in England is also known as
       prep (q.v.).
   (4) In both countries it is slang for *cigarette*. In America (with-
       out any reflection on the English public school system),
       it is synonymous with·*pansy,* i.e., *male homosexual*.

fains I! (sl.)   **n.A.e.**

   Used by children as a magic formula to exempt them from unwanted chores. Example: "*Fains I* washing up! (i.e., "No dish-
   washing for me tonight!"). There would seem to be no equivalent formula in America. Rare, and sometimes *vains I!*

fair do's! (sl.)   **divvy up!**

   Child's slang meaning *share fairly*.

fair-light, n.   **transom**

fair old . . . , adj. (col.)   **quite a . . .**

   Thus, a *fair old* job means *quite a* job (a big chore); a *fair*
   old mix-up is *quite a* mix-up (a snafu of major proportions).

fair's on (col.)   **what's fair is fair**

   To the kind friend who paid for the previous round of drinks, an
   Englishman might say: "*Fair's on* . . . , this one's on me."

fall over backwards   **lean over backwards**

   Uncharacteristically,·in this case the English overstate.

fanny, n. (sl.)   (1) **vulva**
     (2) **(member of) First Aid Nursing Yeomanry**

(1) Delicacy inhibits the inclusion of the American low slang equivalent, which has long been used in England as well, as demonstrated (if need be) by the play on words in *Hamlet* (Act 3, Scene 2). The clinical equivalent is *vulva.* Americans who know and casually apply *fanny* to both sexes as a synonym for *behind* (n.) must be careful to avoid its use in England. Its application to a male person in England would constitute not only a breach of taste but an anatomical paradox. The exact equivalent is not mentioned but is identifiably referred to in a bit of doggerel entitled "Lines on a Book Borrowed From the Ship's Doctor" by Sir Alan Herbert, C. H. (A. P. Herbert), which, after describing the female pudenda in mock-rhapsodic terms, ends with the following quatrain:

> What a pity then it is that, when we common fellows chatter
> Of the mysteries to which I have referred,
> We should use for such a delicate and complicated matter
> Such a very short and unattractive word!

(2) Usually in the phrase *old Fanny.* An acronym (inaccurately doubling the *n*) which developed in World War II, and apparently used in polite society despite its impermissibility with a small *f.*

fare stage   **bus fare zone limit**

In both countries *stage* appears in the phrase "*stage* of a journey," and as part of *stagecoach,* especially in American movies about the Wild West. In England, *fare stages* are the *zone limits* for purposes of computing bus fares.

farthing, n.   **one fourth of a penny**

A coin long since demonetized; but the term is still used figuratively to mean a *bit* in expressions like "It doesn't matter a farthing."

fascia, n.   **dashboard**

A variant, *facia,* means a store sign.

fast, adj.   **express**

Applied to trains and to roads (express highways).

Father Christmas   **Santa Claus**

The English also use *Santa Claus.*

faults and service difficulties   **telephone repair department**

This is what you ask for on your neighbor's telephone when yours isn't working. A faulty telephone is one that is out of order.

feeder, n.   **bib**

feeling not quite the thing (col.)   **not feeling up to par**

felicitate, v.t.   **congratulate**

Used when the subject of good wishes (i.e., the object of the verb) is the lady. One *congratulates* the fiancé or groom but *felicitates* the fiancée or bride.

fender, n.   **bumper**

Automobile term; but American *fender* is British *wing.* Car terminology can be tricky: *see* Introductory Note 26.

fête, n.   **fair**

An important part of English life. Not only churches and organizations like the W.I. (*Women's Institute*—a national women's club with local branches doing excellent charitable work) or the *Young Conservatives Club* (roughly equivalent to the *Young Republicans Club*), but apparently every village in England, down to the smallest, organizes a *fête*. The village *fête* is annual and is a small scale country fair, sometimes preceded by a parade with floats. Attendance at village *fêtes* has been spotty in many cases, and in some villages dire talk of discontinuing the practice is almost as regular as the *fête* itself.

fiddle, n., v.t., v.i. (sl.)   **swindle**

To *fiddle* is to *cheat* and to *fiddle the books* is to *engage in shady dealings*. A *fiddle* is usually a minor cheat. When the offense is of major proportions, the English use *swindle*.

Fiddle

fiddling, adj. (sl.)   **picayune**

A *fiddling business* is a *nickle-and-dime operation,* a *catch-as-catch-can* way of making a living, like street vending or occasional odd jobs. The word is derived from an obsolete slang meaning of *fiddle: sixpence.* Incidentally, *picayune* is an old Southern name for a nickel. *Fiddling* can also have the meaning of *exacting* when it refers to fine work on delicate things like small, complicated machinery or fine watches.

143

file, n.   **loose-leaf binder**

An English schoolboy or university student will keep his notes
in a *file*.

filibuster, n., v.i.   **buccaneer**

Filibuster originally meant the same thing in both countries: as
a verb, to *engage in unauthorized warfare against a foreign
power;* as a noun, a *buccaneer* or *pirate* engaged in that activity. Its use in America now is as a noun to designate an endless
speech in legislative proceedings for the purpose of obstructing
legislative progress in an unwanted direction, and as a verb to
describe the disgraceful activity itself. The naughty legislator
who indulges in the practice is called a *filibusterer.*

fillet, n.   **tenderloin**

This word has many meanings in both languages, among them
the kind of *narrow headband* associated with classical Greek
athletes. On an American restaurant menu the equivalent would
be *tenderloin steak,* or perhaps *filet mignon.*

fill in   **fill out**

The English *fill in* a form; the Americans *fill out* a form. Englishmen also *fill up* a form. Americans use *fill in* intransitively as a
synonym for the verb *substitute,* in the sense in which an under-
study *fills in* for an ailing actor.

fine down (col.)   **thin down**

fingerling, n.   **young salmon**

In America it means anything small and specifically any fish no
longer than your finger.

fire brigade   **fire department**

-fired

The English speak of *oil-fired, gas-fired,* etc., *central heating.*

This is shortened to *oil heat, gas heat,* etc., among the laity in America.

fire-flair, n.   **stingray**

fire-irons, n. pl.   **fireplace implements**

fire office   **fire insurance company office**

fire-pan, n.   **brazier**

fire-raising, n.   **arson**

A *fire-raiser* is a *firebug.*

firewood, n.   **kindling**

Firewood, in America, is a generic term meaning any wood for burning, usually in a fireplace for heat, but also outdoors for cooking. The American term includes *kindling.* In England, where most fireplaces contain grates for the burning of coal, *firewood* denotes merely *wood to start the fire with* and is either gathered outdoors or is bought at the ironmonger's (hardware store) in small wire-bound bundles of thin, short sticks called **pimps** (q.v.).

first, n. (col.)   **summa**

First is a university term which is short for *first class honours* and is roughly equivalent to *summa* in America, which is short for *summa cum laude.* A *second* is a *magna cum laude;* a *third* is a *cum laude.*

first floor   **second floor**

Americans use *first floor* and *ground floor* interchangeably to describe an apartment on the ground level, and *main floor* or *street floor* to describe the ground level of a shop or office building. The English use *ground floor* to describe all of those things, but when they say *first floor*, they mean the next floor up, i.e., the floor above the ground floor, or what Americans call the *second floor*. This difference continues all the way to the top, of course. Though Americans call the floor above the ground floor the *second floor*, inhabitants of that floor are also heard to say that they live *one flight up*. In this difference between the American and English usage, the English are one with the Europeans against their former colony. For example:

	Ground level	One flight up
American	first floor	second floor
English	ground floor	first floor
French	*rez-de-chausée*	*premier étage*
Spanish	*piso bajo*	*primer piso*
Italian	*pianterrano*	*primo piano*
German	*Parterre; Erdgeschoss*	*Erster Stock*

The German usage is highlighted in the title of Johann Nepomuk Nestroy's comedy, *Zu ebener Erde und im ersten Stock* (*Downstairs and Up;* literally, in the American usage, *On the First Floor and on the Second Floor*). One must be careful also to distinguish between *floor* and *storey* (note the *e* in the English spelling) in England: a *two-storey* house has a ground floor and a *first floor*, and so on. Thus, in a fifty-story skyscraper in America, the top floor is the fiftieth. It would be the forty-ninth in England (if you could find one that high). When **pair** (q.v.) is used in the sense of floor (*first pair, second pair,* etc.) remember that *first pair* relates to those dwelling on what would be the *second floor* in America, and so on all the way up.

fish, n.   **fish and seafood**

In England *fish* usually includes *seafood*.

fish, wet, *see* **wet fish**

fishmonger, n.   **fish store**

fish slice (col.)   **spatula**

fit?, adj. (col.)   **all set?**

Usually asked in the form, "are you *fit?*"

fitted, adj.   **wall-to-wall**

Used of carpeting. Synonymous in England with *edge-to-edge* carpeting.

fitter, n.   **plumber; mechanic**

Americans use the phrase *steam fitter* to mean a mechanic who installs or repairs steam pipe systems but do not use *fitter,* as the English do loosely, to mean a *repairman* or *plumber.* In England you send for the *fitter* when your home radiator or your boat engine, as just two examples, is out of order.

fittings, n. pl.   **fixtures**

Store fixtures in America are *shop fittings* in England.

fiver, n.   **five** (app.)

A *fiver* is a *five-pound note,* presently worth $12.00. A *fiver* in America is, of course, a *five-dollar bill.*

fives, n.   **handball**

The games are roughly similar.

fixings, n. pl.   **hardware**

What Americans call the *hardware* on a window, swinging gate, or other such contraption, is called the *fixings* in England.

fixture, n.   **sporting event**

In the English sports world what the Americans call an *event* is called a *fixture.*

Flag Day   **Tag Day**

The day on which people solicit you for contributions to a cause

147

and give you something to put on your lapel to prove you've come through. In England you get little flags; in America you get other little things on the end of a pin. *Flag Day* in America is June 14, which is the anniversary of the day in 1777 when the Stars and Stripes were formally adopted as the American flag.

flan, n.	**sponge cake or pastry with fruit filling**

Usually with a layer of whipped cream as well. In Italy and Spain flan is *crème caramel,* in France, any *custard.*

flannel, n.	**face cloth**

Also known in America as *washcloth* or *washrag.* But when the English talk of a *wash-cloth,* they mean what is known in America as a *dishcloth. See also* **face-glove.**

flannel, v.i. (sl.)	**(1) soft-soap**
	(2) talk one's way out

Sometimes used as a noun to indicate the content.

flapjack, n.	**(1) type of cookie**
	(2) lady's flat compact

Flapjack does not mean *pancake* in England.

flat, n.	**apartment**

A *block of flats* is an *apartment house.* As a slang noun, a *flat* can mean a *dupe.* In England *apartment* means *room* but is now coming into use in the American sense. *See also* **service flat.**

flat out	**full speed ahead**

Flat out to an Englishman suggests a race, particularly a horse race, with the winner (by a nose) going *all out,* using every ounce of power. To an American *flat-out* (sometimes *flat out*) is colloquial or dialect for *flatly,* in the sense of *plainly* or *directly,* as in "I told him *flat-out* what I thought of him."

flatter, n. (col.)   **tenant**

A *flatter* is the *tenant* of a *flat*, that is, one who rents an apartment.

fleck, n. (col.)   **lint**

This term describes the odds and ends that annoyingly cling to dark woolen clothing. It is also called *flick*. Apparently *fleck* popped into the language as the result of an analogy to *flecks* of foam against dark water or *flecks* of cloud against a dark sky. The *flick* must have come about as the result of the literal meaning of that word. Although it is hard to keep up with the volume of lint that collects so rapidly out of nowhere, one does keep attempting to *flick* off the *flecks*. *Fluff* is widely used by the English to describe the same matter. *Lint,* in England, means *surgical dressing.*

fleet, n.   **creek**

Fleet is sometimes also used as an adjective meaning *shallow.*

Fleet Street (col.)   **the press**

See **Threadneedle Street, Wardour Street,** and other street names indicating various businesses and professions.

flex, n.   **electric cord; extension**

Abbreviation of *flexible,* used as a noun.

flick, *see* **fleck; fluff**

flicks, n. pl. (sl.)   **movies**

flipping, adj., adv. (sl.)   **darn**

More or less equivalent to *bloody* but more polite. Pejorative and intensive.

flit, v.i. (col.)   **move**

To change residence (*see also* **moonlight flit**). *Flit* by itself is mainly Scottish.

flog, v.t. (col.)   (1) **push**
                                      (2) **sell illegaly**
                                      (3) **lick** (**vanquish**)

(1) In England *flog* describes the hard sell, whether the insistent effort to *dispose of goods* or to *press an idea.*
(2) Applies to stolen or smuggled goods *flogged* on the black market, for example.
(3) To *flog* one's competitors, whether in sports or competitive examinations, is to *trounce* them, to *beat them all hollow.*

flog it (sl.)   **plod**

In military slang, to *flog it* is to *walk* or *plod.*

floor, v.t. (col.)   **n.A.e.**

When an English schoolboy stands up to recite and isn't prepared, the teacher (master) *floors* him, i.e. tells him to sit down. *Floor* shares the general American colloquial meaning to *overcome* or *shatter* someone with a devastating riposte.

florin, n.   **two shillings**

See Introductory Note 18.

fluff, n.   **lint**

A *bit of fluff* is English slang for *chick* in the sense of *gal.* A *bit of fluff* is not really pejorative; it implies perhaps a wee bit of overdressing or might refer to the relative youth of the female companion of an older man, but no real harm is meant by it. For another use, *see* **fleck.**

fly one's kite (col.)   **send up a trial balloon**

fly-over, n.   **overpass**

fob off   stick ... with
(fool into buying)

Americans and English both (alas) *fob* or *palm* inferior merchandise *off* on people, but the Americans do not describe the victims as being *fobbed off* with the goods as the English do, just *stuck* with them.

fob pocket   watch pocket

Tailor's term.

fogged, adj. (sl.)   befuddled

follow?, v.i.   see?

Usually in the phrase "do you *follow?*," meaning "do you *see?*" or "are you with me?"

fool, n.   n.A.e.

A dessert. Blanch, mash and strain berries or other fruit, mix with custard or cream and serve cold. *Gooseberry fool* is the most common of these desserts, and has nothing whatever to do with **gooseberry** (q.v.) in its colloquial sense of *fifth wheel,* even though that kind of gooseberry would not act that way unless he were a fool.

football, n.   soccer

As the name of a game, *football,* in England, is short for *association football,* the game which Americans call *soccer.* This is the game, which, in England and in most civilized countries except America, attracts audiences which fill those incredibly large stadiums. It is still a relatively minor sport in America but growing in popularity. The nearest equivalent in England to American football is the game called *Rugby football,* or simply *Rugby,* but most commonly called *rugger.* This game is played in uniforms like the ones used in *soccer,* without helmets, padding, nose guards, etc., and how a game of rugger is completed without multiple injuries and even deaths is a great mystery. Rugby is a very old **public school** (q.v.). A kind friend who, like his forefathers, is a Rugby **old boy** (q.v.), has offered the following comment:

"Do you know why a rugger ball, British or American [sic], is oval? Because the original ball was based on a pig's bladder. Have a look at the next pig you see and you will find its bladder oval. The original manufacturer of rugger balls, Gilbert, confirms this and it was so in my father's day at the home of the Rugby game, 1880–83. There is a plaque on the school wall to William Webb Ellis, commemorating his exploit of October 23, 1823, a photocopy of which is enclosed herewith not only for its historical interest but as an example of splendid British understatement:

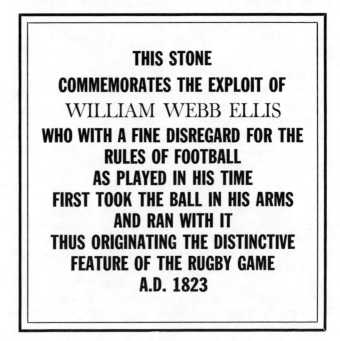

THIS STONE
COMMEMORATES THE EXPLOIT OF
WILLIAM WEBB ELLIS
WHO WITH A FINE DISREGARD FOR THE
RULES OF FOOTBALL
AS PLAYED IN HIS TIME
FIRST TOOK THE BALL IN HIS ARMS
AND RAN WITH IT
THUS ORIGINATING THE DISTINCTIVE
FEATURE OF THE RUGBY GAME
A.D. 1823

The plaque was still up when I was there (1916–20) and is no doubt still there. Father and I went to the Centenary of the October 23, 1823, match when England and Ireland played Scotland and Wales. Quite a match in the lovely original setting, but I do not propose to go to the 400th anniversary of the foundation of Rugby in 1567 by a London grocer. . . ."

footer, n. (sl.)   **soccer**

A schoolboy slang term for *football.*

footplate, n.   **engineer's and fireman's platform**

Railroad term. The engineer (*engine driver* in England) and fireman are known collectively as *footplatemen.*

foot-slog, v.i. (sl.)   **trudge**

A *foot-slogger* is a *hiker;* the word sometimes means *infantryman.*

footway, n.   **sidewalk**

An old-fashioned term, still seen on street signs threatening pedestrians with fines if they permit their dogs to "foul the *footway.*" **Pavement** (q.v.) is the common English term.

forecourt, n.   **front yard**

Applied to a service station, *forecourt* means the *area where gas is pumped.* Thus, a help-wanted ad for a *forecourt attendant,* i.e., somebody to man the gas pumps.

Foreign Office   **State Department**

Now called the Foreign and Commonwealth Office (FCO).

forged, adj.   **counterfeit**

The English speak of a *forged* note, the Americans of a *counterfeit* bill.

fork supper (col.)   casserole meal

This term is applied to a meal that can be eaten without a knife. *Fork lunch* is also used. Roughly speaking, the American equivalent of *fork* in this context might be thought to be *buffet,* as in *buffet lunch* or *buffet dinner,* but at least in the author's experience, there has been many a *buffet meal* in America in which he has had to use a knife and juggle things on his lap. A *fork meal* in England is definitely one in which a knife is superfluous. For the converse of this situation, *see* **knife-and-fork tea.**

form, n.   grade

A school term. Used but rarely in America.

form, n. (col.), *see* on form; what's the form?

for the matter of that   for that matter

And what's more could be used in either country.

fortnight, n.   two weeks

This is a common word in England, very rarely heard in America. *Today fortnight, Monday fortnight,* etc., mean *two weeks from today, two weeks from Monday,* etc. **Week** (q.v.) is used in the same way in England: *today week, Friday week,* etc. *This day fortnight* (or *week*) is still heard, too. "I'd rather keep him a week than a *fortnight*" is a quaint, if mildly callous, way of saying, "He's a big eater."

found, all (or fully), *see* fully found

foundation, n.   founding

The English use *foundation* in the sense of the establishing of an institution, where Americans would use *founding.* Usually, but not necessarily, the English term has in it the connotation of financial endowment in addition to merely getting something started.

ENGLISH   AMERICAN

foundation member   **charter member**

foundation-stone, n.   **cornerstone**

four honours   **100 honors**

A term used in bridge, meaning any four of the top five cards in the trump suit.

fourpenny one (sl.)   **sock on the jaw**

Sometimes a **tuppenny one** (q.v.).

four up, *see* **make the four up**

Four Wents   **four corners** (app.)

This is not a general term meaning *intersection* but rather a very common place name in the English countryside. The *Four Wents,* or the *Four Went Ways,* is always a place name designating a specific intersection. The *four corners* is a classic bucolic general term rather than a specific place name in the American countryside. The *went* in the English expression has nothing to do with the past tense of *going* but is derived from the verb *wend.*

F.P., *see* **old boy**

fraternity, n.   **religious organization**

In America the common meaning of *fraternity* is a *college society* which usually has a name consisting or two or three Greek letters, secret rites, and sadistic initiation ceremonies. *Fraternity* is, of course, an abstract noun in both countries denoting the lovely concept of *brotherliness,* and *fraternité* was one of the three components of the glorious slogan of the French Revolution. But *college fraternities,* which seem to thrive on exclusion rather than inclusion, have been outlawed by a good many American colleges and may become a thing of the past.

free house   **unaffiliated bar** (app.)

Most pubs are tied in with a particular brewery, at least in the
beer and ale department, serving only that brewery's brand.
The brewery owns the premises and leases the pub to the operator, who is known as the **landlord** (q.v.; although he is, legally
speaking, the tenant), or **publican** (q.v.). The pub has its own
historic name (White Swan, Queen's Head, Eight Bells, etc.)
and a standing or hanging decorative pub sign, sometimes
beautifully painted and occasionally ancient, but the effect is
somehow a little marred by the appearance of another sign, attached to the building, of the name of the brewery, which has
the effect of depersonalizing the management. A *free house* is a
pub not affiliated with a brewery. They are few and far between, and serve whatever brands of ale and beer they choose.
All other pubs are *tied houses*.

freehold, n.   **title** (app.)

This term, as opposed to *leasehold*, means *title* to real estate,
whether outright or for life. It implies *ownership* as opposed to
tenancy.

free issue of new shares   **stock dividend**

free line   **wire**

In this sense: you ask your switchboard operator for a *free line*
when you want to dial the number yourself. In America you
would ask her to give you a *wire*.

freight, n.   **cargo**

In England *freight* is applied only to transportation by water. In
America the term is applied to transportation by land or by air,
and *cargo* is the marine term.

French, gin and, *see* **martini**

French beans   **string beans**

fresh butter   **sweet butter**

fresher, n. (sl.) freshman (app.)

An English university term and a little more restricted than *freshman*. *Freshman* applies to the entire first year; *fresher* normally covers only the first term. *Freshman* (despite its second syllable) and *fresher* apply to both sexes. Some universities have their own special terms. At the University of Aberdeen in Scotland, for example, a first year male student is a *bajan* and his opposite female number a *bajanella*.

fret, n. tizzy

People, when agitated, *fret* in both countries. The word is used as a noun in England in the expression *"in a fret"* in situations where Americans would be apt to use *"in a tizzy."*

fridge, n. (col.) refrigerator

Also spelled *frig* and *frige*, but always .pronounced *fridge*. The universal term in England for *refrigerator* or *icebox*. Even the young children in America who have never seen an old-fashioned affair of the sort that actually uses ice seem to prefer *icebox* to *refrigerator*.

friendly society fraternal order

A type of organization whose members provide mutual assistance in illness or old age. An alternative American name for this kind of organization is *lodge*. Examples in America are the Benevolent and Protective Order of Elks (B.P.O.E.) and the Odd Fellows.

frillies, n. pl. (col.) undies

Going out of fashion—the word, that is.

frilling, n. ruching

fringe, n. bangs

Coiffeur term.

Friendly Society

frock, n.   **dress**

The everyday word in England for *dress*.

frock-coat, n.   **Prince Albert**

front, n.   **seaside promenade**

Referring to seaside places, and also called *sea front.* A *front*
or *sea front* is like an American *boardwalk,* except that the
walking surface is not made of wood. People in England do not
talk about going to the *beach* or *shore;* they go to the *sea-side.*
When you get to an English sea-side town, to find the ocean
follow the signs reading *Front.*

front bench

Describes the benches in the House of Commons and the House
of Lords occupied by ministers (cabinet members) and other
members of the government and members of the opposition
shadow cabinet.

frontier, n.   **border**

The word means *border between nations* in both countries, but in England it does not have the special meaning of *outlying settled region,* that part of a country which forms the outer limit of its populated area. In view of England's history, it is understandable that that connotation, having had no application for so long a period, would now be lost. But both countries use the term symbolically, and it is to be assumed that when John F. Kennedy spoke of the New Frontier, Canada did not gird for war.

frosted food   **frozen food**

Sign in Harrods, the great department store (*departmental store*) in Knightsbridge, London: *Frosted Foods*. A refrigerator salesman (*shop assistant* in a *fridge shop*) would point with pride to a large *frosted foods compartment,* which Americans would call a *freezer.*

frowsty, adj. (col.)   **musty**

Frowst is an English colloquialism meaning the *fusty stale heat in a room*. As an intransitive verb, to *frowst* means to *stay in and enjoy frowst,* i.e., to like it stuffy, or to put it another way, to be the opposite of a fresh air fiend. There are people like that. From this colloquial word we get *frowsty,* which describes the way the unfortunate room smells. *Frowsty* is related to the adjective *frowzy,* also spelled *frouzy* in America, which means *close,* in the sense of *musty, fusty,* and *smelly,* and by association *dingy,* but nowadays in either country it is most commonly used in the sense of *unkempt,* and evokes the image of a slatternly woman with her hair in disarray.

frowzy, *see* **frowsty**

fruiterer, n.   **fruit seller**

The *fruiterer's* is a *fruit store.* Not to be confused with *fruiter,* meaning *fruit-bearing tree, fruit-ship* and *fruit-grower.*

fubsy, adj.   **fat and squat**

fug, n. (col.)   (1) **stuffiness** (room)
                                               (2) **fluff** (dust ball)

In addition to these two quite distinct meanings as a noun, *fug* sometimes appears as a v.i. (col.). To *fug* is to like to have it stuffy, in a room, or a car, etc., and is synonymous with *frowst*, (see **frowsty**).

full out   **full time**

In both countries *full out* can indicate *maximum speed,* or *full throttle.*

full stop   **period**

The English do not always use *period*, the little dot at the end of a sentence. Americans use *stop* in dictating cable messages. *Full stop* is peculiarly English, except that Americans do sometimes use *full stop* when reading printed proof aloud.

fully found   **all expenses paid**

"Salary £ 15, *fully found*" means that you get £ 15 per week, and all expenses, like transportation, board and lodging, and so on. *All found* is also used.

funky, adj. (sl.)   **chicken**

This word comes from *funk* (n., v.t., v.i. [sl.] in England and [col.] in America), which, however, is used much more commonly in England than in America. The noun has one meaning in England which it does not have in America: *coward.* "You're a *funk*" would be "you're *chicken*" in America. The adjective *funky* is not commonly used in America in this sense, nor is the slang term *funk-hole* (literally, *trench dugout* of World War I fame) which means figuratively a job that gets you out of military service, or in other words a *draft dodger's dodge.* A *blue funk* is an American expression meaning *in the dumps,* i.e., *a de-*

pression, a situation requiring a visit to a psychiatrist or two martinis.

fun of the fair, *see* **all the fun of the fair**

furnishings, soft, *see* **soft furnishings**

fuss, v.t. (col.)   **faze**

𝕲 | G

gaff, n. (sl.)   **honky-tonk**

Sometimes *penny gaff.* An entirely different English use is seen in the slang expression *blow the gaff,* which means *spill the beans.* An American slang use is found in *stand the gaff,* where *gaff* means *strain* or *rough treatment.* None of these *gaffs* has anything to do with *gaffe,* from the French, meaning *faux pas.*

gaffer, n. (col.)   **(1) old duffer**
                                                        (2) boss

(1) With the implication of the countryside, and humorously affectionate rather than in any sense pejorative.
(2) When used by a gang of unskilled laborers, the *gaffer* means the *man in charge,* the *boss* of the gang, the *foreman,* and, if anything, is mildly pejorative, without the slightest trace of humor or affection.

gall, n.   **rancor**

In America *gall* (apart from its medical implications) is slang for *impudence* or *effrontery.*

gallon, n.   **1 1/5 gallons** (app.)

The standard English *gallon* is the *Imperial gallon,* equal to
277.420 cubic inches. The standard U.S. *gallon* is the old English *wine gallon,* equal to 231 cubic inches. Thus, the English
gallon equals 1.20095, or almost exactly 1 1/5 American gallons, a
fact which makes the English price of gasoline (*petrol*) somewhat less grim for American visitors than the gas tank price signs
indicate. This ratio follows through in liquid measure terms used
in both countries for parts of a gallon, to wit: quart (¼ gallon);
pint (⅛ gallon); gill (1/32 gallon except that a **gill** [q.v.] is not
uniform in all parts of England). And as to terms of dry measure, look out for the English quart, which equals 1.0320, rather
than 1.20095, American dry quarts.

gallop, n.   **equestrian trail**

"Trespassing on these *gallops* forbidden," sign seen on a southern **down** (q.v.).

gallows, n. pl. (col.)   **boom crutch**

A nautical colloquialism.

galoshes, n. pl.   **rubbers**

In America *galoshes* are *overshoes,* waterproof boots that are
worn over shoes and reach to about the ankle. They would be
called *snowboots* in England.

game, n. (col.)   **kind of thing** (app.)

Game is much used in England in a variety of phrases and a
variety of ways. A man says to his much-divorced friend who is
contemplating another plunge, "I should think you'd have had
enough of that *game!*" A *mug's game* (*see* **mug**) is *something
for the birds,* an activity that only a fool would engage in. "I
wonder what her *game* is" means "I wonder what she's *up to,*"
i.e., "what's her *angle?*" *Play the game* means *do the right thing.*

game, v.i.   **gamble**

Americans speak jocularly of the *gaming table,* but rarely if ever use the verb *game.* The verb is not commonly used but is still heard in England.

gamp, n. (col.)   **bumbershoot**

A big one, named after the drunken lady in *Martin Chuzzlewit;* but almost everybody in England says **brolly** (q.v.).

gang, *see* **breakdown gang; navvy**

ganger, n.   **gang foreman**

In charge of a gang of workers. Often applies to foremen in charge of men working on the railroad.

gangway, n.   **aisle**

What the English call a *gangway* in a theatre, a ship, or a shop, would be called an *aisle* in America; but when the English say *aisle* they are referring to the space separating the pews in a church.

garden, n.   **yard** (app.)

Garden is used, in its literal sense, the same way in both countries. But the English use *garden* to mean one's property outside his house, the way Americans use *yard.* Those fairies at the bottom of Beatrice Lillie's garden are, in American prose, simply fairies at the end of her property. Also, the English often use *garden* as a synonym for *lawn.* "How nice your *garden looks!*" is said of your *lawn* even when there isn't a single flower showing.

gasper, n. (sl.)   **butt** (**cigarette**)

Now generally outmoded.

gate, v.t. (col.)   **campus** (app.)

That is, to punish by confinement. To be *gated* is to be *confined* to **college** (q.v.), during certain hours, or in some cases entirely, for a certain period, varying with the severity of the offense committed. The principal aspect of the punishment is the interruption of one's evening social life. The term is derived from the symbolic shutting of the precinct gate against the offender. The term applied originally to Oxford and Cambridge only, but it has been extended to other universities and now even to **public schools** (q.v.), where the punishment would consist of the student's being deprived, for a limited period, of the privilege of leaving the school grounds and going into town. The American equivalent (like the English, a verbal form derived from the noun) would be unintelligible in England, where a campus is called a **quad** (q.v.).

gaudy, n.   **college reunion dinner**

Annual college alumni dinner and celebration. From *gaudium,* Latin for *joy* (and *gaudeo, rejoice*), whence *Gaudeamus igitur, juvenes dum sumus.* The incomparable Dorothy Sayers wrote a novel entitled *Gaudy Night* involving just such a celebration. Literally, *gaudy* means any feast, but it is usually understood in the narrower sense. The dinners themselves are normally anything but gaudy.

gazette, v.t.   **publish** (app.)

There are three official journals for the publication of official notices in the United Kingdom: the *Belfast Gazette, Edinburgh Gazette,* and *London Gazette.* They come out twice a week with official public notices of such things as government appointments, bankruptcies, etc. To *gazette* something is to have it published in one of these publications.

G.C.E.

Stands for *General Certificate of Education. See* **A-levels.**

gear, adj. (sl.)   **cool**

A teenage term, synonymous with *fab* and with *kinky* as used by youngsters.

gearing, n.   **leverage**

gear-lever, n.   **gearshift**

gee, n. (col.)   **horsie**

Gee! and *gee-up!* are used in both countries to urge a horse on. In England *gee-ho!*, *gee-hup!*, and *gee-wo!* are heard, too, and *gee-gee* was originated by children as a juvenile colloquialism equivalent to *horsie*.

gefuffle, n. (sl.)   **tizzy**

I.e., a state of agitation, but also used loosely as synonymous with **shemozzle** (q.v.). *See also* **cuffuffle.**

gen, n. (sl.)   **inside dope**

general election   **countrywide election**

The election of members of the House of Commons (Members of Parliament, usually shortened to *M.P.*s) throughout the country. This must take place at least every five years but can be brought on sooner by the resignation of the Prime Minister. *See also* **go to the country.**

general meeting, *see* **Annual General Meeting**

General Post Office   **main post office
(in London)**

Usually shortened to *G.P.O.* But *general post* means merely *first mail*.

general servant   **maid of all work**

Sometimes colloquially shortened to *general*.

gentle, n.   maggot

As used for fishing bait.

gen up (sl.)   bone up

get across . . . (col.)   **get . . . riled up**

The English as well as the Americans also speak of *getting* a
person's *goat*.

get a duck, *see* **duck** (1)

get a rocket, *see* **rocket**

get one's bowler, *see* **bowler-hatted**

get one's head down, *see* **put one's head down**

get one's head in one's hand (sl.)   **catch hell**

In other words, to get your head chopped off and handed to you.

get one's own back on (col.)   **get back on**

That is, to *get even with,* to *avenge oneself.* Also, *get something
back on.*

get on someone's wick (sl.)   **bug someone**

I.e., to get on his nerves.

get-out, n. (col.)   out

In the sense of an *avenue of escape,* one's *way out* of a jam.

get shot of (col.)   **get rid of**

gett, *see* **gitt**

get the better of   **get the best of**

You *get the better of* (triumph over) somebody in England,
but the Americans use the superlative. Lest you think that

Americans always resort to superlatives, the reverse is true in the following sense: an American says, "I'd *better* leave now"; and the Englishman says, "I'd *best* leave now."

get the push, *see* **push**

get the stick (sl.)   **catch hell**

When a person has been severely criticized, the English say he *got the stick, got a lot of stick,* or *got a bit of stick.* Derived, presumably, from the custom (happily dying) of caning schoolchildren for misbehavior.

get the wind up (col.)   **be jumpy**

In a situation where an American is *nervous about* something, the Englishman *gets the wind up* about it. To *have the wind up* is to be *scared,* rather than merely nervous. To *put the wind up* somebody is to *scare* him. To *raise the wind* is to *make a fuss. Windy,* by itself, means *nervous* or *jumpy.*

getting on for   **well nigh**

Thus: "*Getting on for* thirty years before, Elsie had married into the peerage." Or, "It's *getting on for* one o'clock."

get upsides with   **get even with**

To *turn the tables* on someone, or to *avenge oneself.*

get your knickers in a twist, *see* **knickers**

geyser, n.   **water heater**

Geyser is a geological term in both countries meaning a hot spring which shoots up a column of steaming water at fixed intervals. The most famous of these is Old Faithful in Yellowstone National Park. But to an Englishman the primary meaning of *geyser* is *water heater,* and the word evokes the image of a smallish white cylindrical tank with a swiveling faucet underneath, located on the wall next to the kitchen sink or in the bathroom. To an American coming across an English geyser for the

167

first time, the apparatus looks precarious. However, it is a dependable gadget, and many of them have been working well for so long a time that they, too, deserve the adjectives *old* and *faithful*. In this specialized meaning, the word is pronounced as though spelled *geezer*. *See also* **immersion tank.**

ghastly show, *see* **bad show!**

giddy fit (col.)	**dizzy spell**

giddy-go-round, n.	**merry-go-round**

More commonly *roundabout*. *See also* **carousel.**

gill, n.	(1) **ravine; torrent**
	(2) **¼ pint; ½ pint**

(1) The *g* is hard. Usually a *deep ravine* and wooded. When it means *torrent*, it refers to a *narrow mountain torrent*.

(2) The *g* is soft. When *gill* is used as a liquid measure in England, it usually means ¼ pint (i.e., ¼ of ⅛ of an Imperial gallon) and therefore 1.2 times as large as an American *gill;* but be careful, because in some parts of England it means ½ an Imperial pint, or exactly twice as much as in other parts of England. What is more, in America *gill* can also mean *wench*, and there are American dialects in which it means *creeping ground ivy*. With a capital *G* in England, it is a variant of the female name, *Jill*. *See also* **gallon.**

gin and French; gin and It, *see* **martini**

ginger-nut, n.	**gingersnap**

ginger-up, n. (col.)	**pep talk**

gin-stop, n. (col.)	**gin mill**

Girl Guide	**Girl Scout**

Boy Scouts are Boy Scouts in both countries, but *Girl Scouts* become *Girl Guides* in England.

gitt, n. (sl.)   **jerk**

Occasionally *gett,* and often coupled with a deprecatory adjective, as in "you silly *gitt* . . . !"

give . . . a miss (col.)   **pass . . . up**

One *gives a miss* to a play that has had bad notices or a restaurant where one's friends have had a poor experience. One might do the same thing in the case of the fifth wedding of a dear pal: here Americans might say, "I'll *sit* this one *out!*" But to *give* someone (or something) *a miss* doesn't necessarily imply distaste. One can have seen the Tower of London once too often and decide this time to *give it a miss,* despite past happy experiences there. Or if you've borrowed too often from your friend Tim and have lost again at poker, while you are wondering where to get it this time, you might reflect, "This time I'll *give* Tim *a miss.*"

give . . . a shout (col.)   **sing out**

An Englishman will promise to *give* you *a shout* when he is ready, where an American would promise to *sing out* or let you know.

give . . . best   **bow to . . .**

To *give* somebody *best* is to *admit his superiority,* and in that sense to *bow to* him.

give . . . in charge   **turn . . . in**

I.e., turn a person over to the police. *See also* **charge-sheet.**

give in part exchange   **trade in; turn in**

In England you *give* your old car, television set, or vacuum cleaner *in part exchange* when you buy a new one, in the same way in which you *trade it in* in America.

gives me gyp (sl.)   **hurts me like hell**

give ... the bird   **give ... the gate**

Give Way   **Yield**

Road sign in England, meaning *yield right of way*. In many parts of America there are road signs to the same effect, reading *Yield* in large letters, sometimes followed by *Right of Way* in smaller letters.

glass, n.   **crystal**

Referring to watches and clocks. The term *crystal* is used in England, too, but only in the trade.

glasshouse, n. (sl.)   **stockade**

Military slang for *army prison*. The naval equivalent in both countries is *brig*.

glasspaper, n.   **sandpaper**

Paper coated with glass dust.

go, n.   **turn; try**

If you are caught dozing on your feet during a slow game of croquet on an English lawn when your turn comes around, your adversary will most likely politely notify you, "It's your *go*." If a child is demonstrating his new bicycle to his little English friend, the friend will, after a certain interval, ask anxiously, "May I have a *go?*" In America, he would ask if he might *try* it. *Go* is used in England also in the sense of taking a *shot* at something, like a stuck window or something in your eye.

go a mucker, *see* **mucker**

goat, n. (col.)   **fool**

To act the *goat* or to play the *goat,* or the *giddy goat,* is to play the *fool*.

gob, n. (sl.)   **trap (mouth)**

Slang for *mouth;* thus, "Shut your *gob!*"

go down, *see* **come down**

go-down, n.   **warehouse**

gods n. (col.)   **peanut heaven**

The *gallery* of a theatre, the part nearest heaven. (cf. *le paradis* in France).

goggle-box, n. (sl.)   **boob tube; idiot box**

In both countries affectionately pejorative terms have been invented for the TV.

golden duck, *see* **duck** (1)

golden-knop, n.   **ladybug**

The more common English name for this insect is *ladybird.*

golden syrup   **corn syrup** (app.)

Lyle's Golden Syrup is a proprietary name, i.e., trademark; but *golden syrup* is used generically and is something like American *corn syrup.*

goloshes *see* **galoshes**

go missing (col.)   **disappear**

go nap on, *see* **nap**

gone, v.i.   **become** (app.); **turned**

Used in expressions of time, like "It had *gone* four o'clock by the time Frank arrived." Americans would say "It *was* four o'clock when Frank arrived." More generally, in expressions other than those of time, the American equivalent would be *turned,* for example, in an expression of this sort: "The Dead Sea Scrolls had *gone* all black."

gone for a burton (sl.)   finished (killed)

Originally Royal Air Force slang, describing the men who failed to return from the mission.

gongs, n. pl. (sl.)   medals

No American slang or colloquial equivalent. This is jocular, affectionate military slang, with the accent on understatement and self-deprecation. The *gongs*, usually in miniature form, are worn with military evening dress on festive occasions at places like the Naval and Military Club.

gony, n. (sl.)   dope

In the sense of *dunce*.

Gongs

good innings (col.)   **long life**

One who has had a good *innings* (*innings* is singular in England and simply means *inning*) has had a good *long life*.

good job (col.)   **good thing**

As for instance in a sentence like: "*Good job* it didn't rain during the picnic."

good party? (sl.)   **how'd it go?**

Asked of someone returning from a mission.

good show!   **nice work!**

goods, n. pl.   **freight**

A railroad term. A *goods-waggon* is a *freight car. See also* **covered goods-waggon.**

good value (col.)   **good stuff**

Thus: "That lad is very *good value*."

go off (col.)   **get tired of**

go off the boil (col.)   **quiet down**

Said, for instance, of an official inquiry which starts off like a house afire but turns out to be only a nine-day wonder.

gooseberry, n. (col.)   **fifth wheel** (app.)

The superfluous third party who sticks like glue to the (un)-happy couple who are aching to be alone. To *play gooseberry* is to act as chaperon. All this has nothing to do with *gooseberry*, the fruit, or *gooseberry fool*, the dessert discussed under **fool** (q.v.).

go racing   **go to the races**

ENGLISH   AMERICAN

gormless, adj. (col.)   **dumb; stupid**

A *gormless* person is a *dumbbell.*

go to bath! (sl.)   **go to hell!**

go to bed! (sl.)   **shut up!**

go to the bad (col.)   **go to the dogs**

go to the country   **have a general election**

This is a political idiom. One tests public opinion by *going to the country,* i.e., resorting to a **general election** (q.v.) in a government crisis.

go up   **be promoted**

A school term.

government, n.   **administration**

The English talk about the *Heath government,* the Americans about the *Nixon administration.* Each phrase refers to the people ruling the country at the moment.

governor, n.   **warden**

The head man at a prison is the *governor* in England.

governor, n. (sl.)   **boss; mister**

An English worker might speak of his *boss* as his *governor.* He would address him that way but would always pronounce it *guv'nor,* and that is the way it would appear in the dialogue of a novel. A cab driver might well address his passenger in England as *guv'nor,* and that would be equivalent to the American familiarity *doc,* or *mister.* As a form of address, however, *guv'nor* seems to be going out of fashion in favor of *sir* although one still hears *guv* in London. Old-fashioned Englishmen still use *guv'nor* in the sense of *dad.*

gownsman, *see* **town and gown**

gradient, n.   **grade (hill)**

Gradient can mean *grade* or *slope* in America, too, but it is not as commonly used. *Gradient* would be the more common term in England, as for instance in an automobile instruction book in advising which gear to use when starting up a hill.

graduate, n.   **college graduate**

In America a *graduate* can mean a person who has completed the course at any school, whether elementary school, high school, or college. Used alone, *graduate* in England means one who has graduated from university, or what Americans would call a *college graduate*.

graft, v.i. (sl.)   **knock oneself out**

grammar school, *see* **eleven plus**

gramophone, n.   **phonograph**

granny waggon (sl.)   **jalopy**

grasp the nettle (col.)   **take the bull by the horns**

grass, v.i. (sl.)   **squeal**

grease-proof paper   **waxed paper** (app.)

Not quite the same but generally serving the same functions. The English variety comes not in rolls but in sheets, is more nearly opaque, heavier, and stiffer, and it crackles.

greasy, adj.   **slippery**

Slippery generally not only because of the presence of grease. A wet road or a lawn tennis court after a sudden shower would be described as *greasy*. The same distinction exists in the figurative sense; be just as careful of dealing with a *greasy* Englishman as with a *slippery* American. Americans also use *oily* in the same uncomplimentary sense.

Great Bear   **Big Dipper**

Other English names for the Big Dipper: *Charles's Wain;* the *Plough.*

greats, n. pl. (col.)   **Oxford Finals**

Greats are the final Oxford exams for the degree of *B.A. Great go* is what they call the same thing at Cambridge. Part of a rather complicated system (*see also* **moderations; responsions; smalls** [2]).

Great War   **World War I**

green belt   **no-building zone** (app.)

The *green belt* is the area around an English municipality which is kept green, i.e., where building and development are not allowed, lest the overpopulated little isle develop into one megalopolis.

green fingers (col.)   **green thumb**

greengrocer, n.   **vegetable store**

greens, spring, *see* **spring greens**

greycing, n. (col.)   **greyhound racing**

A portmanteau word: *greyhound* and *racing.*

grid, n.   **map reference system**

The *National Grid,* a system of vertical and horizontal lines superimposed on the map of the country, divides it into lettered squares with numbered subdivisions, providing a reference system for all regional maps.

grill, v.t.   **broil**

A lady who asks her butcher in England for a *broiler* might get a chicken but might instead be referred to the *ironmonger* (*hardware store*). If she wants to be sure to get a chicken for broiling, she should ask for a *grilling-chicken*.

grills, n. pl.   **steaks and chops**

Grills (from *grill* meaning to *broil*) is a common English restaurant sign and is the equivalent of *steaks and chops*. This usage is found in both countries in the term *mixed grill*.

grind, n. (sl.)   **lay**

A crude word usually used pejoratively in the phrase "not much of a *grind*," i.e., an unsatisfactory sexual partner.

grinder, n.   **crammer**

To *grind*, in the sense of *study hard*, is common to both countries; also to *cram*, in the sense of preparing intensively for a particular examination. But where Americans would describe as a *crammer* one who waits until the last moment to *bone up* (**mug** [q.v.] or *mug up* in England), the English call him a *grinder*, the American equivalent of which is not *grind*, because that means (among other things) a student who continually works hard, exam or no exam.

griskin, n.   **lean bacon**

More particularly, the *lean part of the loin*.

grit, n.   **fine gravel**

ground, n.   **field**

A sports area: a cricket *ground*, a football *ground*, etc. *Nevill Ground* in Tunbridge Wells would be called *Nevill Field* in America (one wonders how the *Polo Grounds* in New York got its name).

ground, spare, *see* **spare ground**

ground floor, *see* **first floor**

ground-nut, n.   **peanut**

Synonymous with *monkey nut*.

Grundyism, *see under* **wowser**

guard, n.   **conductor; brakeman**

A railroad term. *Conductor* is used in England to mean the official in charge of passengers on a bus.

guard dog   **watchdog**

guard's van   **caboose**

A railroad term, synonymous with *brake-van*. *Caboose* in England means a *kitchen on the deck of a ship*.

gubbins, n. pl. (col.)   (1) **innards**
                                                           (2) **thingamajig**

(1) The *insides* of something: the *gubbins* of a car—all the bits and pieces mechanics have to get at.
(2) Also used as a vague reference to any old gadget, equivalent to *thingamagig* or *whatchamacallit*.

guggle, v.i.   **gurgle**

The English use *gurgle*, too. *Guggle* appears to be pejorative, as applied to a person in a state of impotent rage or hysterics.

guide dog   **Seeing Eye dog**

guildhall, n.   **town hall; city hall**

The *Guildhall* in London is what Americans would call the *City Hall* if London were an American city. In other municipalities, whether town or city, the English use the expression *town hall* rather than *city hall* to describe the municipal office building.

guillotine, n. (col.)   **cloture**

Limitation of debate in Parliament.

guinea, n.   **one pound, one shilling**

The *guinea* was originally a gold coin created for use in the African trade. It was theoretically pegged at twenty shillings (the same as the pound) but after a certain degree of fluctuation was fixed at twenty-one shillings. This happened relatively recently as British history goes (1717), and the *guinea* was last coined even more recently (1813). Thereafter, no longer the denomination of either a coin or a bill (*bank note* or *note* in England), it became simply a measure of money used in pricing certain goods and services. It appeared on price tags in shop windows and advertisements and on bills (*accounts* in England) sent out by professional people like doctors, lawyers, and such. Stating a price in guineas instead of pounds was a convenient way to keep the numerals down and the prices up. Thus, twenty-one guineas was twenty-two pounds, one shilling (£ 22.1.0). The guinea became obsolete on February 1, 1971, when the English money system was decimalized, eliminating shillings altogether. It may be that the term will be kept alive to denote the new equivalent of one pound, one shilling, which is one pound, five pence. Incidentally, before decimalization, lots of things in England were priced the way they are in America, one penny less than a round amount, to make them seem cheaper. For example, shoes priced at £ 9.19.11 (one penny less than £ 10.0.0), in the same way that they might be priced $29.95 in America. This will now become £ 9.99. *See* Introductory Note 18. *The Guineas* is the familiar name of two of the five classic English horse races, all for three-year-olds, consisting of the "One Thousand Guineas" and the "Two Thousand Guineas," both run at Newmarket in Suffolk each April. The other three are the Derby (pronounced *Darby*), run at Epsom Downs in Surrey on the first Wednesday each June, the Oaks, also at Epsom the following Friday, and the St. Leger at Doncaster in Yorkshire each September.

gum, n.   **mucilage**

If you want something to chew, ask for chewing gum.

gumboots, n. pl.   **rubber boots**

See also **snowboots.**

gump, n. (sl.)   **horse sense**

Short for *gumption.*

gum tree, *see* **up a gum tree**

gutter-crawl, v.i. (sl.)   **cruising for a pickup**

Crawl is used by the English the way Americans use *cruise to*
indicate the slow driving of a car. *Gutter-crawl* describes the
nasty conduct of a motorist on the prowl for women foolish
enough to accept his invitation to hop in. *Kerbside-crawl* is synonymous. (*Kerb* is *curb* in America.)

guy, n., v.t., v.i.   (1) **fright (sight)**
                                            (2) **slip (vanishing act)**
                                            (3) **ridicule**

See also **chap** and the reference there to *Guy Fawkes.* Americans would use *guy* to mean *fellow* where the English would
use *chap,* but *guy* has a number of exclusively English meanings:

(1) As a noun it means a *grotesquely dressed person* in such a
    weird getup that onlookers would call him a *fright,* a *sight,*
    a *scarecrow,* or something of that sort. Literally, a *guy* is a
    scarecrow of a special sort: a limp, shapeless bundle of
    rags often propped up against walls, wearing frightful
    masks and caps, surrounded by street-urchins begging
    "alms for the *guy.*" The word is derived from Guy Fawkes
    and his famous gunpowder plot to blow up King James I,
    the Prince of Wales, and all the Members of Parliament on
    November 5, 1605. Like so many other historical events
    which occurred centuries ago, the gunpowder plot is very
    much alive in English memories as though it were part of
    last week's news. In 1826 handbills were passed out im-
    printed with the following doggerel:

> Please to remember the fifth of November
> Gunpowder treason and plot;
> We know no reason, why gunpowder treason
> Should ever be forgot!

There was a time when every inhabitant of the City of London
(*see* **city**) received a notice on Lord Mayor's Day Eve reading
as follows:

> Sir,
>
> By Virtue of a Precept from my Lord Mayor, in order
> to prevent any Tumults and Riots that may happen on the
> Fifth of November and the next ensuing Lord Mayor's
> Day, you are required to charge all your Servants and
> Lodgers, that they neither make nor cause to be made,
> any SQUIBS, SERPENTS, FIRE BALLOONS or other FIREWORKS,
> nor fire, fling nor throw them out of your House, shop or
> Warehouse, or in the Streets of this City, on the Penal-
> ties contained in an Act of Parliament made in the Tenth
> year of the late King William. Note. The Act was made
> perpetual, and is not expired, as some ignorantly suppose.

This occurs no longer and a word of caution must be added:
American usage of *guy* meaning *fellow* has begun to appear in
England, at least in chic circles. For instance, in a recent advertisement for men's sportswear and under a picture of a very
elegant, casually dressed young man, the copy included the
sentence: "What more could a guy want?" This was, of course,
the American use of *guy* and since it referred to a very elegantly attired person, *guy* in that sentence meant, of course, the
exact opposite of a *grotesquely dressed person!*

(2) In the English slang expression "give the *guy*" to someone,
guy means *slip*, and to do a *guy* is to perform a *vanishing
act*. As an intransitive verb (sl.) to *guy* means to *take it on
the lam*, i.e., to *decamp*.

(3) As a transitive verb, to *guy* is to *exhibit in effigy* and by
extension to *make a monkey of*, i.e., to *ridicule*.

gymkhana, n.   **horse show**

This term is rarely used in America where it means a *sports
meet,* with the emphasis on racing. Technically it means the

181

same thing in England where it has the additional meaning of a *public sports field*. Its most common meaning in England, however, and one little used in America, is *horse show*. You can see signs all over England reading *Gymkhana,* followed by the name of a town or village, a date, and road directions; and if you follow the instructions on such a sign you will wind up attending, or even participating in, a local *horse show*.

gym shoes   **sneakers**

See also **plimsolls.**

gym slip (gym tunic)   **gym suit**

gyp, n.   **college servant**

This is a special term restricted to the universities of Cambridge and Durham. The same functionary is called a *skip* at Trinity College, Dublin, and a *scout* at Oxford.

gyp, gives me . . . , *see* **give me gyp**

ℌ | H

haberdashery, n.   **notions store**

In America a *haberdashery* is a men's outfitter. In England it is one of those shops which are getting harder and harder to find which sell pins, needles, thread, tapes, and a little of this and a little of that.

habit-shirt, n.   **corset cover**

Corset covers must be very rare nowadays, because so few

ladies wear corsets anymore. A good many years ago, Mrs. Abbott Lawrence Lowell, the wife of the then president of Harvard College, told the wife of a faculty member, in hushed tones, that the English word for *corset cover* was *habit-shirt*.

had for a mug, *see* **mug** (1)

haggle, v.i.   **dicker**

Both terms are heard in America but *dicker* is not used in England.

hairdresser's, n.   (1) **barber shop**
     (2) **beauty parlor**

The English term is used for both types of establishment.

hair-slides, n. pl.   **bobby pins**

Also known in England as *Kirby grips*.

half, adv.   **halfpast**

In expressions of time, e.g., *half twelve,* meaning *half past twelve.*

half, n. (col.)   **n.A.e.**

A half pint of beer. Form of address to a **publican** (q.v.).

half a tick (sl.)   **half a minute (right away)**

half-cock, *see* **at half-cock**

half-crown, *see under* **crown**

halfpenny, n.   **n.A.e.**

The old one was discontinued on August 1, 1969, as a step in the decimalization of the English currency system. It used to be worth about one-half cent. Pronounced *hay'-pny*. *See also* **ha'p'worth.** The new one, pronounced as spelled, is worth a little over one cent.

half-term, n.   **n.A.e.**

Brief school vacation. *See* **term.**

half-yearly, adj., adv.   **semiannual; semiannually**

hall, n.   **large public room**

In the context of country gentry, *hall* means the ample residence of a landed proprietor in England. In English universities a *hall* is a building for student living or teaching, and in English colleges a common *dining-room*. Where it is equivalent to *passage* as used in America, it means only an *entrance passage*. In its general American sense *hall* finds its equivalent in the English word *passage*. It is used in America to mean a *public building*, usually in a place name, like Carnegie Hall or Convention Hall, and jocularly in the expressions "hire a *hall!*" and "thanks for the use of the *hall!*"

hall of residence   **dormitory**

In America a student living at college lives in a *dorm*, which is an abbreviation of *dormitory*. In England the term *dormitory* means *multiple bedroom* of the sort found at boarding schools for youngsters (but *see* **dormitory**).

Halt, v.i.   **Stop**

The equivalent of an American *Stop* sign used to be and sometimes still is an English road sign reading *Halt*, but *Stop* is now coming into general use. *See* **arterial road.** Once in a while *Halt* appears coupled with a place name to indicate a railroad stop in the middle of nowhere, but near that place.

hanger, n.   **hillside woods**

This special English meaning is used to describe a wooded area on the side of a steep hill or mountain.

hanging matter (col.)   **serious situation**

Used after a negative, usually in the expression "It's not a *hanging matter*," meaning "It's not *all that bad*," "It's not the *end of the world*."

hang up one's hat (col.)   **settle down**

The context is matrimonial.

Hansardize, v.t.   **confront**

In a very limited sense: to confront a Member of Parliament with previous statements inconsistent with his most recent utterance. From *Hansard,* the name of the official Parliamentary report (analogous to the *Congressional Record*) initiated in 1774 by Luke Hansard (d. 1828) and published ever since by Messrs. Hansard.

ha'p'orth, n. (col.)   **trifle**

Contraction of *halfpenny's worth,* as much as one could buy for a halfpenny in the old days (before August 1, 1969, when the old halfpenny was demonetized); *see* Introductory Note 18.

hard, n.   (1) **sloping road to the sea**
                                (2) **hard labor**

(1) A *hard* is a sloping roadway across the sand of a beach, between the high- and low-water marks.
(2) This is an English slang usage and is simply short for *hard labor*.

hardbake, n.   **almond taffy**

hard cheese (sl.)   **tough luck**

Occasionally *hard cheddar; hard lines*.

hard-cooked, adj.   **hard boiled**

Of eggs, not of people.

hard done by (col.)   **done dirt**

    I.e., ill-used.

hare off (col.)   **vamoose**

hare, put up the, *see* **put up the hare**

hare, start a, *see* **start a hare**

harrow, under the, *see* **under the harrow**

hat trick, n. (sl.)   **triple achievement**

    This is cricket slang which originally described the taking of three wickets by three successive bowls, i.e., putting out three members of the opposing team, each with the first ball bowled against him. The term was then extended to any triple sports achievement, like the scoring of three goals by the same player in one soccer game or the winning of three golf tournaments by the same player in succession. *Hat trick* is still used chiefly in sports talk but can be used figuratively to indicate the bringing off of a series of three notable achievements in a row, like three company acquisitions or a lawyer's winning three successive cases. Although the term is used in technical American sports parlance to mean the scoring by one player of three goals in a single game of ice hockey, there would seem to be no equivalent American generic term covering a multiple triumph, in or out of sports. There are some describing a series of successes in specific sports, such as the *Triple Crown* in racing (winning the Kentucky Derby, the Preakness, and the Belmont Stakes), and the *Grand Slam* in golf (winning the U.S. Open, the P.G.A., the Masters, and the British Open). The term is derived from the practice of presenting the triumphant bowler with a hat— a high hat, like the one worn by cricketers in the old prints.

haulage contractor   **trucking company**

haulier, n.   **truckman**

have a bash at (sl.)   **take a shot at**

To *have a bash at* something is to *give it a try.*

have a doss (sl.)   **take a nap**

have a down on (col.)   **be down on**

have a quid each way (col.)   **bet across the board**

At an American track, you can bet to win, place, or show, or
any combination of the two, or all three. Betting on all three in
America is called *betting across the board.* In American horse
racing, to *place* means to come in second, to *show* to come in
third. In English betting, *place* describes any of the first three
to come in (or in a race with very few horses entered, either of
the first two). At a track in England (incidentally, *track* is
course), if you *have a quid each way* and your horse comes
in, you win two bets: the odds on the winner, plus a proportion
of those odds. In America if you *bet across the board* and have

Hat Trick

picked the winner, you win three bets, at descending odds, for win, place, and show, respectively. *Quid* is also English slang for *pound,* but the *quid* in this phrase is used figuratively, the way Americans use *buck* in an expression like: "Some days it's hard to make a *buck.*"

have a read (col.)   **be reading**

To *have a read* connotes settling in a comfortable armchair, and the common expression is *have a good read,* i.e., be wholly absorbed in that activity.

have a rod in pickle for (col.)   **be laying for**

This is rather ominous stuff. *Pickle* usually evokes the image of cucumber preserved in brine, and there are many varieties in both size and flavor. But that is an extension of *pickle*'s primary meaning in both countries, which is the flavored *brine* or *vinegar* in which the preserving is done. The *rod* in this phrase is the type the sparing of which spoils the child, and presumably one soaked in *pickle* would hurt more than an unpickled one. Since brine is a strong solution of salt, a rod thus treated would both inflict and rub salt into a wound in one quick, easy operation, as they say in the advertisements. To *have a rod in pickle for* someone, then, is to be nursing a grudge against him, aching to punish him, and waiting to pounce on him at the first opportunity; or to put it as Gilbert and Sullivan did, to *have him on your list.*

have a time of it, *see* **rare time**

have everything in the shop window, *see* **shop**

have . . . in one's eye (sl.)   **have . . . lined up**

Referring, for instance, to a better job than the one you are suffering in now.

have jam on it (col.)   **have it easy**

I.e., *be in clover, be feeling no pain,* etc. To *want jam on it* means to *want egg in your beer.*

have no mind to (col.) **not care a rap about**

For example, "He is so old that he *has no mind to* women. (Is anybody that old?)

have no time for **have a low opinion of**

Americans commonly use the expression: "I don't *think much of* him," or "I *have no use for* him," where the English might say "I *have no time for* him." Predictably, to *have a lot of time for* someone is to *have a high opinion of* him. *No time for* is very rarely heard in America; *no use for* almost never in England.

have . . . on, v.t. **(1) have . . . going**
(2) kid along

(1) The American *has* a deal *going;* the Englishman *has* it *on.*
(2) When an Englishman is *having* somebody *on,* he is *kidding* him *along,* or *pulling* his *leg.*

have one over the eight (col.) **get somewhat tight**

When somebody has *had one over the eight,* he is not terribly drunk but is certainly under the influence. The inference may be that one ought to be able to put away eight pints of beer without effect—no mean feat for the inexperienced beer drinker!

have . . . on toast **have cornered**

When an Englishman *has* an adversary *on toast,* he *has him where he wants him;* he has confounded him and has him backed into an impossible situation, by coming up with something that shatters his position. In short, he *has* him.

have . . . put in hand **get . . . started**

If an Englishman needed a secretary, he would mention it to friends, put an advertisement into the newspaper, apply to agencies, and would thus *have* the operation *put in hand;* while an American would *get* it *started.*

have the pull of, *see* **pull**

have the wind up, *see* **get the wind up**

Have you been served?   **Is someone helping you?**

Question asked (or which should be asked) by a salesperson (*shop assistant,* or simply *assistant,* in England). Sometimes, "*Are you being served?*"

hayter, n. (col.)   **rotary mower**

A trademark, like **hoover** (q.v.), but now becoming generic for any rotary mower.

head, n.   (1) **principal; dean**
                                          (2) **top of the bottle**

(1) *Head* is a shortening of *headmaster* or *headmistress,* both of which terms are used in America where, however, *principal* is the common term in secondary schools and *dean* in colleges; whereas *dean,* in England, denotes a church office. *Principal* is seldom seen in England. The Feb. 24, 1967, issue of the *Kent and Sussex Courier,* a weekly rural newspaper, contained an alarming headline: "INFANTS TO GET NEW HEAD." No miracle of surgery constituted the subject matter of the story. The article had to do with a change of staff at the Rusthall Infants' School whose current *principal* was leaving to take up the **headship** (q.v.) at Bishop Down's Primary School, i.e., become *principal* there.

(2) The cream that rises to the top of a bottle of milk is called the *head* in England. As in America, the same word also describes the *froth* on beer.

head boy (head girl)   **top boy (top girl; app.)**

In English schools generally, below the university level, the headmaster (*principal*), with the recommendations of the staff (*faculty*), designates one student as the *head boy* (or *head girl,* as the case may be). This fortunate student is not necessarily the one with the best academic record or the best sports record or the best anything specific, but the one who has made the best all-round contribution to school life. The title is an honorable one and involves the burden of exemplary conduct with no special privileges except that of leading the cheers on the occasion of the visit of a notable personage. Incidentally, leading the cheers has nothing to do with *cheerleading* in the American sense. All it means in England is uttering solo the "hip, hip" part to which the ensemble "hooray" is added.

headed paper   **letterhead**

headlamp, n.   **headlight**

headmaster, *see* **head**

headship, n.   **office of school principal
                                           or college dean**

Heath Robinson   **Rube Goldberg**

Applicable to a mechanical contrivance of amusingly superfluous complexity.

heavy over, come a, *see* **come a heavy over**

helter-skelter, n. (col.)   **carnival slide**

One sits on a mat and travels down a dizzying spiral slide (if one likes that sort of thing).

hemi-demi-semiquaver   **sixty-fourth note**

Musical term. *See under* **breve.**

hemlock, n.   **poison** (app.)

To an American *hemlock* usually evokes the image of a species of evergreen seen all over the country. To an Englishman it means a fatal potion made from a poisonous herb (*conium maculatum—maculatum* means *spotted* and the stems of the plant have *spots*); and to a scholar it calls to mind Socrates, whom the Athenian court sentenced to die by drinking a cup of it in 399 B.C.

hessian, n.   **burlap**

hide, n.   **hiding place**

Of a specialized type—for the observation of wild life. It is sometimes used also to mean *hunting blind*.

hidey-hole, n. (col.)   **hideaway**

highly strung   **high-strung**

High Street   **Main Street**

The English commonly named the principal thoroughfare of their villages and towns *The High Street,* and in referring to it, they still retain the definite article (*see* Introductory Note 25). English *High Streets* are about as common as American *Main Streets*.

high tea   **supper**

Tea would be understood to mean *afternoon tea,* served about 4 P.M. and consisting of tea accompanied by bread and jam and cakes and sometimes scones, biscuits, and the like (*see* **cream tea**). *High tea* includes something cooked: eggs or sausages or Welsh rarebit or any combination of these. It is the equivalent of a *light supper*. It is appropriate to quote from Nancy Mitford's novel, *The Blessing*. Sigi (short for Sigismond) is the small son, brought up in England, of an Englishwoman and a Frenchman. When his parents separate he divides his time between them and is now in Paris with his elegant Gallic father. The following colloquy occurs while the two are dining in Paris:

"In England," said Sigi, "little boys don't have dinner."

"No dinner?"

"Supper. And sometimes only high tea."

"What is this, high tea?"

"Yes, well, it's tea, you know, with cocoa and scones, and eggs if you've got hens and bacon if you've killed a pig, and marmalade and Bovril and kippers, and you have it late for tea, about six."

"How terrible this must be!"

"Oh no—high tea is absolutely smashing. Until you come to supper-time, and then I must say you do rather long for supper."

hip, n. (col.)　　　　　　　　　　　　　　**the blues**

Also used as a transitive verb meaning to *give the blues* to someone, i.e., to *depress* him. As a noun, it is sometimes spelled *hyp,* revealing its derivation (*hypochondria*).

hire, *see* **engage**

hire-purchase, n.　　　　　　　　　**installment plan**

Also known colloquially as the *never-never.* That which is re-possessed is known as *hire-purchase snatchback.*

hit for six, *see* **six**

hit off (col.)　　　　　　　　　　**takeoff** (mimic)

hoarding, n.　　　　　　　　　　　　　**billboard**

hob, n.　　　　　　　　　　　　　　**runner** (sled)

But *see* **on the hob.**

hockey, n.　　　　　　　　　　　　　**field hockey**

To an Englishman *hockey* means *field hockey;* to an American, *ice hockey.* If an Englishman wants to talk about the type played on ice, he calls it *ice hockey.* If the American means the game played on the ground, he says *field hockey.*

hogget, n.　　　　　　　　　　　　**yearling sheep**

Hogget would seem more naturally to mean a *young hog* than a *young sheep.* Its meaning stems from the fact that in certain English country dialects the name *hogget* is applied to a *young sheep* before the first shearing of its coat.

hoist, n.　　　　　　　　　　　　**freight elevator**

In America a *hoist* is a *block and tackle.*

ENGLISH　　　　　　　　　　　　　　　　　　AMERICAN

hold a watching brief, *see* **watching brief**

hold the baby (sl.)　　　　　　　　　　**hold the bag**

hold the ring (col.)　　　　　　　　**stay out of it**

To *hold the ring*, or *keep the ring*, is to *stay out* of a situation, or to *remain on the sidelines*. The ropes forming the prize ring in the old days were not attached to posts but were held by the spectators, thus forming the ring. The derivation then becomes obvious.

hold-up, n. (col.)　　　　　　　　**tie-up** (jam)

In America a *holdup* is a *robbery*. In England a *hold-up* is any kind of bottleneck and particularly a *traffic jam*. Although *holdup* would normally not be used to mean a *traffic jam* in America, Americans do use the verbal form, like being *held up* in traffic.

holiday, n.　　　　　　　　　　　　　**vacation**

An employee in England looks forward to his *holiday*, and while on vacation is a *holiday-maker*. But the university student in England speaks of his *vacations* and the summer recess is the *long vacation*, often shortened to *long vac*. See also **come down.**

home and dry (col.)　　　　　　**safe and sound**

Or *over the hump*, or *home free*, i.e., *doing all right, safe and sound*. Sometimes *home and dried*, and even extended occasionally to *home and dried on the pig's back*.

Home Counties　　　　　　　　**Counties surrounding London**

Middlesex, Surrey, Kent, Essex, Hertford, and Sussex.

home from home　　　　　　**home away from home**

home-farm, n.   **residence farm**

I.e., the farm lived on by a farmer who owns several and rents the rest of them.

homely, adj.   **homey**

Homey is colloquial in America. *Homely* is used in England to mean *simple, unpretentious, nothing fancy.* A *homely* woman in England is a friendly, unassuming, domestic type. *Homely,* applied to the atmosphere of a place, comes close to the German *gemütlich. Homely,* in America, is uncomplimentary and means *not good looking* or even *ugly.* One wonders about the social implications of the evolution in America of the adjective *homely* from the proud noun *home. See also* **plain.**

Home Office   **Department of the Interior**

home run   **homestretch**

Racing term. In America, *home run* is exclusively a baseball term, the slang for which is *homer,* the equivalent of which in cricket is a **six** (q.v.).

hon. sec.   **n.A.e.**

Abbreviation for *honorary secretary,* a noble term bestowed upon long-suffering, unpaid, general factotums of nonprofit organizations.

Honours, Birthday, *see* **Birthday Honours**

Honours, four, *see* **four honours**

Honours List, *see* **Birthday Honours**

hood, n.   **top**

Automobile term. What the Americans call a *convertible* the English call a *drop-head.* The movable roof is called a *hood* in England, a *top* in America. When the Americans say *hood* in talking about a car, they mean the cover of the engine, which in England is called the *bonnet*.

hoo-ha, n. (sl.)   **row**

A *brawl*, a *to-do*.

hook it (sl.)   **take a powder**

The Americans *take a powder, get out of town, take it on the lam,* and do lots of other picturesque things to get away from the police, their wives, and other unfriendly people.

hook off   **uncouple**

Railroad term.

hooter, n.   **(1) schnozzle**
(2) automobile horn
(3) factory whistle

The first two uses are slang, the third quite proper.

hoover, n. (col.)   **vacuum cleaner**

Originally *Hoover* was a trademark, but the word has now become generic, like aspirin, victrola, etc. It is also used as a verb: one hurries home to *hoover* the carpet because guests are coming. The trademark was derived from the name of the pioneer in the field, William Henry Hoover (1849–1932). Most Englishmen would be startled to learn that Mr. Hoover was an American—in fact, he was the first mayor of North Canton, Ohio. He was impressed with a crude prototype put together by a fellow townsman and organized the Electric Suction Sweeper Company. The excellence of the product apparently overcame the dullness of its slogan: "It Sweeps as It Beats as It Cleans."

hop; hop-garden; hopper, *see* **oast**

horses, *see* **come to the horses**

hospital job   **n.A.e.**

When there's a smallish job to be done on your house in no
great hurry, and you ask a friendly local contractor to squeeze it
into his regular schedule from time to time as opportunity arises,
you are giving him a *hospital job*. This was the original usage
and is still the respectable version. But the term has come to
acquire a dishonorable connotation and now much more commonly signifies an unscrupulous worker's conversion of a simple
straightforward assignment into a "career," a sort of malinger-
ing operation: He came to fix a shutter in May and is somehow still around in August replacing perfectly good shingles,
putting up superfluous lattices, and rectifying the traditionally
satisfactory plumbing system.

hospital nurse   **registered nurse**

Still addressed and referred to in England as **sister** (q.v.),
whether or not the hospital or the nurse in question is connected
with a religious order. The order of rank in England is *nurse,
sister, matron;* and *sister* is applied properly only to a nurse of
sister rank, but it is often loosely used to describe or address any
nurse.

hostelry, n.   **inn**

The shorter form *hostel* in both countries indicates a specialized
type of *inn* for young people.

hot ice   **dry ice**

hot on (col.)   (1) **tough on**
                                                         (2) **good at**

(1) Thus: "The boss was *hot on* latecomers."
(2) "He's *hot on* gardening," i.e., expert at it.

house, n.   (1) **building**
                                                         (2) **show**

(1) As part of the title of an office building, with a capital

    H. For instance, the English speak of *Esso House,* the Americans of the *Empire State Building.*

(2) If there are two shows a night, the English talk of going to the first *house* or the second *house,* whereas Americans go to see the first *show* or the last *show.*

housemaid, n.	**chambermaid**

A *chambermaid* in England is a *hotel maid.*

houseman, n.	**intern**

A hospital term.

housewife, n.	**sewing gear kit**

housing estate	**residential development**

How are you keeping?, *see* **keeping**

howler, n. (col.)	**boner**

howzat!	**n.A.e.**

Corruption of *How's that?* The cry, called an *appeal,* to the umpire in a cricket game by one or more of the team (*side*) in the field demanding a ruling that the batter (*batsman*) is out on one technicality or another.

hoy, v.t. (col.)	**drive**

Hoy! is an interjection used in herding or driving cattle. To *hoy* a herd is to *drive* it by gestures and shouts of *hoy!* or whatever else comes to mind.

hum and hah (col.)	**hem and haw**

humane society	**lifesaving service**

A *humane society* man would be called a *lifeguard* in America. A *Life Guard* in England is a member of an elite cavalry regiment attached to the royal household. A *humane society* in America is a benevolent organization for the care and shelter of pets.

humble pie   crow

People eat *humble pie* in both countries, but they eat *crow* only in America. Both terms signify *humiliation,* especially that of *eating one's words,* i.e., having to retract a previous categorical assertion. The *humble* in *humble pie* got there by mistake. It is a corruption of *umbles,* a word now obsolete in both countries, and a variant of *numbles,* an archaic English word for the entrails of a deer. *Umble pie,* long ago, was a pie made of the inferior parts of a deer served to the huntsmen and other servants. The inferior parts included the heart, the liver, and the lights. *Lights* is a little known plural noun meaning the *lungs* of animals, now usually used as food for domestic pets. The confusion between the obsolete word *umbles* and the *humble* status of the servants who were served the pie in the old days is quite understandable, especially in view of the problem certain Englishmen have with the letter *h.* Incidentally, the current English word for *umbles* is the rather nasty sounding word **offals** (q.v.). The pie itself probably tasted pretty good.

hump, n. (sl.)   the blues

And *humpy* means *blue* (*depressed*) or *depressing,* depending upon the context.

humpty, n.   pouf

hundredweight, n.   112 pounds

One hundred and twelve pounds in England; 100 pounds in America. *See also* **stone.**

hunt, v.i. (col.)   skip

If your motor is *hunting* in England, you had better (*had best*) get your spark plugs (*sparking plugs*) looked at (*seen to*).

ENGLISH   AMERICAN

hunt, v.t., *see* **shoot**

huss, *see* Introductory Note 12.

hyp, *see* **hip**

hyspy, n. (col.)   **hide-and-seek**

     A corruption of *I spy.*

𝕴 | I

ice, n.   **ice cream**

     In most English restaurants, *ices* means *ice cream,* and *ices, various* is the name for *assorted flavors* thereof. The English use *sorbet* for *sherbet,* but *sherbet* in England means *powdered candy,* a sweet, sugar-like substance which children suck up through licorice sticks. *Water ice,* meaning *sherbet* in the American sense, is sometimes seen on English menus instead of *sorbet.*

icing sugar   **powdered sugar**

     See also **castor sugar.**

identification parade   **police lineup**

identity disk   **dog tag**

     The Americans prefer the slang expression, for which there is no English slang equivalent.

I'll be bound! (sl.)   **I'll be damned!**

I'm easy about it   I don't care

"I'm easy about it," in answer to a question posing a dilemma or
an alternative (e.g., "Would you rather I came at 10 or 11?"),
means *"I don't care,"* or *"It's all the same to me."* *"I'm easy
about it"* has an English equivalent in *"I don't mind."* Sometimes shortened to *"I'm easy."*

immersion tank   hot water heater

An *immersion tank* is not for a baptism. It heats the water for
the whole house, as opposed to a **geyser** (q.v.), which provides a supply of hot water in a particular room, usually the
kitchen. Often referred to as the *immersion heater* or just the
immersion.

immigrant, n. (col.)   non-white

Used by some as a pejorative synonym for **coloured** (q.v.).
Properly speaking, in either country, any person entering another country to settle there permanently is an immigrant.

imperial, adj. (col.)   terrific

An *imperial balls-up* (*see* **balls**) is *one lousy mess.*

impot, n. (col.)   punishment task

Schoolboy slang. A colloquial abbreviation of *imposition,* sometimes written *impo,* meaning an unpleasant task assigned as
punishment at school, like having to write "I shall not pass notes
during Scriptures" 500 times.

impression, n.   printing

Thus: First published January 1968
           Second *impression* February 1968 . . .
In a book printed in America the *second impression* would be
called the *second printing.*

in a cleft stick (col.)   in a pickle

The two branches of a *cleft stick* are like the *horns of a dilemma.*

in a flap (col.)   **het up**

in aid of   **for** (used for)

Expressing purpose. "What's that *in aid of?*" means "What's that *for?*"—asked by someone pointing to an object whose purpose is unclear. Can also be asked about intangibles like a shout or a trip.

in a merry pin (col.)   **in high spirits**

in a way; in a great way, *see* **way**

in (one's) bad books (col.)   **in dutch with . . .**

Variant: *in (one's) black books.*

in baulk, balk (col.)   **in a spot**

Meaning *in difficulties.*

indent, n., v.t.   **requisition**

Indian meal   **corn meal**

Corn in the American sense is usually called *maize* in England (*see* **corn**), but another English name for it is *Indian corn.* Hence *Indian meal* for *cornmeal.*

industrial estate, *see under* **estate**

ingrowing, adj.   **ingrown**

Referring to toenails. The Americans seem resigned to a *fait accompli.*

inland, adj.   **(1) domestic**
                                                  (2) internal

The English speak of *inland* postage rates and *inland* revenue. The opposite number of an American *internal revenue agent* is the English *inland revenue inspector.*

in low water   (1) **hard up**
                                                     (2) **in hot water**

Financial stress is the usual connotation; *difficult straits* or a
depressed state generally (e.g., the weak position of a political
party out of favor) is the broader meaning, and in this sense its
American equivalent would be *in hot water*. *Low in the water*
is a variant meaning *up against it*. Neither expression indicates
a situation so desperate as **on one's beam ends** (q.v.).

innings,   **inning**

Note the *-s*, which does not make *innings* plural. An American
inning is an English *innings*.

Inns of Court   **legal societies**

These are the four legal societies which alone may admit persons to the bar (in the restricted English sense of allowing them
to practice as **barristers** [q.v.] as distinguished from **solicitors**
[q.v.]). These societies are the Inner Temple, Middle Temple,
Lincoln's Inn, and Gray's Inn. The term *Inns of Court* means not
only those societies but also their buildings in London. In addition to the examination procedures for admission to the bar, the
Consolidated Regulations of Inns of Court (as revised on July
22, 1963) provide for the *Keeping of Terms* (synonymous with
the *Eating of Dinners,* in this context) as follows:

KEEPING TERMS

12. The word "Terms" in these Regulations . . . shall
    mean the Terms fixed by the Inns of Court for the
    purpose of Calls to the Bar. . . . [Four Terms are
    designated, each of twenty-three days' duration.]

13. A student may keep terms by dining in the Hall of his
    Inn of Court any three days in each Term.

    .   .   .   .

15. No day's attendance in Hall shall be available for
    the purpose of Keeping Term, unless the Student
    shall have been present at the grace before dinner,
    during the whole of dinner, and until the conclud-

> ing grace shall have been said, unless the acting
> Treasurer, on any day during dinner shall think fit
> to permit the Student to leave earlier. . . .

The full import of these Regulations would hardly be complete
without the following comment of a friend and barrister, a
member of Gray's Inn, who kindly took the trouble to clarify
some obscurities:

> The clue to these strange customs is that they are a
> survival of the medieval college system, still in full opera-
> tion at Oxford and Cambridge, the college being resi-
> dence, parent, and spiritual home rather than teacher,
> which is the function of the family or "school." The Eng-
> lish attach great importance to belonging to some institu-
> tion with traditional standards of conduct. It makes them
> feel good and even act good (or pretend to, which is near
> enough for practical purposes). Dining in Hall, which is
> the way Terms are kept, is the outward manifestation of
> the inward and spiritual truth of belonging to a sort of
> vestigial university and a far from vestigial profession. Din-
> ners are eaten (and drunk) with some ceremony, particu-
> larly in my Inn, Gray's, and are in fact quite pleasant
> occasions where one gets to know those who are or will
> become one's "learned friends" or, if one reaches the emi-
> nence of the Bench, one's "brothers."
> The teaching and examining functions of the Inns as a
> body are now exercised by the Council of Legal Educa-
> tion, though individual Inns do hold "moots" or mock trials
> which are quite valuable and usually amusing.
> Perhaps I should add, in case it is not clear from the
> documents, that the governing body of an Inn is the
> Benchers (judges and other distinguished lawyers) who
> correspond roughly to the "dons" of an Oxford college.

in one's gift   **at one's disposal**

With particular reference to a **living** (q.v.).

inquiry, *see* **enquiry**

insect, n.

bug

Americans use *insect* and *bug* more or less interchangeably. In England *bug* means *bedbug*. *Bug* has slang meanings in both countries. In English slang a *big bug* is what Americans call a *big gun*, a *VIP*. In American slang a *bug* is a *defect*, something wrong with a piece of apparatus, and manufacturers keep busy trying to get the *bugs* out of new products.

in store, *see* **store**

instruct, v.t.

retain

Term used in the legal profession. In England a client *instructs* a solicitor, that is, *engages* him. In America a client *retains* a lawyer.

intake, n. (col.)

rookies

Those recently *taken in*.

interfere with

criminally assault

I.e., to *rape*. The English circumlocution is even more euphemistic than the American.

interior-sprung, adj.

inner spring

Type of mattress.

international, n.

n.A.e.

An athlete who has represented his country, especially at soccer, rugby, or cricket. In soccer and rugby Britain is not one nation but four—England, Scotland, Wales, and Northern Ireland.

interval, n.

intermission

The pause between acts at the theatre or between the halves of a concert. "Tea in the *interval?*" (at the matinee) or "Coffee in the *interval?*" (at an evening performance) is the courteous and comforting question addressed to members of the audience by English usherettes in most theatres, and if the question is answered in the affirmative, you are served at your seat. Stronger beverages may be procured during the afternoon or evening *interval* at the bar with which every English theatre appears to be equipped.

English	American
in the basket (col.)	**no soap**

When a proposed project is *in the basket,* it's *no soap* (rejected, discarded, nothing doing).

in the cart (sl.)	**in dutch**

in the picture	**au courant**

in train	**coming along**

Sometimes *on train. In train* is not often heard in America, and when it is it sounds rather stuffy and means *in good order* or *in proper form.* In England the phrase is heard quite frequently and is the normal response of merchants or contractors to whom one is complaining about delay: "It is *in train,*" meaning that he has done all he can, and that you must be patient.

in two shakes of a duck's tail	**in two shakes of a lamb's tail**

invalid carriage	**electric tricycle**

Quite common on English roads. They are issued by the Ministry of Health, in some cases, to working people who could not otherwise get around.

invalid's chair	**wheelchair**

Also called **bath-chair** (q.v.) and *wheeled chair.*

inverted commas	**quotation marks**

invigilator, n.	**monitor at school examination**

To *invigilate* is to *keep vigil,* i.e., watch over students during examinations.

ironmonger, n. **hardware store**

item, n. **plank**

An *item* in a political program in England is what Americans would call a *plank* in a political platform.

It isn't true! **That's incredible!**

J | **J**

jack, n. (col.) **odd-job man**

jacket, matinee, *see* **matinee jacket**

jacket potato **baked potato**

Baked potato, when used at all, means *roast potato.*

jack-in-office, *see* **bumble**

jam, n. (sl.) **treat**

A *real jam* is English slang for a *real treat.* A *jam sandwich* in England can mean what it does in America, but it is also a term used to mean the kind of layer cake which has jam between the layers.

jam, money for, *see* **money for jam**

jam on it, *see* **have jam on it**

Janeite, n.   **Jane Austen fan**

Sometimes spelled *Janite.*

jarvey, n.   **hack driver**

jasey, n. (sl.)   **wig**

This word is old English slang, and the wig it describes is usually made of worsted, which in England does not mean primarily the tightly woven material made from woolen yarn, as it does in America, but rather the yarn itself. *Worsted* is derived from a town in Norfolk now spelled *Worstead. Jasey* is probably a corruption of *jersey* and is considered a jocular word.

jaunty, n. (sl.)   **chief ship's cop**

Head policeman on a navy vessel (English naval slang).

jaw, n. (sl.)   **talking to**

A *pi-jaw* (*pi-* is short for *pious*) is one of those lectures or sermons delivered by a schoolteacher or a scout leader on a man-to-man basis when a moral infraction is involved, or to prepare the nervous youngster for life's lurking pitfalls.

jaw-bacon, *see* **chaw-bacon**

jelly, n.   **gelatin-type dessert**

Jelly is used in England as in America, but in an English restaurant if you wanted Jell-O or its equivalent for dessert, you would ask for *jelly.*

jelly-bag cap   **stocking cap**

Jelly-bags are used for straining jelly and are made of the kind of stretchable material associated with what Americans call *stocking caps.*

jemmy, n.   **jimmy**

> English burglars use *jemmies;* their American colleagues use *jimmies. Jimmy* is also used as the English slang name for a dish made from sheep's head.

Jeremiah, n. (col.)   **gloomy Gus**

> Everybody knows (or should know) who Jeremiah was. Does anybody know who Gus was?

jerry, n. (sl.)   **pottie**

> I.e., a *chamber pot*. With a capital *J* it is English slang for a *German*.

jersey, n.   **sweater**

> A *jersey* is a *pullover sweater*.

jib, v.t. (col.)   **buck**

> Normally applied to balking horses and in England, colloquially, to cars as well or even to stubborn persons.

jiggered, adj. (col.)   (1) **pooped**
                                                   (2) **up the creek**
                                                   (3) **damned!**

> (1) After a long day's work, you're *jiggered*.
> (2) In a tough situation, like running out of gas in the middle of the night, you'd feel *jiggered*.
> (3) The exclamation "I'm *jiggered!*" means "I'll be *damned!*" as in, "Fancy meeting you here—I'm *jiggered!*"

jiggery-pokery, n. (col.)   **hanky-panky**

jim-jams, n. pl.   **willies**

jimmy, *see* **jemmy**

Jimmy, dismal, *see* **dismal Jimmy**

job, v.t.   **rent horse and carriage**

The English used to *job* horses and carriages in the old days, the verb being applied to both supplier and user (the way Americans use *rent*). *Jobbing,* in this sense, described an arrangement for a specified period of time, and the supplier was called a *jobmaster.*

jobbernowl, n. (col.)   **dope (fool)**

job of work (col.)   **job**

In the sense of *work to be done.*

joey, n. (sl.)   **threepenny**

After Dr. Joseph Hume (1777–1855), just as *bobbies* got their name from Sir Robert Peel, *bowlers* from a Mr. Bowler, and so on. Hume was a radical politician who served many years in Parliament and was known as "Adversity Hume" for his dire predictions of national disaster. *Joey* (with a lower case *j*) originally meant a *fourpenny* piece, but only until that coin was replaced by the *threepenny* (pronounced *threppenny*), often called *threppenny bit* or *threepence* (pronounced *thruppence*).

John Dorey, *see* Introductory Note 12.

johnny, n. (sl.)   **guy**

Usually pejorative. For the English meaning of *guy, see* **guy.**

John Thomas (sl.)   **cock**

Low slang for the male member. Sometimes abbreviated to *J.T.*

joiner, n.   **carpenter**

Technically speaking, *joiners* in both countries, as distinct from *carpenters,* engage especially in interior light carpentry (doors, shelves, etc.) and cabinet making. The English appear often to use the terms interchangeably, but *joiner* is rarely heard in ordinary American conversation.

joint, n.   **roast**

In England that tasty leg of lamb or roast of beef or loin of pork is known as a *joint*. Popular for Sunday lunch, hence the *Sunday joint*.

jolly, adv. (col.)   **mighty (very)**

jotter, n. (col.)   (1) **steno pad**
      (2) **notebook**

J.T., *see* **John Thomas**

jug, n.   **pitcher**

In England it is the milk *jug* or water *jug* which is placed on the table.

juggins, n. (sl.)   **dope (fool)**

Synonymous with *muggins*.

jumper, n.   **pullover**

This term is used to describe a woman's *pullover* sweater. In America a *jumper* is what the English would call a *pinafore*, i.e., a one-piece sleeveless dress, usually worn over a blouse.

junction box, *see* **box**

junk   **worn-out rope**

Old, worthless stuff, rubbish, which is called *junk* in America, is generally referred to as *rubbish* or **lumber** (q.v.) in England, where *junk*, though now extended to mean *rubbish* generally, is still more especially a nautical term meaning *worn-out hawsers* or *cables* which are either discarded or picked apart for use as calking material or in making swabs.

jurist, n.   **legal scholar**

In America *jurist* is synonymous with *judge*. Unfortunately not all *jurists* (in the American sense) are *jurists* (in the English sense).

just a tick!   **right with you!**

just going   **just about**

Used in expressions of time of day: "It's *just going* twelve" means "It's *just about* twelve," or *practically* twelve. The expression *just on* is used by the English in the same way: "It's *just on* nine o'clock," i.e., it's *not quite* or *just about* nine.

just here   **right here**

just on, *see* **just going**

𝕶 ┃ K

K., n. (col.)   **knighthood**

To get one's *K.* is to be *knighted* (*see* **Birthday Honours**).

keenest prices (col.)   **biggest bargains**

Often seen in advertisements: "For *keenest prices* shop at So-and-So's."

keen on, *see* **dead keen on**

keep, v.t.   **raise**

An Englishman who *keeps* pigs is not simply having them as pets; he is in the business and in America would be said to be *raising* them.

keep cave, *see* **cave**

keeper, n.   custodian; guard

When Americans use the word *keeper* they think in terms of a prison, an insane asylum, or a zoo. *Keeper* is the usual English term for a *museum custodian* or *guard*. To an Englishman *guard* would normally evoke the image of a sentry or member of an elite regiment.

keeping, *see* **How are you keeping?**

keep one's terms, *see* **eat one's dinners; Inns of Court**

keep the ring, *see* **hold the ring**

keep your eyes skinned (col.)   **keep your eyes peeled**

Keep your pecker up! (c.)   **Chin up!**

In this expression, *pecker* means *spirits* or *courage*. This connotation of *pecker* is probably derived from its original meaning of a *bird that pecks* (cf. *woodpecker*), and by extension, that with which it pecks, i.e., its beak, which became slang for *nose*. It is obviously impossible to *keep your pecker* (in this sense) *up* without simultaneously *keeping your chin up*.

kerbside-crawl, *see* **gutter-crawl**

keyless watch   **stem-winder**

kick the beam (sl.)   **lose out**

kick-up, *see* **dust-up**

kidney, n. (col.)   **stripe**

Both Englishmen and Americans use *kidney* figuratively in the sense of *type* or *temperament*, in expressions like a *person of that kidney,* or a *man of the right kidney;* but the English do not use *stripe* that way.

213

Kilkenny cats (col.) squabblers

Based on an old Irish legend about two cats who fought each other so long and so murderously that finally there was nothing left but their tails. Kilkenny is a county in southeast Eire, and also the name of its capital; it was the scene of long and ancient internecine struggles between the Anglo-Irish and the original Irish which began in the thirteenth century and went on. If there were a real free-for-all going on, it might be referred to as a *donnybrook*, from Donnybrook Fair, an annual event which used to take place in the town of Donnybrook, also in Ireland, and was famous for the drinking of much whiskey and riotous fighting. The Kilkenny cats of the legend were pretty murderous, too, but figuratively the phrase means a group of people who really do not get along well at all and whose disagreement is audible or at least noticeable.

kinky, adj. (sl.) (1) oddball
(2) cool

(1) *Kinky*, as used by grownups, often implies odd sexual tastes. There is also a slang noun, *kink*, which has its American equivalent in *kick*, as in the phrase "I'm on a new kick," i.e., involved in a new interest.
(2) As English teenage slang, *kinky* is the rough equivalent of *cool* in American adolescent slang.

kiosk, *see* call-box

kip, n., v.i. (sl.) (1) rooming-house
(2) room in a rooming-house
(3) bed
(4) sleep
(5) turn in

The *house*, the *room* in the house, the *bed* in the room, the *sleep* in the bed; sometimes seen in the expressions *go to kip* or *take a kip*, meaning to *turn in*.

kipper, n. (sl.)   **kid** (tot)

Synonymous with a like-sounding English slang word—*nipper.*

Kirby grips, n. pl.   **bobby pins**

Also known in England as *hair-slides.*

kissing gate   **cattle gate** (app.)

Kissing gates found in rural England are gates hung with the side away from the hinge swinging within a V-shaped or U-shaped enclosure in such a way that people can get through but cattle can't. You push the gate away from the nearside of the "V" or "U," step into the latter, slide over to the other side, and push the gate back. This quaint device acquired its romantic name (one is told) because it was often the place where a swain said goodnight to his lady love, and a certain amount of lingering and incidental activity was in order.

kiss your hand, *see* **as easy as kiss your hand**

knacker's yard   **boneyard**

knave, n.   **jack**

In playing cards.

knickers, n. pl.   **ladies' underpants, elasticized top and bottom**

In America *knickers* would be understood as short for *knickerbockers,* which is the English term for *plus fours,* an article of wearing apparel still seen there. *See also* **cami-knickers.** To *get your knickers in a twist* is to *make a great fuss.*

knife-and-fork tea (col.)   **light supper** (app.)

A **high tea** (q.v.), at which meat or fish is served and a knife is required. The converse of a **fork supper** (q.v.).

knob, n. (sl.)   scab (strikebreaker)

knobble, *see* **nobble**

knock, n. (sl.)   hit (success)

But *see* **bit of a knock.**

knock, v. (sl.)   wow (impress)

To *knock* someone in American slang is to *disparage* him, but in English slang it means to *impress* him greatly, i.e., to *knock him dead,* and is probably short for *knock for six* (*see* **six**).

knock acock (col.)   bowl over

To *astonish,* to present with the unexpected.

knocker, *see* **up to the knocker**

knocker-up, *see* **knock up** (1)

knock for six, *see* **six**

knock oneself up   knock oneself out

I.e., to *overdo it.*

knock-out, n.   (1) **practice session**
                                                (2) **elimination contest**

(1) A tennis term, synonymous with **knock up** (2).
(2) Competition resulting in the elimination of losers.

knock up   (1) **wake up; look in on**
                                                (2) **tennis warm-up**
                                                (3) **throw together**

(1) The use of this term by Englishmen in America is fraught with danger; like the use of **fanny** (q.v.) by Americans in England. A respectable American will take great pains to avoid *knocking up* a lady friend, as he understands the

term, because in his country it is an indelicate expression
for getting a lady into a delicate condition. In England
knocking people *up* is a far less serious matter. All it
means there is to *wake* people *up*. The *knock* in the
phrase refers simply to knocking on the door of somebody
who wasn't expecting you, and if it is at a late enough
hour, arousing the captive host. This may be inconsiderate,
but the damage done by that kind of knocking up is far
more easily repaired. *Knocker-up* in England is a term denoting a special type of arouser, one whose function it is to
summon sleeping railroad workers to their jobs.

(2) A wholly unrelated use of *knock up* as a colloquial noun
is as the equivalent of the American term *warm-up* as
used in tennis, meaning the practice of knocking the ball
back and forth for a while before starting the match in
earnest. Synonymous with *knock-out*.

(3) A further wholly unrelated English meaning is *throw together*, as for instance: "Don't stand on ceremony, come
along, we can always *knock* something *up* in a hurry," referring, of course, to getting up a hurried impromptu lunch.

Knocked Up

Knock up is used also in the sense of providing a make-shift facility of one sort or another under urgent circumstances, as for instance, to *knock up* a little place in the barn for an unexpected artist guest as a temporary studio. A jocular use in this same general area has been seen in such expressions as *knock up* an heir, meaning to manage to get a baby started, referring of course, to a previously childless couple. A further meaning is to *eke out* or *scratch together* (a living, an existence) by precarious employment as in the case of a struggling author or a person living by his wits. *See also* **knock oneself up,** where the reflexive use introduces an entirely different meaning.

ENGLISH	AMERICAN
know the form (col.)	**have the inside dope**
knuckle-duster, n. (col.)	**brass knuckles**
K.O.	**kickoff**

An English football abbreviation. Thus, on a poster advertising a **football** (q.v.) game, "*K.O.* 3 P.M." It also means *knock-out,* a boxing term, as in America.

𝕷 | L

ENGLISH	AMERICAN
label, n.	**sticker; tag**
labourer, *see* **agricultural labourer; casual labourer**	
labour exchange	**state employment office** (app.)
lacquer, n.	**hair spray**

ladder, n.   **run**

This term applies to ladies' stockings. *Ladder-proof* hose are advertised in England just as *run-proof* stockings are advertised here, but the ladies remain skeptical on both sides of the Atlantic.

ladybird, n.   **ladybug**

Also called a *golden-knop.*

Lady of Threadneedle Street, *see* **Old Lady of Threadneedle Street**

lag, n., v.t.   (1) **insulate**
                                                     (2) **insulation**

To wrap a pipe with insulation against loss of heat. As a noun it means the *pipe covering* and is sometimes lengthened to *lagging.*

lag, n., v.t. (sl.)   **jailbird**

A *lag* is a *jailbird* and the word is usually found in the expression *old lag.* To be *lagged* is to be *sent up,* although *lagged* sometimes means merely *pinched* (*arrested*), whether or not the unfortunate is eventually *sent up.* A *lagging* is a *stretch.* There exists an organization called the *Old Lags Brigade,* which consists of hardened criminals placed on last-chance probation before they are imprisoned. It was founded in the fifties by a London judge named Reginald Ethelbert Seaton.

lambs' tails (col.)   **catkins**

Lambs' tails in England, in addition to making good soup, also refer to *catkins* hanging from certain trees such as the hazel and willow, and *catkins* in both countries are *downy flowerings* or *inflorescences.* The word *catkin* is a rather cloying diminutive of *cat* (formed like *manikin, pannikin,* etc.) and was invented because of the resemblance of those inflorescences to *cats' tails.* In any event, none of this is to be confused with *Lamb's Tales,* which are synopses of Shakespeare's plays by Charles and Mary Lamb.

| **lame duck** (sl.) | (1) **hard-luck guy** |
| | (2) **stock exchange defaulter** |

(1) A person *in difficulties, unable to cope.* The narrow American usage, describing an incumbent political official or body still in office after losing an election but only because the winner has not yet been seated, is a highly restricted application of this English meaning.

(2) This term also has the meaning of one unable to meet his obligations on the London Stock Exchange.

land agent   **real-estate broker**

Synonymous with *estate agent.*

landed with (sl.)   **stuck with**

landing, n.   **upstairs hall**

Americans use *landing* to mean the area at the top of a flight of stairs where you stop to catch your breath before continuing upwards. A *landing* in an English home is a *hall* on an upstairs floor.

landlord, n.   **pub keeper**

In addition to its wider general meaning in both countries, *landlord* has the special English meaning and flavor of *innkeeper.* Many **pubs** (q.v.) were once real inns and a few still have rooms for rent, but some which no longer let rooms still have names which include the word *hotel,* such as the Eight Bells Hotel and the Queen's Head Hotel. The keeper of such a pub (who used to be a *landlord* in the literal sense when rooms were available) is nonetheless still called *landlord* and is so summoned and addressed by clients not familiars of the establishment who don't feel privileged to address him by name. *Publican* is synonymous with *landlord* in this sense and comes

from *public house,* a term still in use but far less common than
its shortened form *pub. See* **free house** for a discussion of the
landlord's business arrangements.

land of the leal   **heaven**

Leal is a literary form of *loyal.*

landslip, n.   **landslide**

larder, n.   **pantry**

lasher, n.   **pool**

Particularly, one formed by water spilling over a **weir** (q.v.).

lashings, n. pl. (sl.)   **scads**

laugh like a drain (sl.)   **horselaugh**

lavatory roll   **roll of toilet paper**

Delicacy, like the American use of *tissue.*

Law Society   **Bar Association** (app.)

There is a national *Law Society* and many local ones in England, just as there is a nationwide *Bar Association* and many
local ones in America. In certain areas such as the setting of
ethical standards in conduct, the furtherance of legal education,
and so on, the functions of the English and American bodies
coincide. Membership in *law societies* is confined to **solicitors**
(q.v.) only. **Barristers** (q.v.) have their own group which is
known as the General Council of the Bar. No such dichotomy
exists in America. In neither country is membership compulsory.

layabout, n.   **loafer; hobo**

lay-by, n.   **rest area**

Roadside parking space. When you see a road sign reading
lay-by as you drive along in England, you know that up ahead

on your left, there will be a turn-out which broadens into a
parking area. People use it for momentary parking, e.g., to take
a nap, to look at the view, or as a picnic area. The English are
very fond of stopping by the side of the road and having a picnic lunch or high tea complete with folding chairs, folding table
with tablecloth, tea kettle, and very elaborate outdoor eating
equipment generally, to say nothing of all that good food. If
there is no *lay-by* handy, any old *verge* (*shoulder*) will do.

lay on   **provide; arrange for**

Very commonly seen in the participial form *laid on*, meaning
provided for in advance. Thus, office quarters can be rented in
England with or without a secretary *laid on.*

laystall, n.   **rubbish heap**

lea, *see* **ley**

leader, n.   (1) **editorial**
                                                                  (2) **chief counsel**
                                                                  (3) **concert master**

This word has three distinct English meanings which are not
found in America:
(1) It means *newspaper editorial,* especially the principal one.
    There is a related (and rather unattractive) word *leader-
    ette,* which has nothing to do with female leaders but
    means a *short editorial paragraph* which follows the main
    one.
(2) Another meaning is that of *leading counsel* on a team of
    lawyers trying a case.
(3) Finally, it means the *concert master* of an orchestra, i.e.,
    the first violinist who sits to the conductor's left and is his
    right-hand man, acting as his liaison with the rest of the
    players. This meaning sometimes confuses Americans, be-
    cause *leader* is popularly used in America to mean *con-
    ductor* when it refers to a small orchestra (as opposed to a
    symphony orchestra), and also because *leader,* in America,
    is properly used to describe the *baton-wielder* in a band,
    large or small.

lead for the Crown   **act as chief prosecuting attorney**

    See also **leader** (2).

leasehold, *see* **freehold**

leat, n.   **open watercourse**

leaver, n.   **graduating student**

    One about to complete the curriculum at a **prep school** (q.v.) or **public school** (q.v.) at the end of that term. During that final term the student is known as a *leaver*. On the completion of the term the *leaver* becomes an **old boy** (**old girl;** q.v.).

leave the metals, *see* **metals**

leave well alone   **leave well enough alone**

left luggage office   **baggage room**

left-on, adj.   **left-handed**

    To describe a left-handed bowler (app. cricket counterpart of a pitcher); but a left-handed batsman (batter) is called *left hand.*

legitimate drama   **classical drama**

    This phrase means very different things in the two countries. In England it refers to dramatic works of established merit as opposed to melodrama or farce, no matter how well-known, e.g., *Hamlet* vs. *East Lynne,* or *The Rivals* vs. *Charley's Aunt.* In America the *legitimate theatre* means the *stage* as opposed to any other form of dramatic representation, and *legitimate drama* includes any play produced on the stage, or in today's idiom, *live.*

legpull, n. (col.)   **gag (joke)**

lengthman (lengthsman), n.   road maintenance man

A *lengthman* is a laborer charged with the duty of keeping a certain *length* of road in good condition. The word developed in the old days before the creation of a countrywide system of hard-surfaced roads requiring the services of teams of road workers equipped with all kinds of heavy machinery and evokes the image of the solitary worker equipped with only a spade, a high degree of independence, and a noble sense of responsibility. As used today it can sometimes be taken only as synonymous with *streetcleaner*. There is a highly specialized category of *lengthman*, however, which relates to the maintenance of England's inland waterways or canals. These wonderful canals are quite a story in themselves, one which has been beautifully written by L. T. C. Rolt, and in his second book on the subject, *The Inland Waterways of England* (George Allen and Unwin, Ltd., London, 4th ed., 1966, pp. 110–111), he writes of the canal lengthman in the following prose, which is offered for the reader's delight:

> If a canal overflows or bursts its banks the consequences may be serious as it may run upon embankments high above thickly populated areas. . . .
>
> In October 1939, 3 inches of rain fell in one night in the Daventry area, and despite every effort to discharge the surplus flood water, a breach occurred in the Weedon embankment of the Grand Union Canal. The local lengthman, who had been on duty all through the night, was aware of this danger-point, discovered the breach almost as soon as it carried away in the early hours of the morning, and dropped the stop planks. Only minor local flooding occurred and damage to property was negligible, but had it not been for this prompt action, fifteen miles of waterway could have poured out through an ever widening gap.
>
> Of all the many never-ending jobs upon which the security and comfort of our lives and property depend, that of the canal lengthman is probably the least known or appreciated. When we sweep to the north in a night Scotch express or awaken from sleep to hear a locomotive

whistle and the clash of buffers we do occasionally remember the signalman's vigil in his lonely cabin or the
endless work of shunters and train crews on the steel webs
of the marshalling yards. We sometimes hear the roar of
night lorry traffic on a trunk road, or flick a switch in the
small hours and think of those who tend the turbo-alter-
nators and switchgear in some distant power station. But
when a great storm lashes rain against the panes and
booms in the chimney it merely induces, by contrast, a
sharpened sense of comfort and security. Yet a quarter of
a mile away there may be a canal whose water level is
higher than our roof top, and we do not realize that we
are only being saved from a catastrophic flood by the vig-
ilance of one man. He may have forfeited a night's sleep
to plod, storm lantern in hand through the blinding rain
along the towing path watching his levels, regulating his
paddles, looking for danger signs. He is often a solitary
taciturn old man, accustomed to keeping his own company, for his little red-brick cottage dating from the day
the canal was built is often remote even from the vil-
age by-road, accessible by land only along the towing path
or by a footway over the fields. Sometimes if you are walking the towpath in the daytime you will meet him, a slow-
moving, heavy-booted figure bow-hauling his small punt-
shaped boat with a load of hedge trimmings or some clay
puddle to stop a small leak in the bank. You may perhaps
see his weather-beaten face in the village pub of a night,
the beer froth whitening the fringe of his heavy mous-
tache. He may not talk to you about his job, for he is seldom a conversationalist, preferring a contemplative pint,
but even in these surroundings you can generally recog-
nize him by the queer little hump between his shoulder-
blades. It is caused by the end of the lock windlass which
he habitually carries tucked over the shoulder under his
coat. He is a countryman just as the canal has become a
part of the countryside, and yet in a sense he stands apart
from the village being a member of that unique amphib-
ious community of the canals. Probably he gets his winter
coal by water, and if he ever moves house he will do so by

boat. His job of regulating the water over a wide area calls for considerable local knowledge, a knowledge which he inherited from his father before him, a knowledge of sluices, weirs, culverts and streams of which his mind is often the only chart. The canal is his life and his first thought. When his time comes, and he must make way for a generation whose first thought is the contents of the weekly pay packet, it is probable that much of this inherited knowledge will go with him. So much the greater will be our loss.

let, *see* **engage**

letter box   **mailbox**

See also **pillar box; post box.**

letter post   **first-class mail**

The terms *first-class mail* and *second-class mail* are now current in England to indicate priorities for delivery.

let the shooting, *see* **shooting**

level, adj.   (1) **even**
                                                       (2) **close**

(1) When players are *level* in a game, it means that they are *even*.
(2) However, a *level* race is not a *tie* but only a *close* race.

level crossing   **grade crossing**

level pegging, n., adj. (col.)   **even**

A term borrowed from cribbage, in which the score is kept by advancing *pegs* along a series of holes in a board. It applies to equal scores in games or mutual obligations between friends or businessmen which wash each other out.

levels (A-levels; O-levels), *see* **A-levels**

ley, n.   **temporary pasture**

Ley-farming is the system of putting a given area into grazing pasture for a few years, then "catching the fertility," as they say in East Anglia and using that area for a particular crop. A *ley* is a *rotating pasture;* variant of *lea.* In Cambridge The Leys is the name of a well-known private school.

licensed, adj.   **having a liquor license**

Sign seen on most English hotels and restaurants.

lick, n. (col.)   **dab**

Term used in house painting, meaning a *light wash.* Cf. *lick* in a *lick and a promise.*

lido, n.   **public open-air swimming pool**

The *Lido* is Venice's famous bathing resort. A *lido,* in England, is a *public swimming pool (swimming-bath).* One sees the term *corporation swimming-bath,* meaning *public swimming-bath. Corporation* in that phrase is the equivalent of the American term *municipal.* A *deck lido* is a *ship's swimming pool.*

lie doggo (sl.)   **lie low**

Literally, to *lie doggo* is to *lie motionless,* the way a dog does; to play dead. Figuratively it means to *lie low,* to *bide one's time.*

lie down under (col.)   **buckle under**

I.e., to *give way* to the other party, to *kowtow.*

life-belt, n.   **life preserver**

In England a **life-preserver** (q.v.) is a *blackjack.*

Life Guard   **member of a regiment of household cavalry**

The household involved is the royal household. Properly speaking, a member of this elite cavalry regiment is called a *Life Guardsman*. *Lifeguards* in the American sense (people who save other people from drowning) are called *humane society men*.

life-preserver, n.   **blackjack**

In America, a *life preserver* is an instrument of mercy called a *life-belt* in England.

life vest   **life jacket**

The English say *jacket*, too, but B.O.A.C.'s pamphlets and signs remind you that there is a *life vest* under each seat.

lift, n.   **elevator**

To go higher in a building (without walking) the English use *lifts*, the Americans *elevators*. To stand up higher, the English put *elevators* into their shoes, the Americans *lifts*.

like a dog's dinner (col.)   **dolled up**

To be *got up like a dog's dinner* is to be *dressed to kill*, i.e., all *dolled up*.

like one o'clock (col.)   **to a "T"**

"Does that suit you, sir?" "*Like one o'clock!*"

li-lo, n.   **air mattress**

Li-lo is in fact a trademark for a particular make of air mattress. There are other brands, but *li-lo* is becoming generic, like **hoover** (q.v.) for *vacuum cleaner*. The nonbrand English equivalent for *air mattress* is *air bed*.

limb, n. (col.)   **little devil**

Limb is a shortening of the phrase *limb of the devil* or *limb of Satan* and is used to mean a *mischief-making youngster*, the way *little devil* is used in America.

limb of the law   arm of the law

limited company   corporation

Also called *limited liability company,* more usually just **company**
(q.v.). The essence of this form of business organization in
either country is the *limitation* of its liability to the value of its
net worth, so that individuals can regulate, i.e., *limit,* the
amount of their investments in a corporate enterprise without
risking their other assets. The abbreviation *Ltd.* is the English
equivalent of the American *Inc.* (for *Incorporated*). A *company* in America may be a corporation but need not be. In
America, *Joseph Smith & Company, The Joseph Smith Company,* or *Joseph Smith Associates* very often means just plain
Joe Smith, doing business all by himself.

Like a Dog's Dinner

line, n.   track

Americans use the word *line* to mean a whole *railroad company,* rather than the *track* itself. Passengers in America are warned not to cross the *track.* In England it is the *line* one mustn't cross, according to the signs.

liners, n. (col.)   **underpants**

Worn under **knickers** (q.v.).

lines, marriage, *see* **marriage lines**

lining, n.   **striping**

Term used in painting, e.g., the painting of automobiles.

lino, n. (col.)   **linoleum**

The English almost always use the colloquial shortening. *Linoed* means covered with *linoleum.* A *linoed* floor is a *linoleum* floor.

lint, n.   **surgical dressing**

listening room   **control room**

Where the engineer of a radio station sits.

list office   **calendar clerk**

Legal term.

little-go, n. (col.)   **first B.A. examination
at Cambridge**

little Mary (col.)   **tummy**

live in cotton wool (col.)   **be born yesterday**

Cotton wool is *absorbent cotton,* used here as a metaphor for careful packing to provide insulation from the traumas of life in this harsh world.

live like fighting cocks (col.) **gorge**

To eat not wisely but too well. The phrase implies that the food is not only plentiful but rich.

liverish, adj. (col.) **bad tempered**

livery, n. **costume**

Livery has a number of historical and distinctly English meanings having to do with ancient London City companies or guilds called *Livery Companies* which used to have distinctive costumes or *liveries*. *Livery* is still used generically in both countries to describe certain types of uniform, such as those worn by chauffeurs. In England it is now also applied to characteristic *color schemes* like those of the various divisions of the British Railway System.

living, n. **benefice**

Used in church positions such as those of a rector, vicar, etc.

loaf, n. (sl.) **bean (head)**

Short for *loaf of bread,* cockney rhyming slang for *head,* but now adopted as general slang as in such expressions as "Use your loaf!" *See* Introductory Note 13.

local, n. (col.) (1) **neighborhood bar**
(2) **native**

(1) Englishmen often talk of nipping down to the *local* (*local pub*).
(2) Usually heard in the plural, the *locals* is a rather affectionate term meaning the *natives,* the people in a particular community who look as though they haven't just moved out from the city, have been around a while, really belong there, and are going to be around for some time to come.

locum, n. (col.)   **doctor covering for**
another

The term is also applied to mean a *clergyman's temporary re-*
placement. Locum is a colloquial shortening of *locum tenens.*
Locum is the accusative case of *locus,* which is Latin for the
noun *place,* and *tenens* is the present participle of *teneo,* which
is Latin for the verb *hold.* In the phrase *locum tenens, locum* is
the object of *tenens,* and *tenens* is used as a substantive, i.e., a
person holding. A literal translation of *locum tenens,* then, would
be *one holding a place,* and by inference, a *person taking*
somebody else's place, i.e., a *replacement. Lieutenant* (pronounced *leftenant* in England) was taken over intact from the
French, in which language *lieu* means *place* and *tenant* is the
present participle of *tenir, to hold,* and somebody *tenant*
somebody else's *lieu* becomes a *lieutenant,* so that it is easy to
see how that word acquired not only its military connotation, but
even more particularly its general meaning of one's *deputy,*
substitute, and at times, *replacement.* Be all that as it may,
while your English doctor is off on a Scottish salmon fishing holiday or just playing village cricket that afternoon, his *locum* will
take good care of you.

lodger, *see* **boarder**

loft, n.   **attic**

lofty catch   **pop fly** (app.)

A cricket term.

lolly, n. (sl.)   **dough (money)**

A *piece of the lolly* means *some of the gravy.* A *lolly* in England (reminiscent of *lollipop*) is also ice cream or water ice on
a stick.

Lombard Street (col.)   **money market;**
Wall Street (app.)

London's money market, named symbolically after its principal street for banking and finance; analogous to *Wall Street* used that way. But **the City** (q.v.) is the more usual colloquialism for the financial community generally.

long chalk, *see* **not by a long chalk**

long firm (col.)   **set of deadbeats**

long-head, n. (col.)   **smart cookie**

The adjective is *long-headed.*

long odds on   **heavy favorite**

This is a sports term, used as a noun.

long pull (col.)   **extra measure**

In America the *long pull* signifies the *future,* the *years to come* in a particular situation. Thus, one buys securities and holds them for the *long pull.* The English use it quite differently: In a pub, the *long pull* is a measure of beer or other liquid refreshment over and above the quantity asked for; in other words, a drink with a built-in dividend. Sometimes the *long* is omitted, so that *a pull* means the same thing as a *long pull.*

long sea outfall   **remote sewage disposal pipe**

This awkward phrase describes a sewage pipe that sticks way out into the ocean in order to dispose of the effluent of a seaside town without polluting the beaches.

long-sighted, adj.   **farsighted**

In England *far-sighted* is hardly ever used literally to describe corporeal optical capacity. It is almost always used in the figurative sense of *looking ahead,* which figurative use is shared with America. The English term for *nearsighted* is *short-sighted,* which is always used figuratively in America to describe a person who doesn't plan ahead, this figurative use being shared with England. In other words, the English use *long-sighted* and *short-sighted* literally where the Americans would say *farsighted* and *nearsighted*. The English use *far-sighted* figuratively, as the Americans do; and the Americans use *shortsighted* figuratively, as the English do.

long vac, *see* **come down; holiday**

loo, n. (col.)　　　　　　　　　　　　　　　　　　　　**john**

I.e., *bathroom* or *lavatory* or *washroom* or *powder room*—the euphemisms are many. The English unashamedly use the word *toilet,* a term usually avoided by Americans as indelicate. But Evelyn Waugh, in "An Open Letter to the Hon'ble. Mrs Peter Rodd (Nancy Mitford) on a Very Serious Subject," says that *toilet* is "pure American" and that *lavatory* is the English euphemism. If Mr. Waugh was right when he said that, the whole thing somehow managed to change completely around in the meantime. In any event, the author has been assured that *loo* is a corruption of *l'eau* (French for *the water*) as used, in the good old days, in the expression *"Gardez l'eau!"* (*"Watch out for the water!"*), shouted down at pedestrians by people throwing slops out the window. Another source advises that *loo* is a truncated pun derived from *Waterloo* (cf. the *water* in *water closet*). But a more trustworthy derivation would appear to be as follows: The French euphemism, used in hotels, consists of putting the number *100* on the door of the toilet, as a variant of the letters *w.c.,* which stand for *water closet. Numéro cent* and *w.c.* (pronounced *dooblevay say*) are used interchangeably in French by the anxious guest looking for the facility. It is easy to see how the Englishman returning from a visit to France could have misinterpreted the number *100* and come back with *loo.*

looby, n.　　　　　　　　　　　　　　　　　　　　**simpleton**

loofah, n.　　　　　　　　　　　　　　　　**sponge** (app.)

There is an inedible member of the cucumber family called *luffa aegyptiaca,* whose pod dries out after the fleshy part rots, leaving a spongelike skeleton which is used like a sponge in the bath. Somewhat abrasive.

look out   (1) **pack**
                                                      (2) **select**

Look out has a good many English uses shared with America, but there are two not so shared:
(1) While watching you pack for a trip, your English friend might say, "*Look out* your woolies; it's cold where you're going." (*Woolies* are sweaters in England, *heavy underwear* in America.) *Look out*, in that sense, means *pack*, and your friend is advising you to *take along* a few sweaters. Better follow the advice.
(2) One can also *look out* facts in reference works while engaged in a research project. Here, *looking out* means *looking up*, and then *selecting* the data you find for use as authority to prove whatever it is you're trying to prove.

look-out, n. (col.)   **outlook**

I.e., *prospect*, as in stock market forecasting: "The *look-out* for that group of companies is bleak." It also has the connotation of *lot* or *fate* when it refers to something then future, now past: "To die at 18—that had been a *poor look-out*," i.e., a *sad fate*. *Look-out* has the ordinary American colloquial meaning as well (*responsibility, concern*), as in: "Keeping petrol in the car is your *look-out*." Conversely, the standard American meaning of *lookout* (no hyphen), a *point* from which one gets a wide view of the landscape, is often **view-point** (q.v.) in England, which of course (again without a hyphen) refers to things abstract rather than concrete in America.

look 'round   **look**

As a noun: a *good look*, an inspection.

look slippy! (sl.)   **get going!**

look-up, v.t.   **look . . . up**

"I *looked-up* myself in *Who's Who*," said a famous man. An American celebrity would have said, "I *looked* myself *up*. . . ."

loopy, adj. (sl.)   **loony**

loose-box, n.   **horse stall**

loose chippings   **loose gravel**

That over which the motorist is enjoined, in both countries, to drive slowly, please.

loose covers   **slipcovers**

loose waterproof   **slicker**

lords and ladies   **jack-in-the-pulpits**

Also called *cuckoo pints*.

lorry, n.   **truck**

To *lorry-hop* or *lorry-jump* is to *hitchhike*. An **articulated lorry** (q.v.) is a *trailer truck*.

lost property office   **lost and found**

lot, n. (col.)   (1) **the works**
                         (2) **group**
                         (3) **bunch**

(1) The *lot* means the *whole lot*, the *whole kit and caboodle*, the *works*. Thus, "They gave me a beautiful room, marvelous food, wonderful service . . . the *lot!*" Or, "He caught cold, got the mumps, sprained his ankle . . . the *lot!*" The *lot* also means *all* of something. At a sale, there are three dresses hard to choose from. You ponder and ponder and finally say (recklessly), "I'll take the *lot*," i.e., *all of them*.

(2) It also has the meaning of *group*. In an American Chinese

restaurant, they are fond of arranging dishes into Group A, Group B, etc. They do it in England, too, and there you would say, "We'll have two from the first *lot,* three from the second *lot,* etc.

(3) *Lot* means *group* in another sense, too, the sense in which Americans use the slang term *bunch.* Thus, if an Englishman saw a group of unsavory-looking characters on a street corner, he might remark: "I don't like the looks of that *lot,*" where an American would refer to them as "that *bunch." You lot* means *the lot of you,* i.e., *all of you,* in addressing a group of people, and might come out in America as "Hey, *you guys.*"

lot on one's plate | **lot to do**

Or *enough on one's plate (plenty to do).*

loud-hailer, n. | **bullhorn**

lounge, n. | **living room**

lounge bar | **n.A.e.**

Synonymous with **saloon bar** (q.v.). *Lounge* means *living room. Lounge bar* is sometimes used instead of *saloon bar* to indicate the fancier and more exclusive part of a pub.

lounge suit | **business suit**

love, n. (col.) | **honey** (app.)

Widely used as a very informal term of address in the north of England; by men only to women, but by women without distinction as to sex. Its nearest American equivalent would be *honey,* which used to have a particularly southern flavor, but by now has spread all over the country.

lovely! adj. | **fine!**

Lovely! is heard all the time in England and is by no means the exclusive property of the cultured. It means *fine!* or *great!* A

237

gnarled old parking lot (*car park*) attendant of distinctly pro-
letarian mien and attire, guiding you into a narrow space will
say, "Cut to the left, cut to the right, straighten out, back a little
more, stop, that's it. *Lovely!*" The same exclamation would be
used by a friend to whom you had just announced the news of
your daughter's engagement. *Lovely!* covers a multitude of ex-
pletives: *fine! great! wonderful! marvelous! terrific! that's it!*
and even *wow!*

low in the water, *see* in low water

£ s.d.   dough (money)

Spelled *£.s.d.* and meaning *pounds, shillings, pence*. These
three letters are the initials of the Latin ancestors of those three
words: *librae, solidi,* and *denarii*. All this stems from the Roman
occupation of Britain, which indeed was a good many years
ago, but the symbols remain and will continue to do so even
though the English have put their money on the decimal system (*see* Introductory Note 18). Spoken (pronounced *ell-
ess-dee*), the phrase is an English colloquialism whose American equivalent is *dough*. L. S. *Deism*, meaning *money worship*,
is a pretty good English pun. Nothing to do with the drug.

lucern (lucerne), n.   alfalfa

lucky bargee, *see* bargee

lucky-dip, n.   grab bag

luge, n. (col.)   toboggan

A word taken over from Swiss dialect.

luggage, n.   baggage

Englishmen *register luggage*, Americans *check baggage*. On an
English train, it goes into the *luggage van;* on an American
train, into the *baggage car*.

lugs, n. pl. (sl.)   **ears**

No American slang equivalent.

Luke's Little Summer (col.)   **Indian summer**

Other English names: *St. Luke's Summer; St. Martin's Summer.*

lumber, n., v.t.   (1) **superfluous**
                                   possessions
                         (2) **clutter**

Lumber is old furniture, stuff, doodads, and general junk around the house not good enough to use or be seen by your guests, not bad enough to throw away; you never really want to see it again but you can't bear to part with it. So you put it into your *lumber-room* (*storage room; see also* **box-room**), the way Americans stuff their attics, and wish with all your heart but none of your mind that you had never been **lumbered with** (q.v.) it. The English use *lumber,* especially *lumber up,* also as a verb. To *lumber up* a room is to *clutter* it *up.* Incidentally, the English use *clutter* also as a noun meaning *miscellaneous junk* or *gear. Lumber,* in common usage, has none of these connotations in America where it means only *wood* for use in carpentry, which is called *timber* in England. But *timber* in America usually connotes *standing timber,* i.e., living trees grown for eventual cutting and use as *lumber* in the American sense. Old beams, especially the hand-hewn variety found in old buildings, barns, and ships, are called *timbers* in both countries, just to complicate matters. A beautiful example of the English use of *lumber* is found early in chapter 3 of Jerome K. Jerome's classic *Three Men in a Boat.* The three neophyte sailors have made a list of theoretically indispensable accoutrements for a proposed river trip, but it becomes clear that "the upper reaches of the Thames would not allow of a boat sufficiently large" to accommodate the list. Then George reflects: "We must not think of the things we could do with, but only of the things we can't do without." "I call that downright wisdom," says the author, "not merely as regards the present case, but with reference to our trip up the river of life generally." Then follows a ruminative passage, quite a long one, which the author himself must never have intended, for at the end he says to the reader: "I beg your pardon, really. I quite forgot." The passage is all about lumber:

How many people, on that voyage [the trip 'up the river of life generally'] load up the boat till it is ever in danger of swamping with a store of foolish things which they think essential to the pleasure and comfort of the trip, but which are really only useless lumber.

How they pile the poor little craft mast-high with fine clothes and big houses; with useless servants and a host of swell friends that do not care twopence for them and that they do not care three ha'pence for; with expensive entertainments that nobody enjoys, with formalities and fashions, with pretence and ostentation, and with—oh, heaviest, maddest lumber of all!—the dread of what will my neighbour think, with luxuries that only cloy, with pleasures that bore, with empty show that, like the criminal's iron crowns of yore, makes to bleed and swoon the aching head that wears it!

It is lumber, man—all lumber! Throw it overboard. It makes the boat so heavy to pull, you nearly faint at the oars. It makes it so cumbersome and dangerous to manage, you never know a moment's freedom from anxiety and care, never gain a moment's rest for dreamy laziness—no time to watch the windy shadows skim lightly o'er the shallows, or the glittering sunbeams flitting in and out among the ripples, or the great trees by the margin looking down at their own image, or the woods all green and golden, or the lilies white and yellow, or the sombre-waving rushes, or the sedges, or the orchis, or the blue forget-me-nots.

Throw the lumber over, man! Let your boat of life be light, packed with only what you need—a homely home and simple pleasures, one or two friends, worth the name, someone to love and someone to love you, a cat, a dog, and a pipe or two, enough to eat and enough to wear, and a little more than enough to drink; for thirst is a dangerous thing.

You will find the boat easier to pull then, and it will not be so liable to upset, and it will not matter so much if it does upset; good, plain merchandise will stand water. You will have time to think as well as to work. Time to drink in life's sunshine—time to listen to the Aeolian music that the wind of God draws from the human heartstrings around us—time to—

I beg your pardon, really. I quite forgot.

lumbered with (sl.)	**stuck with**

lumber-room, n.	**storage room**

See also **box-room.**

lumme! (**lummy!**), interj. (sl.)	**whew!**

Corruption of *love me!*

lumper, n. (col.)	**contractor**

A middleman who takes on a piece of work as a whole and parcels it out in sections.

M

ma'am, n.	**n.A.e.**

A highly specialized use of this contraction of *madam* is used as the proper form of addressing the Queen, and when it is so used it is pronounced *m'm* by servants and *mam* by all others. You ought to know this, just in case. . . .

241

mac, n. (sl.)   **raincoat**

Short for *macintosh* (sometimes *mackintosh*), a waterproof material patented in the early nineteenth century by one C. Macintosh.

macadam, n.   **tar**

After J. C. McAdam, who late in the eighteenth century invented the building of roads with layers of crushed stone.
Tarmac (q.v.), short for *tar macadam,* added tar to the crushed
stone layers. But since tar is almost universally added to the
crushed stones these days, *macadam road* is used in England
the way Americans use *blacktop road.* The English also use the
expression *made-up road* to mean the same thing. *See also*
metalled road.

machinist, n.   **machine operator**

This term, used by itself in England, can mean *sewing machine
operator.* The English also use the term *machine-minder*
where Americans would say *machine operator.*

made-up road, *see* **macadam**

mad on (col.)   **crazy about**

Americans also say *mad about* and the English also say *crazy
about,* but only the English say *mad on,* and when an Englishman wants to be emphatic, he says *mad keen on,* or sometimes
dead keen on.

maffick, v.i.   **exult**

Mafeking is a small town in Cape Province, South Africa. During
the Boer War it was besieged by Cronje and defended by
Baden-Powell from Oct. 13, 1899 to May 17, 1900, when the
siege was raised by Mahon and Plumer. The relief of Mafeking
was cause for great rejoicing and the populace of London and
elsewhere celebrated the happy event with great extravagance
and exultation. The *-ing* ending was mistakenly believed by the

general public to indicate a gerund, and *maffick* came to mean, to the many who had never heard of the place, *celebrate hilariously*, usually with the assistance of alcoholic stimulants. However, you can't *mafek;* you must *maffick*. Somehow in the back-formation from the supposed gerund, the spelling went wrong, too.

mag, n. (sl.)   **halfpenny**

maiden over   **n.A.e.**

A cricket term which like so many other cricket terms has crept into the general language. In cricket there are two bowlers. Each bowler bowls to the opposing batsman six times, which constitutes an *over*. If the batsman fails to make a single run during an *over*, the result is called a *maiden over*, and the bowler is said to have *bowled a maiden over*—an expression which lends itself to an obvious pun. *Maiden* is used differently from its use in such a phrase as *maiden voyage*. In *maiden over*, *maiden* evokes the Victorian image of *virgo intacta*, the idea being that the score was not touched either. Applied to life in general, rather than cricket in particular, *maiden over* can be used as an elegant and dramatic way of describing a *successful ordeal*, one in which the chief protagonist comes through unscathed.

maid of honour   **lady in waiting**

An English *maid of honour* is an unmarried woman who attends a queen or a princess. (It is also a type of *cheesecake*, the edible kind.) In America, where there are no queens or princesses to attend, the one attended is a bride.

main drainage, *see* **drains**

mains, n. pl.   **electric power source**

I.e., the outside (light and power company) source. Thus, directions on an electric appliance: Disconnect *mains* before adjusting controls.

maize, n. **corn**

Corn (q.v.) is the generic English term for *grain*.

maizie, n. (col.) **flower frog**

An improvised *flower frog* consisting of a ball of crushed chicken wire.

major, adj. **elder**

Used after a surname. In an English **public school** (q.v.) the eldest of three or more students then attending who have the same surname has *maximus* (the superlative form of the Latin adjective *magnus,* meaning *large* or *great*) placed after his name; thus, Smith *maximus,* i.e., Smith *the eldest,* to distinguish him from the other Smiths then at the school. The youngest would be Smith *minimus* (*minimus* being the superlative form of *parvus,* Latin for *small*). The corresponding Latin comparatives, *major* and *minor,* are used when there are only two with the same surname. Sometimes English cardinal numerals, rather than Latin comparatives and superlatives, are used: thus, *Smith One, Smith Two, Smith Three,* if there were three Smiths at the school. In such a case, the smaller the numeral, the older the Smith. At some public schools, *major* has been used to mean *first to enter,* even if an older Smith enters the school later, while the first Smith is still attending; and at other schools *maximus* and *minimus* have been used to refer not to age but to academic standing. These various terminologies are used not only by public schools but also by some English **prep schools** (q.v.). These varying uses, like so many other carefree English departures from uniformity in practice, can be confusing, but the safe assumption is that these Latin adjectives (or English numerals) following youngsters' surnames indicate seniority in years rather than priority in enrollment or academic rank.

majority, n. **plurality**

A voting term. When the English use the term *majority* in discussing an election they mean what the Americans call a *plural-*

ity. If they want to indicate an arithmetical majority (i.e., more than fifty percent), they use the term *clear majority.*

major road, *see* **arterial road**

make a balls of (sl.)	**mess up**

See also **balls** (2).

make a dead set at (col.)	**make a play for**

make a (the) four up	**make a fourth**

For instance, at bridge or tennis doubles.

make all the running (sl.)	**go the limit**

Refers to the degree of sexual intimacy permitted by the lady. Not to be confused with **make the running** (q.v.).

make a pair of spectacles, *see* **duck** (1)

make hay of (col.)	**make hash of**

I.e., *muddle up, make a mess of.* Sometimes the meaning is closer to *make short work of:* Someone goes on and on trying to prove a point, you come up with a decisive refutation and *make hay of* his thesis.

make old bones (col.)	**live to a ripe old age**

Gloomily enough, seen almost exclusively in the negative: "He'll never *make old bones.*"

make the running (col.)	**take the lead**

In a competitive situation; but to *make some running* (not in common usage) would mean to *make some headway.* For another kind of headway, *see* **make all the running.**

make up	**fill**

English chemists (druggists) *make up* prescriptions rather than *fill* them.

malicious wounding

crimes of violence

Term from criminal law.

manager, n.

producer

In speaking of the theatre in England, *manager* is the equivalent of *producer* in the American theater. *See also* **producer.**

managing director

executive vice president (app.)

In an English company, the offices of **chairman** (q.v.) and *managing director* can be combined in one person. This is not common and the division of functions and authority, as between these two offices, will vary from company to company, as it does between *chairman of the board* and *president* in American corporations. Roughly speaking, the *chairman* makes policy, while the *managing director* runs the show day by day.

manhandle, v.t.

handle by hand

The English use this the way it is used in America to mean *handle roughly, deal roughly with,* but it has also the more literal meaning in England shown above.

marching papers (col.)

walking papers

Also *marching orders.*

marge, n. (col.)

oleo

Each country has its own way of abbreviating *oleomargarine.*

mark, n.

type (sort)

The phrase *of much this mark* means *very much like this.* Thus an Englishman might be heard to say, "At school we slept in beds *of much this mark.*"

mark, v. (col.)

cover

A term used in **football** (q.v.). In the English game, a player is said to *mark* an opposing player who may be receiving the ball;

in the American game that would be called *covering* the receiver.

market, n.   weekly market

Many English towns have a *weekly market day*, a particular day of the week on which a market, usually open-air, is held for the sale of all kinds of wares, arranged in stalls. As might be expected, these markets, which constitute normal commerce among the natives, seem like fairs to the visitor for they crackle with the festive air of a bazaar. Such a town is called a *market town*. A number of English *market towns* still have names which include the word *market:* Market Drayton, Market Harborough, Market Weighton, etc. But the names of most towns with weekly markets do not reveal the fact: Stourbridge (market day on Friday), Guisborough (market day on Saturday), etc. Occasionally, as in the town of Stone, the market is held only once every other week. In Stratford-on-Avon, however, there are markets three days a week: Tuesday, Wednesday, and Friday. The A.A. Book (the handbook issued to each member of the Automobile Association in England), which practically every English motorist keeps religiously in the **cubby** (q.v.) of his car, gives all sorts of miscellaneous information about the towns it lists, including the market day (MD). The Royal Automobile Club issues an almost identical handbook.

market garden   truck farm

And a *market gardener* is a *truck farmer*.

Marks & Sparks (col.)   Marks & Spencer

A joke name for Marks & Spencer, a chain store (*multiple shop*) reminiscent of J. C. Penney.

Mark Tapley   Pollyanna

One who sees only the bright side. See *Martin Chuzzlewit* by Dickens.

marquee, n.   **large tent**

A *marquee* to Americans generally means a rigid canopy pro-
jecting over the entrance to a theater or other public hall, and
the word evokes the image of large illuminated letters spelling
out the names of stage and movie stars, double features, and
smash hits. This significance is never attributed to the word in
England, where it means a *large tent* of the sort used on fair
grounds and brings to mind England's agricultural fairs (*see*
agricultural show), village **fêtes** (q.v.), the Henley Regatta,
and all those garden parties of Katherine Mansfield's childhood.
At the annual regatta at Henley-on-Thames, for example, there
are little marquees for staff, sanitation facilities, and that sort of
thing, middle-sized marquees for champagne and that sort of
thing, and what must be one of the largest marquees in history
for luncheon. *Marquee* is sometimes used in America, too, in the
same sense in connection with outdoor wedding receptions and
entertainments.

marriage lines   **marriage certificate**

The American term is now common.

marrow, n.   **squash** (app.)

A kind of oversized *zucchini*. The English do not use the term
zucchini (except possibly gourmets at Italian restaurants in
Soho) and do not ordinarily say *pumpkin* (except when telling
their children at bedtime the story of Cinderella or possibly
each other the sad tale of Whittaker Chambers and Alger Hiss);
they might say **courgettes** (q.v.); and when the English say
squash, unless they are using it as a sports term, they mean a
soft drink, usually lemon squash or orange squash (*see* **squash**).
Americans rarely use *squash* to mean a soft drink. When they
say *squash,* they are usually referring to either a vegetable or
the subway rush hour.

martini, n.   **vermouth**

If you ask for a *martini* in an English pub, you will get a glass of
vermouth. Whether it is dry or sweet will depend upon chance,

but in either event it will be warm. If you ask for a *dry martini,* you will get a glass of *dry vermouth.* If you want a *dry martini* in the American sense, ask for a *gin and French,* specify extremely little French, and that it be served very cold, by stirring the mixture over *blocks of ice* (*ice cubes*), but further specify that the blocks be removed (unless you want it on the rocks); and furthermore, if it would grieve you terribly not to find an olive or a piece of lemon rind in it, you had better remain in America. A *gin and It* (*It* being an abbreviation of *Italian vermouth*) is still occasionally ordered and shouldn't be.

mash, n. (col.)   **mashed potatoes**

More elegantly, *creamed potatoes* in England. A Camberwell pub used to present "sausages and mash" in the public bar at three shillings and "sausages and creamed potatoes" in the saloon bar at four shillings, sixpence. Same dish.

match, n.   **game**

Two *sides* (*teams*) play a *match,* rather than a *game,* in England.

match, test, *see* **test match**

matchcard, n.   **scorecard**

mate, n. (col.)   **buddy**

Matey is a slang adjective for *chummy,* i.e., *buddies.* A *penmate* is a *pen pal.*

maths, n.   **math**

matinee jacket   **baby cardigan**

matron, *see* **sister**

maximus, *see under* **major**

May Week

commencement week (app.)

May Week is a Cambridge University function which lasts several days longer than a week and is celebrated in June. It is a festive period after finals are over, the principal festivities being a series of balls and *bumping-races. Bumping-races* are boat races among eights representing the various colleges (*see* **college**) in which a boat which catches up with and touches another (called *bumping*) scores a win. A *bump-supper* is held to celebrate such a win. The English are pretty casual in their use of approximations like *May Week.*

maze, v.t.

bewilder

Related to *amaze* but now archaic in America.

M.B.E., *see under* Birthday Honours

M.C.C., *see under* the Ashes

m.d. (col.)

retarded

Stands for *mentally deficient;* no slur on the medical profession.

mean, adj.

stingy

In America *mean* is most commonly understood as signifying *cruelty* and *ill temper;* in England as expressing *stinginess.*

meant to

supposed to

An Englishman asks, for instance, "Are we *meant to* throw rubbish in that bin?"

mear, *see* mere

meat safe

food cupboard

Built of wire mesh and fast becoming obsolete, giving way to the refrigerator. Although it is called a *meat safe,* it can be used to preserve any food.

mediatize, v.t. **annex**

This very rarely seen verb means to annex a smaller country, usually a principality to a larger one. The former ruler retains his title and may be permitted to keep some governing rights. Hence, the expression *mediatized prince.*

Member, n. **congressman; representative** (app.)

The English opposite number of a *congressman* is a *Member of Parliament,* colloquially abbreviated to *M.P.* and commonly shortened to *Member.* The area represented by an *M.P.* is known as a **division** (q.v.) or a **constituency** (q.v.), while a *congressman* represents a *Congressional district.* An Englishman is the Member *for* his division, e.g., the Member *for* Putney; the American is the representative *from* his district, e.g., the representative *from* the Second Congressional District.

memorandum and articles of association **corporate charter**

mend, v.t. **repair**

You may hear Englishmen talking about having their shoes, flat tires (*punctures*), and chairs *mended* but their cars, plumbing, and television sets *repaired.* The distinction would appear to be arbitrary. Nowadays the upper classes tend to have most things *repaired* rather than *mended,* though really old-fashioned types, especially in the country, still tend to have many things *mended.* Thus in the villages, you often hear references to the *shoe mender,* the *watch mender,* and so on.

mental, adj. (col.) **off one's rocker**

An American will speak of a disturbed person as a *mental case.* The English content themselves with the adjective alone.

mercer, n. **textile dealer**

Usually designates an exclusive shop, dealing in expensive high-style fabrics, with emphasis on silk.

mere (mear), n.   **lake**

Or *pond;* almost never used in America. A rather poetic term, one often applied to the Norfolk Broads. Another meaning of *mere* is *boundary* or *boundary marker,* but this is country dialect and rare.

mere vapouring (col.)   **hot air**

mess-up, n.   **mess**

metalled road   **paved road**

The English speak of *metalled roads* and *unmetalled roads.* Americans call a *metalled road* a *paved road, tar road,* or a *blacktop road* and an *unmetalled road* a *dirt road.* The English speak of *unmetalled, unpaved, unmade,* and *dust roads,* all synonymous. *Road-metal* is an English term for the crushed stone which constitutes the layers of macadam roads (*see* **macadam**).

metals, n. pl.   **rails**

When a train *leaves the metals* in England, it has been *derailed.*

meteorological office   **weather bureau**

And the much reviled official whom the Americans call the *weatherman* is the *clerk of the weather* in England.

methylated spirit   **denatured alcohol**

middle name (col.)   **nickname** (app.)

In America John Henry Smith has a *first* name, a *middle* name and a *last* name. In England he would commonly be said to have two *Christian* or *given* names and a *surname.* John Henry Samuel Smith would be said to have two *middle* names in America, three *Christian* or *given* names in England. The term *middle name* itself may also be used either jocularly or bitterly in both countries but usually in somewhat different ways. In America (rarely in England) a wife speaking of her husband's favorite dish (or sport) might say about him, "Apple pie (or hockey) is his *middle name!*" In England a person complaining of another's hypocritical conduct might say, "His *middle name* is Heep!" (after the knavish Uriah in *David Copperfield*). The corresponding colloquialism in America would be: "He's a regular Uriah Heep!"

milk float   milk truck

Probably so called because of its stately gait, required to prevent churning. Not a good vehicle to get behind at the beginning of a long, winding hill.

milliard, n.   billion

An English *billion* is a *million million* (*See* **billion**).

mince, n.   chopped meat

The common name by which an English housewife orders from her butcher what her American opposite number would ask for as *chopped meat* or *hamburger*. Sometimes the English use the term *minced meat* instead. *Mincemeat* generally means, in both countries, the mixture of chopped apples, raisins, candied orange rind, suet, etc., etc., which goes into mince pie.

mincemeat tart   mince pie

Mince pie would be understood in England to mean a small individual one.

Mincing Lane (col.)   tea trade

An actual street in London, which has given its name to the *tea trade,* just as other London streets have become symbols and nicknames for other lines of endeavor.

mind, v.t., v.i.   (1) watch out for
(2) care
(3) mind you

(1) When a train stops at a curved platform at an English railroad station, there are attendants who say, or signs

which read, "*Mind* the gap!," or where there is an unexpected step, you will be enjoined to *mind* the step, i.e., to *watch out* for it. In "*Mind* you do!" *mind* means *make sure*.

(2) In America, "I don't *mind*" means "I don't *object*." In England it means "I don't *care*," in the sense of indifference when an alternative is offered. Thus, if asked, "Would you rather stay or go?" or "Do you want chocolate or vanilla?" an Englishman who would be happy either way says, "I don't *mind*." *See also* **have no mind to.**

(3) In the imperative, *mind* often omits the *you* in England: "I don't believe a word of it, *mind!*"

mineral, n.   **soft drink**

One sees *"minerals"* on signs in English restaurants, tea rooms, etc. They are not trying to sell you iron, steel, or copper—all they are offering is soft drinks. This use of the term is related to the term *mineral water* which one still hears in America.

mingy, adj. (col.)   **tight (stingy)**

A portmanteau word: combination of **mean** (q.v.) and *stingy*.

mini-budget, *see* **budget**

minim, n.   **half note**

See under **breve.**

minimus, *see under* **major**

minister, n.   **cabinet member**

A term relating to government officials. The officials whom Americans describe as *cabinet members* are known as *ministers* in England.

minor, *see under* **major**

missing, *see* **go missing**

miss out   skip

I.e., to omit. If you don't like artichokes, for instance, you *miss them out* at the dinner table.

mithered, adj. (col.)   **hot and bothered**

Of Lancashire origin. *See also* **moider.**

mixed bag (col.)   **conglomeration**

mixture as before (col.)   **same old story**

When you have a prescription renewed in England, the label often bears the expression "The *mixture as before.*" The phrase is jocularly applied to situations which amount to the *same old story*, as when delegates to labor negotiations or peace conferences return after an interval and present each other with nothing new.

mobile police   **patrol cars**

mod. con., *see* **amenities**

moderations, n. pl.   **first exams for B.A.**
                                                       degree at Oxford

Often abbreviated to *mods.* The examiner is called a *moderator. See also* **greats; responsions; smalls.**

moderator, n.   (1) **officer presiding over**
                                                math tripos (q.v.)
                                            (2) **examiner for**
                                                moderations (q.v.)
                                            (3) **Presbyterian minister**
                                                presiding over church
                                                group

moider, v.t. (col.) **bother**

Moidered is north of England dialect for *hot and bothered*. *See also* **mithered.**

mole, n. **little hill**

money for jam (col.) **like taking candy from a baby**

Description of a task embarrassingly easy.

money-spinning, n., adj. (col.) (1) **money raising**
(2) **moneymaking**

(1) A *money-spinning* event is one which enriches the treasury of a do-good organization.
(2) A *money-spinning* play is simply a hit which is raking it in.

monial, n. **mullion**

monkey, n. (sl.) **£25**

monkey nut **peanut**

Synonymous with *ground-nut* and thought by some to be slang or at least mildly jocular.

monomark, n. **registered identification mark**

An arbitrary symbol, consisting of letters, numbers, or both, for purposes of identification.

moonlight flit (col.) **(nocturnal) powder; night escape**

To do a *moonlight flit* (or *shoot the moon*) in England is to *blow town at night* with all your belongings, with no forwarding address, in order to get away without paying the rent or settling with your creditors. It is like *doing a bunk* (*see* **bunk**) but at night.

moped, n.   **motorized bicycle**

Two syllables: *mó-ped*. The *mo* is from *motor*, the *ped* from
pedal. To get the motor going, you pedal a few turns. Sometimes going up a steep hill you help the motor along by pedaling.
Sometimes the motor rebels and you just keep pedaling, and
you have a **push-bike** (q.v.), and you *mope,* a word which some
future etymologist may one day trace, by back-formation from a
supposed past tense, to *moped.*

mop up   **sop up**

That which Frenchmen do in public, and most other national-
ities do in private, in order to gather up that irresistible last
bit of gravy on the plate.

more power to his elbow (col.)   **more power to him**

morning coffee, *see* **elevenses**

most secret   **top secret**

Mothering Sunday   **fourth Sunday in Lent**

Traditional day to visit parents with gifts.

motion, n.   **bowel movement**

motor coach   **bus**

motorway, n.   **turnpike**

Americans call their great highways *turnpikes, thruways, free-
ways, expressways,* and perhaps a brand new name is being invented at this very moment for the kind of road that saves so
much time and creates such interesting traffic death statistics.

mouch, mooch, v.i. (sl.)   **hang around**

To *mouch round* or *mouch about* a place is to *hang around* it or
in juvenile American slang to *hack around* in it. *Mouch* also ap-

257

pears as a noun in the expression *go for a mouch* meaning the same thing.

mount, n.   **mat**

The border, usually made of pasteboard, placed between a picture and its frame.

move house   **move**

The English also use the shorter American form for *change residence.*

M.P., *see* **Member**

Mrs. Grundy, *see* **wowser**

much of this mark, *see* **mark**

muck, n., v.i.   **mess**

The English government makes a *muck* of things, in about the same way the American government makes a *mess* of things, and in the same way in which all the other governments seem to be making whatever-it-is-they-call-it these days. Whereas Americans *mess around,* Englishmen *muck about.*

mucker, n. (sl.)   (1) **spill**
                               (2) **spending spree**

(1) To *come a mucker* is to *take a spill.*
(2) To *go a mucker* is to *go on a spending spree* or *throw your money around.*

muff, n.   **oaf**

Muff is used in both countries as a verb meaning *miss.* One can *muff* any kind of opportunity, in life generally. In sports, one *muffs* a catch. From this the English have developed the noun *muff,* meaning an *awkward, stupid fellow.*

muffetee, n.   **knitted wrist cuff**

muffin, n.   **small spongy cake**

This has nothing whatever in common with what Americans call
English muffins, which are unobtainable in England. Instead, it
is a light, flat, round, spongy cake, served toasted and buttered. The word *muffin* means something entirely different in
America: a *quick bread,* baked in a cup-shaped pan. *Muffins*
in America can be made of various types of flour, bran, corn,
etc., and are often studded with delicacies like raisins or blue-
berries.

mug, n., v.i. (sl.)   (1) **dope (fool)**
                                                           (2) **grind (bookworm)**
                                                           (3) **quiz**

(1) To be *had for a mug* is to be *taken in,* i.e., taken for a
    dope. A *mug's game* is *something for the birds; my idea
    of nothing at all;* a *foolish endeavor.*
(2) The English also use *mug* and *mug up* verbally, meaning
    bone up, e.g., for an examination (*see also* **sap; swot**).
(3) A school term, now obsolescent.

mull, n., v.t., v.i.   **mess; mess up**

To *mull* (or *mull over*) in America is to *ponder* or *cogitate,* an
activity which often winds up in a *mull* in the English sense.

multiple shops   **chain store**

mummy, n.   **mama; mommy**

Also *mum. Mummy* and *mama* start in childhood, but *mummy*
lingers on longer in England than *mama* does in America, where
it usually becomes *mother.* The Queen Mother is affectionately
called the *Queen Mum* and sometimes preciously, but still affectionately, *Queenie Mum.*

259

ENGLISH   AMERICAN

mump, v.t. (sl.)   **cadge**

To *mump* something is to get it by begging, to *cadge* or *wheedle* it out of someone. The same verb, used intransi'ively, has two separate meanings in standard English: (1) to *mope,* and (2) to *go begging,* from which the slang transitive use is clearly derived. *Mumping* is an English police term, of which the nearest American equivalent is *free-loading,* the practice, sternly disapproved by the majority of the force, of accepting minor gifts from people on the beat, like a cup of tea in the back room of a shop, or petty graft in the form of discounts on goods or services.

mum's help   **mother's helper**

music hall   **vaudeville theater**

A *music hall turn* is a *vaudeville act. Variety* is the usual English term for *vaudeville. Vaudeville* is the name of a famous theatre in London and is not commonly used as a common noun.

muslin, n.   **cheesecloth**

The term *muslin* in America is equivalent to the word *calico* in England. *See* **butter-muslin; calico.**

mutes, n. pl.   **professional pallbearers**

muzz, v.t. (sl.), *see* **muzzy**

muzzy, adj. (sl.)   **woozy**

The implication in *muzzy* is that the unfortunate condition it describes is the result of too much drink. The slang English verb *muzz* means to make *muzzy,* i.e., to put somebody *hors de combat,* not in one fell swoop by slipping him a micky, but in nice, easy stages.

my old dutch (col.)   **my dear old wife**

A term of endearment. *See also* **dutch.**

𝔑 | N

NAAFI, n. (sl.)   servicemen's canteen organization

Pronounced *naffy* or *narfy* and standing for *Navy, Army, and Air Force Institutes,* an organization which operates canteens and service centers for members of the British armed forces.

nailed on (sl.)   **all set**

Means the same thing as the American slang expression *nailed down.*

nail varnish   **nail polish**

nannie, n.   **child's nurse**

Nanny is the dictionary form but *nannie* appears frequently.

nap, n. (sl.)   **tip (on the races)**

To *go nap* is to *bet your stack.* A *nap selection* is a racing expert's list of betting recommendations. *Nap* is an English card game and a *nap hand* has come to have the figurative meaning of being in the position where one is practically sure of winning if he takes a risk. *Nap* is also, if rarely, used as a transitive verb, meaning to *recommend* (*give a tip* on a horse). The association of *nap* with *winner* results from *nap*'s being an abbreviation of Napoleon, who was a winner for a while but appears not to have done so well at the end. A wholly coincidental American association between Napoleon and horses is seen in the old vaudeville ditty, "Giddyap, Napoleon, it looks like rain." *See also* **pot.**

nappy, n. (col.)   **diaper**

A corruption of *napkin.* No American colloquialism for this useful article.

nark, n. (sl.)   **stool pigeon**

narked (sl.)   **sore**

In the sense of *angry:* to be *narked* is to get *sore.*

nasty bit of work (col.)   **perfect horror**

An unspeakable person.

national income   **constructive income**

A bit of income tax terminology to indicate income payable to one, but taxable to another, or income received in one year but taxable in another year, for reasons too technical to go into here.

nation of shopkeepers, *see* **shop**

natter, v.i. (col.)   **gab**

Natter is also used as a noun meaning *gabfest.* Don't be misled by *natterjack,* which is not a male gossip but rather a yellow striped toad indigenous to England.

naught, *see* **nought**

navvy, n.   **construction worker**

Especially a road, railway, or canal worker. A *gang of navvies* is a *construction crew.* Nowadays mechanical excavating machines are operated by gasoline or diesel fuel. In the old days when they were operated by steam, they were known as *steam-navvies.* The term *navvy* reflects a bit of English history. England has a complex and beautiful inland waterway system dating back to the eighteenth century (but, alas, of uncertain future). The earliest canals, dug with pick and shovel, were called *navigations* and the hordes of diggers *navvies.*

N.B.G. (col.)   **N.G.** (app.)

The *B.* stands for *bloody.*

near-side lane   **left lane**

Since traffic keeps to the left in England, and the *near* refers to
the edge of the road, the *near-side lane* means the leftmost one
for regular driving. The one nearest the center is called the *off-side lane,* and is used for passing.

near to the bone   **close to the mark**

neat, adj.   **straight**

Applied to undiluted alcoholic drinks: the English say *neat,* the
Americans *straight.* A Planter's Punch might be described by an
Englishman as gaudy but not neat.

neck, n. (col.)   **nerve**

In the sense of *cheek* or *gall,* i.e., impudence.

neck and crop (col.)   **headfirst**

The way people get thrown out of the barrooms in western
movies.

nervy (sl.)   **jumpy**

Englishmen express themselves as feeling *nervy* or describe
someone as looking *nervy.* In each case, the American equivalent would be *jumpy.* The American slang meaning *cheeky* is
not shared with England. A less common English slang meaning,
not shared with America, is hard to describe by a one-word
equivalent but is used to describe something that gets on your
nerves. In other words, a *nervy* person in England can be *jumpy*
or *wearing,* depending on the context. Come to think of it,
there is no reason why the same person cannot be both at the
same time.

neuter, v.t.   **castrate**

See also **doctor.**

never-never, n. (sl.) **installment plan**

The serious English equivalent for *installment plan* is *hire-pur-chase*. The *never-never* is popular, wistful, jocular slang.

Newmarket, n. **tight-fitting overcoat**

Newmarket is a horseracing town. It is also the name of a card game. A *Newmarket* or *Newmarket coat* is a *tightfitting overcoat* for either sex.

newsagent, n. **newsdealer**

news editor, n. **city editor**

newspaper post **second-class mail**

Second-class mail now refers in England to non-priority letters sent at a cheaper postal rate than *first-class mail.*

news-room, n. **periodical room**

The reading room in a library where newspapers and magazines are kept. *News room* in America is a newspaper term meaning the news section of a newspaper office.

New Year's Honours, *see* **Birthday Honours**

next turning, *see* **beyond the next turning**

nice bit of work (sl.) **quite a dish**

Other complimentary slang in the same vein: *nice bit of crum-pet* (*see* **crumpet**); *nice bit of stuff; nice bit of skirt.* Appar-ently, a nice bit of almost anything would do. *Nice bit* is often *nice piece* in these expressions.

nice to hear you **nice to hear your voice**

A common telephone phrase. Americans say, "How nice to hear your voice," or "How nice to hear from you."

nick, n. (sl.)
(1) **station house**
(2) **shape**

   (1) I.e., police station.
   (2) In the sense of *physical condition.* Usually in the phrase *in the nick,* sometimes *in good nick,* meaning *in the pink.*

nicker, n. (sl.)   **pound (£)**

   Unit of currency, not weight. Low-class, petty criminals' cant.

nide, n.   **pheasant brood**

night-cellar, n. (sl.)   **a dive**

night on the tiles (sl.)   **night on the town**

   This phrase is derived from the custom among cats of having

Night on the Tiles

fun at night on rooftops, which in England are often made of tiles.

night sister, *see* **sister**

nil, n. nothing

Used in game scores where Americans would use *nothing*, e.g., *six to nil. See also* **nought.**

nineteen to the dozen (col.) a blue streak

Usually seen in the expression *talk nineteen to the dozen.*

nipper, n. (sl.) kid (tot)

Sometimes *kipper.*

nippy, n., adj. (sl.) (1) quick
(2) waitress

(1) "Look *nippy!*" means "Make it *snappy!*"
(2) As a noun, *nippy* is slang for *waitress.* The term was confined originally to the nimble girls at Lyons Corner Houses (a restaurant chain), but then became generic.

nip up (col.) run up

To *nip up* somewhere is to make a hurried trip there and back.

nit, n. (sl.) dope

Short for *nitwit.*

nix! cheese it!

"*Nix!*" is an interjection used in England to warn one's colleagues that the boss is snooping around. As in America, it is used also to signify a strong "*No!*", i.e., "*Nothing doing!*" "*Cheese it!*" (or "*Cheezit!*") has become rather old fashioned in America. There would seem to be no modern equivalent, perhaps because people are so much less afraid of the boss these days. *"Look busy!"* (in a hoarse whisper) is probably the closest equivalent.

nob, n. (sl.)   **swell**

nobble, v.t. (sl.)   (1) **tamper with**
         (2) **fix**
         (3) **scrounge**
         (4) **nab**
         (5) **rat on**

Sometimes spelled *knobble.* In any of its meanings, a thoroughly unpleasant bit of English slang:
(1) One *nobbles* a racehorse to prevent its winning.
(2) One *nobbles* a jury to get the desired verdict.
(3) *Nobble* also means *scrounge,* get something away from somebody through sly, dishonest maneuvering.
(4, 5) To *nobble* a criminal is to *nab* him, or get him *nabbed* by *ratting on* him.

noddle, n. (sl.)   **noodle (head)**

Often shortened to *nod.*

no effects   **insufficient funds**

Banking term; for the more up-to-date term, *see* **refer to drawer.**

no entry   **do not enter**

Road sign indicating one-way street.

nog, n.   **strong ale**

Once brewed in Norfolk; sometimes spelled *nogg.* In America *nog* is used as short for *eggnog* and means generally any alcoholic drink into which an egg is beaten.

nonconformist, n., adj.   **non-Anglican**

As a noun, synonymous with *dissenter; see* **chapel.**

non-content, n.   **nay-voter** (app.)

One who votes against a motion in the House of Lords.

nonillion, *see under* **billion**

nonresident, n.   **transient** (app.)

One often sees a sign in front of an English hotel, or attached to its wall, reading "Meals Served to *Nonresidents,*" or words to that effect. In that use, *nonresident* is used in the sense of a *person not living at the hotel.* The term thus used has nothing to do with national domicile.

no reply   **no answer**

A telephone term. In America the operator exasperates you by saying, "They *don't answer.*" In England the unhappy formula is, "There's *no reply.*"

Norfolk capon (col.)   **red herring**

A false issue.

Norfolk dumpling (col.)   **Norfolk type**

Synonymous with *Norfolk turkey,* meaning a native of the county of Norfolk.

norland, n.   **north**

Norland is a common noun and is simply short for *northland.* Norland with an upper case *N* is the name of a training college for children's nurses (*see* **nannie**), which turns out a very superior product who eats with the family.

nose to tail (col.)   **bumper to bumper**

nosey-parker (col.)   **rubberneck**

Sometimes used as an intransitive verb meaning to be a *rubberneck* or *busybody*, i.e., to take much too great an interest in other people's affairs.

not a sausage (sl.)   **not a damned thing**

not best pleased   **not too happy**

not by a long chalk (col.)   **not by a long shot**

note, n.   **bill**

Referring to paper money: a one-pound *note*, a five-pound *note*, and so forth.

notecase, n.   **billfold**

See also **pocketbook.**

notepaper, n.   **stationery**

not half (col., sl.)   (1) **not nearly**
                                                        (2) **not at all**
                                                        (3) **terrifically**

One must be extremely careful in interpreting the expression *not half*. The first two meanings are colloquialisms:
(1) When an Englishman says to a departing guest, "You haven't stayed *half* long enough," he means *not nearly* long enough.
(2) When an Englishman criticizes his friend's new necktie and describes it as *not half* bad, he means *not at all* bad, i.e., quite satisfactory.
(3) *Not half* has a peculiar slang use as well. Thus, in describing the boss's reaction when he came in and found everybody out to lunch, an English porter might say, "He didn't *half* blow up," meaning that he did blow up about as completely as possible. In other words, *not half* is used iron-

ically, meaning *not half—but totally*. As an expletive, by itself, *"not half!"* might find its American equivalent in *"not much!"* meaning, of course, the exact opposite: *"very much! (and how!)* Thus: "Would you like a free trip to California?" *"Not much!"*

nothing else for it   **no alternative**

In less elegant words, *no other way out* or *nothing else to do about it.*

nothing starchy (sl.)   **no fuss or feathers**

nothing to make a song about (col.)   **nothing to write home about**

notice, v.t.   **review**

In England a book can be spoken of as *reviewed* or *noticed*. *Noticed* implies that the review was brief.

notice board   **bulletin board**

For instance, the one at railroad stations listing arrivals and departures. *See also* **board.**

not much cop (sl.)   (1) **not worth a damn**
                                           (2) **not much fun**

(1) Referring to persons or objects.
(2) Referring to a job or task, i.e., tough.

not my line of country (col.)   **not my kind of thing**

An English alternative would be *not my cup of tea,* or in Mayfair, *"It isn't madly me."* An American alternative might be *not in my line* or *"It ain't for me."*

not on (col.)   **not done**

In addition to the concept of impropriety, it might also mean *not in the cards* or *hopeless.*

ENGLISH	AMERICAN

not so dusty (col.)   **not so bad**

not to worry (col.)   **don't let it bother you**

nought (naught), n.   **zero**

It is used in scoring—*ten to nought*. In that sense Americans would probably use *nothing* instead of *zero*. As a term in arithmetic, an English synonym is *cipher*. *See also* **nil.**

noughts and crosses   **tick-tack-toe**

nr.   **near**

A term used on envelopes in addressing letters: thus, Sandhurst, *nr.* Hawkhurst, to differentiate that Sandhurst (which has nothing whatever to do with the military academy) from Sandhurst in Surrey. *Nr.* in Scotland becomes *by:* thus, Giffnock *by* Glasgow.

nullity, n.   **annulment**

Term in matrimonial law. If you can't stand your spouse but have no grounds for divorce, your American lawyer can look into the chances of obtaining an *annulment*. His opposite number in England would determine whether you had grounds for a *nullity suit*.

number plates   **license plates**

Number 10 Downing Street   **White House** (app.)

Usually shortened to *No. 10*. The seat of executive power and residence of the prime minister. Like the White House, it is not only an address but is also used figuratively to mean the chief executive himself.

nurse, v.t.   **fondle**

A use not met with in America: to hold a baby on one's lap caressingly. The verb is also used to describe the attentions of a

politician to his constituency to convince the voters of his devotion to their interests.

nursing home   private hospital

Also *convalescent home.*

nutcase, n. (sl.)   nut; case

The Americans refer to a nutty person as a *case* or a *nut*. The
English make sure of being understood by using a combination
of the two words.

Ⓞ | O

oast, n.   hops kiln

The *oast* (the *kiln* itself) is housed in an *oast-house,* a red brick
tower almost always cylindrical like a silo. The oast-house is
topped by a cone-shaped vented cap, painted white, which is
rotated by the action of the wind pushing against a protruding
vane. The part of southeastern England known as the **Weald**
(q.v.), particularly the hilly Kent and Sussex countryside, is
dotted with hundreds of these structures, usually single but often
in pairs or clusters of several, lending a special character to the
landscape. A native of this part of England returning to his
homeland feels he has arrived when he spots his first oast-
house. Occasionally an oast-house is decommissioned, as it were,
and converted to a private dwelling, usually attached to the
original farmhouse and making for a most attractive structure.
The county of Kent is known as the Garden of England because
of the many fruits and particularly the concentration of hops
grown there in the hop-gardens. Early each September the

countryside comes alive with the picking of the hop vines, called *bines,* which are carted to the oast-houses. There they are stripped of their greenish-white blossoms, which are then dried in the oasts. In the old days, thousands of Londoners, mostly **cockney** (q.v.)—and the majority of those from London's **East End** (q.v.)—invaded that part of the country to have a few days of *hopping* (*hop-picking*) holiday in the open air and to drink up their wages in the local pubs. Nowadays the London *hoppers'* (*hop-pickers'*) annual invasion is largely history. Local housewives and children get temporary work picking the bines, instead of the individual blossoms, and feeding them to ingenious machines which strip them of the blossoms. And still another picturesque country custom has become lore.

O.B.E.

See *under* **Birthday Honours.**

oblique, n.   **slash line**

Sometimes called *oblique stroke.* The line between *and* and *or* in the abominable *and/or.*

O.C.   **C.O.**

Officer Commanding.

occupier, n.   **occupant**

In England one who occupies a house is its *occupier.* One occupying a room, railroad compartment, etc., is an *occupant* in both countries. *Occupier* always refers to a dwelling.

octillion *see under* **billion**

octingentenary, n.   **800th anniversary**

America still has some years to go until even the bicentenary of its independence from the mother country, which can indulge in words like *octingentenary.*

odd, adj.   **peculiar**

Odd is used much more in England than in America to describe
a person as *peculiar* in the sense of *eccentric*. The English, generally speaking, like to regard themselves as *odd* in that sense.
Americans conform a great deal more than Englishmen, despite
a lot of nonsense to the contrary.

odd sizes   **broken sizes**

I.e., not all sizes available (referring to merchandise for sale).

off, adj. (col.)   **bad form**

Thus: "It was a bit *off* to be doing her nails at the restaurant
table."

offal, n.   **viscera**

A butcher's term covering liver, kidneys, tongue, etc., or animal
insides generally. It would seem to appear only in the singular
in American usage, and its usual meaning in that form is *excreta*.
See also **humble pie.**

office block, *see* **block**

offices, n. pl.   **conveniences**

Synonymous with another English word which has a meaning
unknown in America—**amenities** (q.v.) in the sense of *conveniences,* as applied to a house. A real-estate agent's term:
"All the usual *offices,*" i.e., electricity, hot and cold running
water, kitchen, lavatory, etc., etc.

off licence   **bottled liquor license** (app.)

Sign on shops indicating that they can sell liquor all day long
(not merely **during hours** [q.v.]) to be taken *off* the premises rather than drunk thereon.

off-load, v.t. (col.)   **bump**

Meaning to *displace* an ordinary airplane passenger in favor of a VIP—usually the victim is a civilian and the VIP is military or government personnel.

off one's chump (sl.) .   **off one's rocker**

off one's dot (sl.)   **off one's rocker**

off one's feed (sl.)   **out of sorts**

Literally, a person *off his feed* is *without appetite.* Conversely, an American might say, "Something's eating *him.*"

off one's onion (sl.)   **off one's rocker**

off one's own bat (col.)   **on one's own**

Used in expressions indicating doing things without anybody else's help. A term derived from cricket.

off-peak, adj.   **non-rush hour**

It costs less to ride on *off-peak* trains in England. Term and practice now being adopted in America.

off-putting, *see* **put . . . off**

off-side lane   **right lane**

The passing lane; the one nearest the center of the road. *See also* **near-side lane.**

off-the-peg, adj.   **ready-to-wear**

old, adj. (col.)   **n.A.e.**

A more or less slangy term used especially in addressing intimates (or persons you would like to be intimate with), coupled with a variety of nouns, thus: *old man, old chap, old bean, old thing, old fruit, old egg, old top;* but *old boy* (not as a form of address) has the special meaning of *alumnus* (*see* **old boy**).

old basket (sl.)   **old geezer**

old boy; old girl (col.)   **alumnus (alumna)**

In the frame of reference of secondary education, *old boy* would be *alumnus* or *graduate* in America. When you get to the university level, *old boy* becomes *old student;* it would remain *alumnus* or *graduate* in America in formal terms, but *old grad* colloquially. The American term *old grad* is a much narrower term than *old boy,* connoting unduly intense college patriotism, especially with respect to religious and vociferous attendance at football games. *Old boy contacts* often referred to as the *old boy network,* which are so terribly important in England, would come out in America as *old school connections,* but compared with the English variety they are so tenuous as to be almost academic, figuratively as well as literally. In Scotland, an *old boy*

Old Boy

is referred to, with rather more dignity, as a *Former Pupil,* sometimes abbreviated to *F.P.*

old cock (sl.)   **old man**

Used vocatively.

old dutch, *see* **my old dutch**

old-fashioned (col.)   **precocious**

This is said of a youngster who is *fashioned* like an *older* person, and has nothing to do with the usual sense of the word.

Old-Fashioned

old girl, *see under* **old boy**

Old Lady of Threadneedle Street (col.)   **Bank of England**

A colloquialism derived from its address.

old man of the sea (col.)   **unshakable bore**

old party (col.)   **old-timer**

Describing a not-quite-doddering old thing; affectionate pejorative.

old stager (col.)   **old hand**

old sweat (col.)   **old soldier**

O-levels, *see* **A-levels**

omnium gatherum (col.)   (1) **mixture**
                                                       (2) **open house**

Mock Latin. *Omnium* is the genitive plural of *omnis,* Latin for *all; gatherum* is a phony Latinization of *gather.* Applied to:
(1) Any motley collection of persons or things.
(2) A party open to all comers.

on, prep.   **over**

A poker term used in the description of a full house. Thus, aces *on* knaves, which in America would be aces *over* jacks.

on a piece of string (col.)   **tight spot**

A bad place to be, on either continent. Usually in the phrase to *have someone* there.

on appro (col.)   **on approval**

Describing merchandise taken but returnable at the customer's option. *Appro,* unlike approval, is accented on the first syllable.

once in a way·   **once in a while**

A favorite usage of the author Anthony Powell.

oncer, n. (sl.)   **once-a-Sunday churchgoer**

A *twicer,* literally, is a newspaper worker who doubles as both typesetter and printing press operator; but in slang it means a *twice-a-Sunday churchgoer.* One searches in vain, in both dictionary and church, for a *thricer.*

one-eyed village

one-horse town

Also known in America as a *whistle stop.*

on form

in form

Preposition usage is tricky; see Introductory Note 8 on this. Thus, *on* form meaning *in* form, but *in* Regent Street as opposed to *on* Fifth Avenue.

on heat

in heat

In season is used in both countries.

on one's beam ends (col.)

on one's last legs

A ship *on her beam ends* is *on her side* and in danger of capsizing. A person *on his beam ends* is *in a bad way, on his last legs, in extremis.* The condition need not be physical. It might, for instance, be that of a bank teller who had sincerely intended to put the money back.

on one's tod (sl.)

on one's own

on second thoughts

on second thought

How singular of the Americans! But they do *have* second thoughts.

on the cards

in the cards

on the cheap (col.)

on a shoestring

on the hob (col.)

on the wagon

on the loose (col.)

wild

In the sense of lax morals rather than merely *fancy-free,* which the expression connotes in America. Americans do talk about *living a loose life* or *living loosely,* however.

279

on the pictures   **in the movies**

on the stocks (col.)   **in the works**

Already started, describing any project on which work has already begun. Borrowed from shipbuilding.

on the telephone   **having a telephone**

In America *on the telephone* means *speaking on the telephone.* In England if you want to get in touch with someone and want to know whether or not he has a phone, you ask him, "Are you *on the telephone?*" In America you would ask, "Do you *have a phone?*"

on the tiles, *see* **night on the tiles**

on the up and up (sl.)   **going places**

Quite a different meaning in England! Describes a person or company getting on.

on thorny ground   **in trouble**

on tick (col.)   **on the cuff**

on train, *see* **in train**

oof (sl.)   **dough**

In the sense of *money.* This word is at the least old fashioned; it may now be obsolete. It is short for *ooftish,* a Yiddish corruption of *auf dem Tisch,* which is German for *on the table.* In other words, *money on the table,* also known as *cash on the barrel.*

operating-theatre, n.   **operating room**

oppidan, n.   **noncampus Etonian** (app.)

At Eton there are seventy **collegers** (q.v.), also known there as *scholars* or *foundation scholars,* and 1,030 (or thereabouts) *oppidans* (from *oppidum,* Latin for *town*). The *collegers,* or *scholars,* are the privileged few who live in **college** (q.v.). The *oppidans* attend the same courses but live in school boarding houses in town.

opposite prompt   **stage right**

Short for *opposite prompter* and often abbreviated to *o.p.* This archaic circumlocution was based on the position of the prompter's box in the old days. *Prompt* (short for *prompt side,* often abbreviated to *p.s.*) naturally means *stage left.* Maddeningly enough these terms sometimes mean the exact reverse, particularly in the older theaters, where the prompter's box was located on the other side of the stage.

ops room (col.)   **operations planning room**

A military colloquialism. A *tour of ops* is an RAF term meaning the number of missions to be completed in order to earn a rest period.

orderly bin   **street litterbox**

order paper   **calendar**

An *order paper* is the Parliamentary equivalent of an American Congressional *calendar.*

order to view   **appointment to look at**

Term used in house hunting.

ordinary call   **station-to-station call**

Telephone call. In England a *person-to-person* call is known as a *personal* call.

ordinary shares   **common stock**

ordnance datum   **sea level**

Above sea level is commonly seen in England; *above ordnance datum* is never seen in America.

organize, v.t. (col.)   **round up**

As in "It's too late to *organize* a baby sitter," when you get a last-minute invitation to play some bridge. Colloquially, to *organize* somebody or something is to *get hold of,* to *arrange for,* the person or thing that fills the need.

other place, *see* **another place**

outdoor relief   **aid given by a poorhouse to an outsider**

Also known in England as *out-relief.*

out for a duck, *see* **duck** (1)

outgoings, n. pl.   **expenses**

This English word is used to cover not only *household expenses* but also *business overhead.* Note that *overhead* is *overheads* in England, a real plural taking a plural verb.

overall, n.   **smock**

The English use *overall,* or *boiler suit,* in the sense of a one-piece work garment and also to describe what Americans would call a *smock.*

overdraft, n.   **bank loan**

In America *overdraft* is a rather dirty word; it means the act of drawing a check on your account in excess of the existing balance, and it usually results in a stern reaction from the official in charge. In England *overdraft* implies the bank's consent and simply describes a method of borrowing.

overleaf, adj.   **reverse side of the page**

Overleaf is synonymous with another English injunction, **P.T.O.** (q.v.), which stands for *please turn over,* shortened in America to *over.*

282

overspill, n., adj.   **surplus population**

An *overspill* city is a new English sociopolitical phenomenon. It is a made-to-order city designed in accordance with blueprints drawn up under the New Towns Act to take care of surplus urban population. Thus, there exist the New Towns of Crawley, Stevenage, Basildon. Milton Keynes in north Buckinghamshire will include many existing villages and towns and if plans work out will provide homes and jobs by 1981 for 70,000 souls now living in London. This particular *overspill* city is being named after one of the little villages it will engulf which, last time the Author looked, had a population of 159.

overtake, v.t.,v.i.   **pass**

A traffic term. *Do not overtake* is the English road sign equivalent of *No passing.*

over the eight, *see* **have one over the eight**

over the road   **across the street**

Oxbridge, n.   **Oxford and Cambridge**

Obviously a portmanteau concoction. Used when contrasting Oxford and Cambridge with the provincial universities such as Birmingham, Manchester, and Sheffield, which are referred to as the **redbrick universities** (q.v.), originally a pejorative term. The image of these universities, however, has been greatly enhanced. No comparable term is yet current to describe a third group of new universities which has recently been established. Of several terms heard, the most pleasant is the *Shakespearean universities,* so-called because their names (Essex, Sussex, Warwick, Kent, Lancaster, York) suggest the dramatis personae of his historical plays. Also heard is the term *plate-glass universities,* reflecting their contemporary architecture.

Oxford bags, *see* **bags**

𝔓 | P

p. a.   **secretary**

Abbreviation of *personal assistant,* a rather lofty title now in vogue in the British Diplomatic Service for long-suffering secretaries. The title *secretary* would be confusing because of hierarchical semantics.

pack, n.   **deck**

In the expression *pack of cards. Deck* is rare in England.

packed out with (col.)   **packed full of**

For instance, a popular restaurant in London is *packed out with* people at lunch time.

packet, n.   **package**

The delivery man in England leaves a *packet* at the door; in America this would be a *package.* Applied to cigarettes, the American term is *pack. Pay packet* is the English equivalent of *pay envelope. Packet* has a number of slang uses as well. If you win a lot of money at an English track or on the London Stock Exchange, you *make a packet.* The American equivalent of this would be a *pile.* A *proper packet* of something is a *great big bunch* of it. If you have been having all kinds of unpleasant experiences, for instance while making the rounds looking for a job, you might announce at the end of such a day, "I've had a *packet,*" meaning a *bellyful.* One thing not to do with a *packet* is to catch one, because *catch a packet* means *stop a bullet.*

pack up, (sl., col.)   **conk out; give up**

Or *pack it up.* Another American slang equivalent is *fold.* It depends on who or what is doing the *conking out.* Thus, in America, an unsuccessful business *folds;* a person giving up an unequal struggle would be said to *conk out.* In its most extreme sense to *pack up* is to *croak* or *kick the bucket.* Those passing on can be said to *kick the bucket* in England, but *croak* is not heard. *"Pack up!"* has an entirely different sense: *"Shut up!"* Other English forms of the same injunction are *"Belt up!,"* *"Put a sock in it!"* The English use the expression *pack up* or *pack in* transitively, to describe the *giving up* of an activity. Thus one *packs up* or *packs in* gardening because of a sore back. *Pack in* is used where the cessation is intended to be permanent; *pack up* is more common where an activity is suspended for the time being.

paddy, n. (col.)   **tantrum**

Paddywhack is a variant. *Paddy* is a nickname for *Padraig,* which is old Irish for *Patrick,* and there are so many Patricks in Ireland that Patrick or Pat is usually the chief protagonist in Irish jokes. Apparently Irish tempers are shorter than English ones, because somehow *paddy* came to mean *tantrum.*

page, n.   **bellhop**

Pagett M.P.   **whirlwind tourist**

Pagett M.P. is a Kipling character who thinks he gets to know all about a foreign country by visiting it for a short time. It is used generically to designate that type of tourist, in the same way that the name of the Sinclair Lewis character *Babbitt* has come to mean the businessman whose bible is the mores of his social group, and who is embarrassingly wanting in cultural pursuits.

pair, n.   **floor (of a building)**

In addition to its other English uses as a noun, shared with the American language, *pair* is used on building directories to indicate what *floor* a tenant occupies. A person on the *third pair* means a person *three flights up.* Presumably *pair* is used this way in situations where there are only two tenants on a floor. Old-fashioned building directories usually put the number of the *pair* first, followed by the name of the occupants. One must be careful to remember that if Mr. Jones occupies the *third pair* he is *three flights up* and is therefore on what in America would be called the *fourth floor*, because although English and Americans both mean the same thing when they talk about the *ground floor*, the next floor up in England is the *first floor*, whereas in America it is the *second floor* (*see* **first floor**).

pair of tongs, *see* barge pole

panache, n.   swagger

Panache has the literal meaning of plume, as on a helmet. It is found in England in phrases such as *professional panache*, describing, for instance, a doctor or lawyer who acts as though he were very sure of himself.

panda car   police car

A familiar sight all over England is the light blue Morris 1000 coupé with a broad white stripe down the middle and a large POLICE sign on the top, driven by a **bobby** (q.v.).

pannage, n.   pig food

pantechnicon, n.   moving van

Technically a *pantechnicon* is a furniture storage warehouse, and *pantechnicon van* is the equivalent of *moving van;* but popularly the *van* is dropped so that *pantechnicon* has come to mean the van rather than the storage house. *See also* **removals**.

pantomime, n.   n.A.e.

Sometimes *panto* for short. This is a peculiarly English form of show, produced during the Christmas season, based on fairy tales or legends, involving singing, dancing, clowning, topical humor, and almost anything but the silence which is associated with the word in its ordinary sense. Adults are admitted if accompanied by children.

pants, n. pl.   **underpants**

The English equivalent of American *pants* is *trousers.* In England pants are *underwear,* usually men's shorts; but *pants* in England can also include ladies' *panties.*

parade, n.   **promenade**

A *shopping parade* is a *line of shops* along a street, especially where there is an arcade or colonnade. The English also use *parade* the way the Americans do, complete with brass bands and martial music.

paraffin, n.   **kerosene**

The English equivalent of *paraffin,* as the word is used in America, is *white wax.*

parish, n.   **town** (app.)

Besides its original religious connotation, this word, used alone, is understood in the proper context as *civil parish,* meaning the subdivision of a county constituting the smallest unit of local government, regulated administratively by the *parish council.* The American approximation of *parish* in rural areas would be *town.* A *town* in England is larger than a *parish. Town* (without the definite or indefinite article) always means *London* in the **Home Counties** (q.v.).

parking bay   **parking space**

The space covered by a parking meter, or an outdoor parking space for rent.

parky, adj. (sl.)   **snappy**

Meteorological slang meaning *chilly.*

parson's nose (col.)   **pope's nose**

That part which goes over the fence last.

part exchange, *see* **give in part exchange**

parting, n.   **part**

Both English and Americans *part* their hair, but the result is known as a *parting* in England and a *part* in America.

party candidate   **straight ticket** (app.)

When Americans go to the polls they vote for all sorts of offices, from president down to dogcatcher, and they either vote the *straight ticket* or *split their ticket*. An Englishman votes only for his *M.P.* (*Member of Parliament*), and if his vote is based on party rather than choice of individual, he votes for his *party candidate*.

pass, n.   **passing grade**

Referring to school examinations: thus, *O-level pass, A-level pass*, etc. *See* **A-levels.** A *pass degree* is a lower level of academic distinction than an *honours degree*.

passage, n.   **hall**

An American variant is *hallway*.

pass a message   **leave a message**

passing, n.   **passage**

Referring to a bill in Parliament.

passman   **college graduate**

Not a common word; it means a person who takes a degree at a university.

past a joke (sl.)   **not funny**

I.e., *intolerable*. Describes a situation which can no longer be laughed off.

288

pasty, n.   individual pie

The only one-word American approximation (very approximate) is, in certain parts of the country, *knish.* The most famous *pasty* of all is the *Cornish pasty,* which originated in the duchy of Cornwall but is now ubiquitous in England and is always filled with meat. *Knishes* are usually filled with mashed potatoes, which would seem to make for a very unbalanced diet indeed. *Pasties* can be filled with almost anything—there are *jam pasties* and *fruit pasties* as well as *meat pasties.*

Paternoster Row (col.)   **n.A.e.**

The *publishing industry.* The English often use a street name metaphorically to indicate a profession centering about that location. Cf. *Throgmorton Street, Fleet Street,* etc. Americans do it too: *Wall Street, Broadway,* etc.

patience, n.   **solitaire**

Name for the endless varieties of card game played by a lone (and usually lonely) player. *Patience* is the English name and *solitaire* the usual American name, although *patience* is occa-

Patience

sionally heard among older people in America. The game *solitaire* in England describes a game played by a lone player with marbles on a board containing little holes into which the marbles fit.

Patrol, n.   **school zone** (app.)

Along the road one sees signs reading *Patrol 150 yards, Patrol 125 yards,* etc., often with a picture of a child. These are the equivalent of *School Zone* signs in America.

pavement, n.   **sidewalk**

Sidewalk is not used by the English. *Crazy pavement* (sometimes *crazy paving*) means irregular-shaped, sometimes varicolored·flat stones used in the building of garden paths, patios, etc. *Pavement artists* make very elaborate colored chalk drawings in London and other cities on sidewalks and hope for tips from passersby. In London, where it rains so often, this would seem to be a particularly ephemeral medium.

pay, v.t.   **waterproof**

A nautical term. The usual materials are tar and pitch.

pay-box, n.   **box office**

P.A.Y.E.   **pay as you go**

These dreary initials stand for *pay as you earn,* which is the English name for the income-tax system which provides for the withholding of income tax by employers, banks paying interest, companies paying dividends, and so on.

pay for the call   **accept the charge**

This is the term used by the operator in the process of putting through a *collect call* (*reverse charge call* in England). The American operator asks the person at the other end of the line, "Will you *accept the charge?*" The English operator asks, "Will you *pay for the call?*" (Especially in matters of money, the English are much more direct and tend to avoid euphemisms.) There are many differences between the two countries in telephone idiom (*see* **caller; ordinary call; personal call; through; trunk enquiries**). Incidentally, Americans often have difficulty at first in understanding one word used by English operators while attempting to place the call: *trahnkneckchew.* This is English operator-ese for *trying to connect you,* the oft-repeated placatory term they use to soothe the nerves of the impatient caller.

pay one's whack, *see* **whack** (3)

pay packet	**pay envelope**

pay the earth	**pay a fortune**

Americans also *pay an arm and a leg,* a particularly gruesome expression happily not used by the English. The English do not say *pay a fortune,* but things in England can *cost a fortune,* as well as *costing the earth.*

P.C., *see under* **Birthday Honours**

peak hour	**rush hour**

pearlies, n. pl. (col.)	(1) **costermongers' attire** (2) **costermongers**

Costermongers' clothes are heavily studded with mother-of-pearl buttons, hence *pearlies.* In addition to describing their clothing, *pearlies* is used colloquially to mean the costermongers themselves. *See also* **coster.**

pebbledash, n.	**pebble-coated stucco**

A not very good looking and all too frequent building surfacing in England. It gets dirty rather quickly and appears to be totally unwashable because of the rough texture. Whole industrial villages of *pebbledash* structure are seen here and there, often in the Midlands, apparently covering up bad brickwork,

and one wonders how in the world this miserable invention ever
came about. Luckily as far as present construction is concerned,
its day is over.

peckish, adj. (col.)   **empty** (app.)

Peckish means *faintly hungry,* wanting a snack, hankering after
a little something to fill the void, but not by any means a real
meal. Undoubtedly, *peckish* is derived from *peck* in the sense
of *pecking* at food, a little of this and a little of that, the way a
chicken eats.

pedestal, n.   **toilet bowl**

Sometimes *w.c. pedestal,* a terribly polite euphemism for *toilet
bowl,* seen, for example, in lavatory signs on certain British railroad cars requesting passengers not to throw various objects into
the *w.c. pedestal.*

pedlar, n. (col.)   **blabbermouth**

Pedlar is spelled *peddler* in America. Its literal meaning is the
same in both countries, evoking the image of a *pack-carrying*
or *wagon-driving hawker* of small and extremely miscellaneous
merchandise—an image which is fast vanishing from the landscape. In England it has a figurative meaning: *gossip* (as indeed
most *pedlars* must have been, since they saw everything that
was going on). *Pedlars' French* is English slang for *thieves' jargon,* or more generally, *underworld lingo.*

peeler, *see* **bobby**

peep-behind-the-curtain, *see* **Tom Tiddler's ground**

peg away (col.)   **work away**

To *stay with* a job, no matter how tired you get.

peg out (sl.)   **kick the bucket**

pelmet, n.   **valance**

penny, n.   **n.A.e.**

See Introductory Note 18.

penny dreadful (col.)   **dime novel**

Sometimes called a *penny blood* or a *shilling shocker.*

(the) penny dropped   **I (he, etc.) got the message**

I.e., *something clicked.* Used to describe the situation where the protagonist is at first unimaginatively unaware of the significance of what is going on, can't take a hint or two, and then—finally—the veil lifts: *it dawns on him; he gets the point, it clicks.*

penny-farthing, n. (col.)   **high-wheeler**

Primitive bicycle.

penny gaff, *see* **gaff**

penny plain (col.)   **simple**

As opposed to **twopence coloured** (q.v.). The meaning is *unadorned, without frills.*

penny reading   **n.A.e.**

An old-time show consisting of a series of short skits and sketches, usually comic. The price of admission was a penny. The practice is kept alive at some of the **public schools** (q.v.). Despard Murgatroyd, in *Ruddigore* (Gilbert and Sullivan), was a "**dab** [q.v.] *at penny reading.*"

pepper castor   **pepper shaker**

pepper pot   **pepper shaker**

perambulator, n.   **baby carriage**

But practically always shortened to *pram.*

pergola, n.   **trellis**

Pergola, in America, evokes the image of a rather rustic garden
house to escape into out of the rain or for children to play house
in or adolescents to daydream in. Technically it means an *arbor*
or *bower.* But in England, especially in the country, it is the
name for a *trellis* running in a straight line and usually constructed of slim tree trunks as uprights and branches as cross-
pieces and Y-shaped supports, all still wearing their bark, and
forming a frame for the training of climbing roses.

period return, *see* **return**

perish, v.t.   **destroy**

Perish is, of course, common in and to both countries as an intransitive verb. The transitive use is very rare in America and is
now heard only in dialect. In England one still is *perished* by
(or with) cold, thirst, etc. This does not mean one has died of it
but merely been distressed or at least made *seriously uncom-
fortable.* When heat or cold *perishes* vegetation, it does mean
destroyed. Perishing can be used in England as an adverb, as
in *perishing cold.* It's *perishing,* which means *terribly cold,* is
another English way of saying *bloody cold. Perisher* is synonymous with *blighter,* and both are English slang which originally
described a person of low character (*bounder* or *cad*) but now
are not so pejorative as formerly. *Perisher* is derived from the
transitive use of the verb.

perks, n. pl. (sl.)   **gravy** (app.)

Slang shortening of *perquisites.*

permanent way   **roadbed**

Railroad term. It means the *roadbed* or the *rails* themselves. In
view of the shutting down of one branch line after another in
England (as well as in America), the *permanent* seems naive.
An echo from a happier time when all good things, like rail-
roads, were going to endure forever.

perry, n.   **pear cider**

A fermented pear juice drink which the author has never heard
of in America.

personal call   **person-to-person call**

petrol, n.   **gasoline**

petrol pump   **filling station**

pewter, n. (sl.)   **loot**

Nothing stolen—used in this context it means only *prize
money,* the kind of *loot* you bring home from a church bazaar.

p.g. (col.)   **boarder**

Stands for *paying guest,* a euphemism for what Americans would
call a *boarder* and Englishmen call a *lodger. Paying guest* would
seem to be close to a contradiction in terms.

pie, n.   **deep-dish pie**

An ordinary American *pie* would be called a *tart* in England.
In much of England *pie* connotes *meat pie* (*see* **pasty**), rather
than something involving fruit. We are familiar with the expression, *as American as apple pie.* The writer has never heard
as English as meat pie, but it may well be time to invent that
expression. *Pie* used by itself in America would never suggest a
filler of anything but fruit.

piece of cake (sl.)   **cinch**

Meaning an easy thing to do; like rolling off a log.

pig it (sl.)   (1) **live like a pig**
                                                    (2) **shovel it in**

pi-jaw, *see* **jaw**

pillar, n.   **post**

Automobile term: the *post* between two doors of a four-door sedan (*saloon*). When you trade in the Rolls for a Cadillac, you go from pillar to post.

pillar box   **mailbox**

See also **letter box; post box.**

pimp, n., (col.)   **small bundle of kindling**

Sign in a Kentish hardware store (**ironmonger's** [q.v.]) window: "Pimps—2½ pence." In the county of Kent and neighboring sections of Sussex, a *pimp* is a small, cylindrical roll (also called *bung* because it is shaped like a big stopper) of kindling, usually called *firewood* in England.

pinafore, n.   **jumper**

Jumper, in England, means a *pullover,* a type of sweater.

pinch, v.t. (sl.)   **swipe**

Pinch and *swipe* meaning *steal,* and *pinch* meaning *arrest,* are used in both countries; but in the meaning *steal, pinch* is favored in England, *swipe* in America, where *pinch* more commonly means *arrest.* In America you're *pinched* if you are caught *swiping;* in England, you're *nabbed* if you are caught *pinching.*

pink, v.i. (col.)   **knock**

Referring to automobile engines.

pint, n.   **beer** (app.)

If an Englishman asks for a *pint* he means a *pint of* **bitter** (q.v.). (As a unit of liquid measure, the *pint* in question is an Imperial pint of twenty oz., as opposed to the sixteen oz. American pint.) If his thirst or budget is of more modest proportions, he will ask for a *half,* or *half a bitter,* which means *half a pint,* i.e., ten oz. The two sizes of glasses are standard pub equipment, hanging on row after row of ceiling hooks or lined up on shelves and always spotless. Since *bitter* is usually of two grades, *ordinary bitter* and *best bitter,* the regular client, whose taste in the matter is a known quantity, need not specify. Otherwise he will volunteer the grade, or the person behind the counter will ask. Standing by itself, in this context, a *pint* in England means about the same thing as a *beer* means in America.

pip-at-the-post, v.t. (col.)   **nose out**

The post referred to is the winning post in a horse race.

pip emma   **P.M.**

Ack emma is *A.M.* Both now generally outmoded.

pissed, adj. (sl.)   **tight (drunk)**

Usually reserved for cases of advanced inebriation.

pit, n.   **rear of orchestra**

What is called (strangely enough) the *orchestra* in America turns up in England as the **stalls** (q.v.). The *pit* used to be the name for the rear of that part of the theatre, and a *pittite* was never, as the sound of it might imply, a member of an ancient Semitic tribe, but only a rarely used word for a person occupying a seat in the *pit.*

pitch, n.   **cricket field**

Technically the *pitch* is the narrow grass strip between wickets along which the batsmen run. But *pitch* has come to mean, generally, the whole field, and what is technically the *pitch* is often called the *wicket.* There is, of course, enough material in cricket terminology to constitute (perish the thought) Volume II of this work. *Pitch* has come to have a more general meaning and can be a *football pitch* (*soccer field* in America) as well as a *cricket pitch. Pitch* is sometimes used colloquially, like **wicket** (q.v.), to mean *situation:* to be *on a good pitch* (or *wicket*) is to be *in a good spot.*

pitch upon (col.)   **pick on**

Not in the sense of *nag* but rather in the sense of *select*. Thus: The police *pitched upon* him as the likeliest suspect.

placeman, n.   **office holder**

With the strong implication that the appointment was motivated by self-interest and produced a rubber stamp.

plain, adj.   **homely**

It is entirely possible to be quite attractive in England and **homely** (q.v.) at the same time. It is likewise possible to be quite attractive in America and *plain* at the same time. Watch these adjectives in dealing with women.

plain as a pikestaff   **plain as the nose on your face**

plait, n., v.t.   **braid**

Pronounced *plat*. Girls *plait* their hair or have their hair in *plaits* in England. In America they *braid* it or put it into *braids*. Same difference in usage with respect to horses' tails.

planning permission   **building permit**

Short for *town and country planning permission*. A *town and country planning commission* is the English opposite number to an American *zoning board*.

plaster, n.   **adhesive tape**

play a straight bat (col.)   **know your business**

A term from cricket meaning *know what you're doing.*

play for one's side (col.)   **be on one's side; side with one**

play for safety   **play safe**

play the game, *see* **game**

play . . . up (col.)   (1) **play up on** (go wrong)
                                           (2) **pester**

  (1) In England your trick knee or your hi-fi *plays* you up; in
       America it *plays up* on you.
  (2) Pupils who deliberately annoy their teachers are said to *play*
       them *up*.

please close the doors!   **all aboard!**

  Heard in railroad stations and often followed by "Train is about
  to depart!" In England, the one-time maritime power, the
  nautical term is still reserved for nautical situations.

pleasure   **don't mention it**

  A common response to any expression of gratitude. Americans
  and English both say *"you're welcome!"* or *"don't mention it!"*
  or *"not at all!,"* but *"pleasure!"* (short for *"it's a pleasure!"*) is
  exclusively English.

plimsolls, n.   **sneakers**

  Another English term is *gym shoes. Plimsolls* is the common
  English word for *sneakers,* so named after Samuel Plimsoll, who
  also lent his name to the expression *Plimsoll's Mark* (or *Plimsoll
  Line*), which is the line showing how far a ship is allowed by law
  to be submerged when loaded. In addition, he is known as one of
  the moving forces behind the British Merchant Shipping Act of
  1876. This connection between Mr. Plimsoll and shipping leads
  to the conclusion that *plimsolls* got their name from the fact that
  they were the kind of cheap canvas soft-soled shoes worn on deck.

Plough, n.   **Big Dipper**

  Other English names for the *Big Dipper* are *Charles's Wain*
  and *Great Bear.*

plough, v.t. (sl.)   **flunk**

That is, to *flunk* a pupil, not an exam. Undoubtedly short for *plough under.*

ploy, n. (col.)   (1) **job**
                                                      (2) **toy**

The second meaning given above refers specifically to *educational toys,* and looks like a portmanteau formation of *play* and *toy,* which was probably helped along by the first meaning: in other words, a *toy* that keeps the kids busy with a *job,* like fitting things together. In America, at least since the appearance of Stephen Potter, *ploy* means a move like a gambit in chess, a feint in boxing, a calculatedly misleading step in the business world, or an act of one-upmanship at a party: anything calculated to get results by outwitting or upsetting the other fellow.

plum duff (col.)   **plum pudding**

The *duff* is *dough* pronounced like *rough.*

po, n. (sl.)   **pottie**

Short for the *pot* in *chamber pot,* and pronounced like the *pot* in *pot de chambre.* The French pronunciation is supposed to make it amusing and therefore less clinical.

pocketbook, n.   (1) **pocket notebook**
                                               (2) **billfold**

In England a lady's handbag is always called a *bag* or a *handbag,* never a *pocketbook.* That term is reserved there for a *pocket notebook* or a *folding wallet,* which the English also call a *notecase. Pocket books* are small *paperbacks* in both countries. *Pocketbook* is used figuratively in America to mean *financial resources.* Thus: "A luxury cruise is too much for my *pocketbook.*" The English use *purse* in the same way.

podge, n. (col.)   **fatty**

Podge gives rise to the adjective *podgy,* which has its American equivalent in *pudgy.*

pogged, adj. (sl.)   **stuffed**

After too much food: "I'm *pogged!*" A bit of Yorkshire slang.

point, n.   (1) **electrical socket**
                                                 (2) **railroad switch**

In use (1), *point* often appears as *electrical point* or *power point.* Sometimes it is used in combination with another word, as in *razor point,* thus indicating an electrical outlet to be used for a particular purpose.

pointsman, n.   (1) **traffic policeman**
                                                 (2) **switchman**

(1) *Point-duty* is the *traffic detail* and a *policeman on point-duty* is a *traffic cop.*
(2) The railroad man in charge of switches.

poker school   **poker session**

policy, n.   **landscaped ground**

The landscaped part around a country house. Usually in the plural, the *policies,* and more commonly seen in Scotland than in England.

politician, n.   (1) **government official** (app.);
                                             (2) **political scientist**

Perhaps not necessarily one actually in power at the moment, but in any event a person skilled in the science of government and politics generally. The term has none of its pejorative implications as in America, where it immediately suggests the scheming and manipulating characteristic of party politics and unenlightened self-interest. In America the terms *politician* and *statesman* are almost antithetical in popular usage. Not so in England, where a *statesman* is merely a higher order of *politician* in the English sense, the recognition of whose experience, wisdom, and resulting power entitle him to the more eminent label.

Pompey, n. (sl.)   **Portsmouth**

Affectionate slang for the naval base.

ponce, n. (sl.)   **pimp**

A much fancier English synonym is *souteneur,* taken over from the French, in which language it literally means *protector,* indicating something or other about certain French attitudes.

pong, n. (sl.)   **stink** (app.)

No colloquial American equivalent. Used, for eaxmple, about Emmenthal cheese—"Tangy without the *pong.*"

pontoon, n.   **twenty-one**

A card game. *Pontoon* is a corruption of the French name for the game, *vingt-et-un.* The English apparently made the common mistake of omitting the *et* in *vingt-et-un, trente-et-un,* etc., and then proceeded to corrupt the corruption phonetically.

pony, n. (col.)   **£25 (twenty-five pounds)**

poop, n. (sl.)   **dope**

Short for *nincompoop.*

poor tool (col.)   **total loss**

To be a *poor tool* at such and such an activity is to be a *total loss* at it, a *bust.* Thus: He's a *poor tool* at providing for his family.

pop, n., v.t. (sl.)   **pawn**

Popshop is slang for *pawn shop.*

poplin, n.   **broadcloth**

In England, *broadcloth* describes a special kind of woolen material.

popper, n.   **snap**

To fasten articles of apparel. *See also* **press stud.**

poppet, n. (col.)   **sweetie**

A term of endearment used especially in describing little ones and pets.

popsie, n. (sl.)   **cutie**

Most commonly heard as the name for an old man's darling.

porch, n.   **overhang over outside door**

The word has an altogether different meaning in America—*veranda*. Older readers may remember the American popular song "Last Night on the Back Porch," indicating a location for that type of goings on which would have been rather difficult using *porch* in the English sense. One wonders what the English thought the lyrics meant.

porridge, n.   **oatmeal**

To *keep your breath to cool your porridge* is to *keep your advice for your own use* or to *practice what you preach.*

porter, n.   **doorman**

Americans think of *porters* as uniformed red-capped baggage carriers in railroad stations where they are usually known and addressed as *redcaps,* or at airports, where they are called *sky-caps.* Americans still call them *porters* at ship docks. A *red cap,* in England, is a *military policeman,* usually referred to in America as an *M.P.,* which of course stands for *Member of Parliament* in England. *Porter* is not used in America to designate a *doorman, doorkeeper,* or *gatekeeper.* The English often use *hall porter* to distinguish a *doorman* from a *railway porter. Porterage* is used to describe the services of a doorman. Where an American would say that his apartment house has a *doorman,* the Englishman would say that there is a *porter* at his *block of flats* or *porterage* is *laid on with his flat. Porterage* in America is a rarely used word meaning the services of a porter or the charge for his services.

portmanteau, n.   **blended word**

The figurative meaning is that of a made-up word combining the sounds and meanings of parts of two other words, like *squarson,* combination of *squire* and *parson; mingy,* combination of *mean* and *stingy; smog,* combination of *smoke* and *fog,* etc. One would guess that Lewis Carroll's *slithy* toad must have been not only *slimy* but also *lithe.* He invented this usage of portmanteau in *Through the Looking-Glass:* "You see, it's like a portmanteau—there are two meanings packed into one word."

posh, adj. (sl.)   **swanky**

From the initials *P.O.S.H.,* which stand for *port out, starboard home,* i.e., the north side of ships traveling between England and India. It was the shady, and therefore the preferable, side. (There are some authorities who vigorously contest this etymology.)

position, n.   **situation**

Position has two English uses which one almost never hears in America: it means *situation,* in the sense of *location,* of a house or other building. The other English meaning is also *situation* but in the figurative sense of the *way things stand.* For instance: "The *position* is that the company is insolvent," or, "Do you understand the *position?*"

post, n., v.t.   **mail**

See also **general post office; letter post; newspaper post; recorded delivery.**

postal van   **mail car**

Railroad term.

postal vote **absentee ballot**

post box **mailbox**

The smallish red iron boxes bear the initials of the sovereign in whose reign they were erected. An Englishman will announce with pride that the box near his home is a V.R. box! Occasionally called *posting box* or *letter box. See also* **pillar box.**

poste restante **general delivery**

Permanently borrowed from the French. Literally it means *mail remaining* (waiting to be picked up). The French have a pun for what so often happens when one follows the dangerous course of asking another to mail a letter for him: *poche restante* (*poche* means *pocket*).

post free **postpaid**

postman, n. **mailman**

post mortem **autopsy**

More commonly used in England.

pot, n. (sl.) (1) **boodle**
(2) **favorite (horse racing)**
(3) **various slang uses**

(1) Used alone or in the expression *pots of money.* To *put the pot* on a horse at an English race course is to *shoot your wad* or *bet your stack* at an American track. The English also use the expression to *go nap* on a horse to describe the same vice (*see* **nap**).
(2) The *pot* is also English slang for the *favorite* in a horse race.
(3) An English slang usage sometimes heard (occasionally lengthened to *pot-hunter*) is to describe a person who enters a contest not for the sport of it but only for the prize. Another English slang use is in the expression to *put* someone's *pot on,* which means to *squeal on* him, or *spill the*

beans, for which the English also use the expression *blow the gaff.* A *big pot,* however, means something entirely different—*VIP.*

pot-boy, n.   **bartender's assistant**

Potman means the same thing. Literally, someone who helps out in a pub, but sometimes used figuratively in the sense of *prat boy* as a pejorative term meaning somebody at anybody's beck and call. *See also* **dog's body.**

pot-house, n. (sl.)   **pub**

Slang for a **public house** (q.v.).

potsherd, n.   **broken fragment of earthenware**

Convenient for covering drainage holes in flowerpots. Pronounced *pot-sherd.* The *sherd* part of the word (sometimes *shard*) is said to be archaic standing by itself, but the author has heard it from the lips of more than one English country gardener. Also commonly used by archeologists.

pouf, pouffe, *see* **puff**

pour with rain   **pour**

It would be hard to know what else the impersonal it *could* pour with. The *rain* is assumed in America.

power point, *see* **point**

pram, n. (col.)   **baby carriage**

Short for *perambulator.*

prang, v.t. (sl.)   (1) **crash land** (an aircraft)
(2) **bomb** (a target)
(3) **lay** (a girl)

(1) and (2) are presumably onomatopoeic; but (3)?

praties, n. pl. (col.)   **spuds**

Borrowed from the Irish, and according to some authorities, given back.

prawn, n.   **small shrimp**

Small in American terms, because *shrimps* in England are generally tiny things compared to what Americans mean by the term. An Englishman would consider a *prawn* a large, rather than a small, shrimp. What Americans think of as shrimps are generally called *scampi* in England, a term usually confined in America to cooked shrimps in restaurants with continental cuisine. Sorry it's so complicated.

prefect, n.   **monitor** (app.)

A school boy or girl who attains a quasi-official position to help keep order.

preference shares   **preferred stock**

premium bond   **government lottery bond**

Monthly lottery drawings are held with cash prizes going to the holders of the bonds with lucky serial numbers. They bear no interest. In America the same phrase describes regular interest-bearing corporate bonds callable before maturity, on short notice, for redemption at a premium.

prep, n. (col.)   (1) **homework** (app.)
                                             (2) **study hall**

Short for *preparation. Prep* is the name for both (1) the work the student does to *prepare* for the next day's (or less frequently, that afternoon's) classes and (2) the session at boarding school at which he does it. *Prep* is usually supervised by a **prefect** (q.v.) or master who not only keeps order but is available to help the struggling student. The work itself in America is called *homework,* the session *study hall,* and the teacher who supervises serves only as monitor, not as tutor. Work to be done at home is called *homework,* even in England.

prep school   pre-preparatory school

In this phrase, *prep* is an abbreviation of *preparatory*. A *prep school* is a private school for boys or girls who enter at the age of eight and remain for five years. It is called a *prep school* because it *prepares* the children for **public school** (q.v.) which they enter at thirteen and where, too, they usually stay for five years. A *public school* is known in America as a *prep school,* and there it enjoys that name because it *prepares* the boys and girls for college. These usages make intelligent conversation between Englishmen and Americans about education practically impossible, especially since **college** (q.v.) does not mean the same thing in both countries. To make matters worse (if possible) the English do use the expression *private school* sometimes in the same way in which it is used in America, i.e., a *fee-charging school.*

presenter, n.   newscaster

Or *commentator* generally. Sometimes heard as a credit at the end of a television program.

presently, adv.   in a minute

Presently, used in this sense, would sound pompous in America. Everybody uses it in England.

press stud   snap

To fasten articles of apparel. Synonymous with **snapper** (q.v.).

pricey, adj. (col.)   high

In the sense of *high-priced.*

printed paper rates   third-class mail

prise open   pry open

Also spelled *prize.*

private, adj.   **personal**

On envelopes, meaning that nobody but the addressee is to open.

private bar, *see* **pub**

private school   **n.A.e.**

The author has been informed that Etonians use the expression *private school* exclusively for *prep school* (in the English sense). *See* **prep school; public school.**

private treaty   **contract**

In advertisements of real estate for sale, one often sees the phrase *for sale by private treaty,* which means that the common English practice of putting up real estate for sale at auction (*by auction* in England) is not being followed in that case.

Prize Day, *see* **Speech** Day

P.R.O.   **PR man**

The English call them public relations *officers* for some strange reason.

proctor, n.   **college monitor** (app.)

A *senior proctor* and a *junior proctor* are selected each year at Oxford and Cambridge as officials charged mainly with disciplinary matters. To *proctorize* is to exercise that function. The word is used in somewhat the same sense in some American colleges, with the emphasis on dormitory and examination discipline, but the American verb is *proctor,* same as the noun. The English have a special use of the word in *King's* (or *Queen's*) *Proctor,* designating an officer who may intervene in certain lawsuits, mainly matrimonial, where collusion or other skullduggery is suspected.

producer, n.   (1) **director**
                                                                   (2) **producer**

(1) In the English theatre *producer* and *director* are both used to mean *director* in the American sense, and *theatrical manager* means *producer* in the American sense.

(2) In the film industry *producer* and *director* are used as in America.

prog, n. (sl.)   n.A.e.

Slang for **proctor** (q.v.).

programme, n.   platform

What Americans call the *platform* of a political party is called its *programme* in England.

prompt, n.   stage left

See **opposite prompt.**

propeller shaft   drive shaft

Automobile term.

propelling pencil   mechanical pencil

proper, adj.   real

Used by the English as an intensive. If a pal should see you sipping lemonade in a pub, he might ask you why you're not having a *proper* drink, i.e., a *real* drink, an *honest to goodness* drink. A *proper pushing lad* is a *real go-getter*. Less complementary is an expression such as a *proper fool,* where the adjective emphasizes the degree of folly.

property, n.   real estate

A *property dealer* would be called a *real-estate operator* in America.

P.T.O.   over

Placed at the bottom of the page and indicating *please turn over*. The English also use the expressions *overleaf. See* **overleaf; over.**

pub, n. (col.)   bar (app.)

Very approximate—the institution of the English *pub* being so dismally, nay, tragically lacking in American life. *Pub* is short for *public house.* Everybody in England has "his" *pub.* A synonym for *pub* is the *local,* which is, of course, short for the *local pub.* (Note that *local* can also mean *native; see* **local.**) Every *pub* has at least two bars: the *public bar* and the *saloon bar.* The latter is somewhat more elegant and drinks served in that room cost a little bit more. One is apt to find a carpet on the floor of the *saloon bar,* but the darts board, the bar-billiards table, and the shove-halfpenny board would normally be found in the *public bar. See also* **free house; tied.**

pub-crawl, n., v.i. (col.)   make the rounds (of pubs)

To *pub-crawl* is to visit (and presumably give one's custom to) one pub after another, and *pub-crawl* is also the noun describing this deplorable activity.

publican, n.   saloon keeper (app.)

The *publican,* also known as the **landlord** (q.v.), is the *proprietor* of a *pub.*

public bar; public house, *see* pub

public convenience   comfort station

A battle of euphemisms, both meaning *public toilet;* a municipal institution which still flourishes in English towns and villages but seems to be disappearing in America.

public prosecutor   district attorney

public school   **private school** (app.)

In some ways a closer approximation might be *prep school,* but one must be careful to remember that in England **prep school** (q.v.) means *pre-prep school* in the American sense. The *public school* derived its name not, as did the American *public school system,* from the fact of public, i.e., government support, but rather from the fact that, centuries ago, certain gentlemen thought it preferable to have their children educated in a group away from home, rather than by private tutors at home. Hence the term *public school* in the sense of *group* (rather than *solo*) *education.* The English public schools are specially endowed and though highly individualistic in their traditions have organized a type of association and in common subscribe to certain standards. They are *private schools* in the American sense; but in England, too, there are also certain fee-charging schools which are called *private schools* but are not *public schools* and are therefore not *public* in either the English or the American sense. Very confusing, but it seems to work.

pudding, n.   **dessert**

But *see* **dessert** and **sweet.**

pudding club (col.)   **pregnancy**

In the pudding club means *pregnant.*

pudsy, adj.   **plump**

puff, n. (sl.)   **pansy**

I.e., male homosexual. Also *pouf* and *pouffe.*

pukka, adj.   **first class**

Of Hindu origin, occasionally spelled *pucka* or *pukkah;* synonymous with *super* and *smashing,* and there may be other words, all of them being equivalent to the American *great* or *swell.*

pull, n.

(1) **extra measure**
(2) **advantage**

(1) When you get more beer (or other liquid refreshment) than you ask for in a pub, you get a *pull,* also known as a *long pull.*

(2) To have a *pull* of someone is to have an *advantage* over him.

pull down   **tear down**

House-wrecking term.

pull one's socks up (col.)   **get going**

I.e., to *start moving,* to *show more stuff:* "He'd better *pull his socks up* if he wants to keep his job."

pull-up, n.   **diner**

Diners, in America, can be anything from shabby to magnificent. *Pull-ups* are usually quite shabby shacklike establishments.

pun, v.t.   **tamp**

Pun appears to be a variant of *pound.* A *punner* is a *tamper,* i.e., a tool with which one tamps the earth, rubble, etc.

punch-up, *see* **dust-up**

puncture, n.   **flat**

Puncture would sound old fashioned or at least pedantic in America. *Flat* is slowly being adopted by the English.

punner, *see* **pun**

punnet, n.   **small fruit basket**

A *small basket* for vegetables or fruit, woven of thin pieces of wood which are known in England as **chip** (q.v.). Strawberries and raspberries are sold in England by the *punnet,* which comes in one-pound and half-pound sizes.

punter, n.   **bettor**

Technically, to *punt* is to *bet against the house* in a card game; but colloquially it means to *bet on a horse race;* and the usual meaning of *punter* in this context is such a *bettor.*

purchase, hire, *see* **hire purchase; never-never**

purler, *see* **come a purler**

push, n. (col.)   **gate**

Meaning *dismissal.* Some *give the push,* some *get the push,* and it's all very sad.

push-bike (col.)   **bike**

As distinguished from *motor-bike.* Also *push-bicycle* and *push-cycle.*

pushcart, n.   **baby carriage**

Usually **pram** (q.v.). *Pushcart* in the American sense is **barrow** (q.v.).

push chair   **stroller**

push pin   **thumbtack**

Synonymous with *drawing pin.*

push the boat out (sl.)   **treat**

Usually heard in the expression "so-and-so's turn to *push the boat out,*" meaning that it is his *treat,* i.e., his turn to pay, e.g., for the next round of drinks or this trip to the movies.

put . . . about (col.)   **be a nuisance**

"I hate to *put you about,* but I really need the stuff this minute."

put a foot wrong (col.) **slip up**

Happily enough seen almost exclusively in the negative: "He'll never *put a foot wrong*," indicating a meticulous person. Sometimes one sees *put a foot right*, also in the negative: "I can't *put a foot right* today" means "*I shoulda stood in bed.*"

put a sock in it! (sl.) **stow it!**

The equivalent of "*Belt up!*" or "*Pack up!*" in England or "*Shut up!*" in America.

put down (1) **put to sleep**
(2) **charge**

Two wholly unrelated meanings:
(1) Euthanasia of pets. Sad. The English expression has now become common among professional dog breeders in America.
(2) "*Put* it *down*, please," is the way the customer asks the shop to charge it. Alternatively he might have said, "Please *book* it to me" or "*Book* it to my account" (*see* **book**).

put in hand, *see* **have ... put in hand**

put ... in the picture (col.) **bring ... up to date**

put it across ... (col.) **let ... have it**

I.e., to *punish*. The teacher became angry at the obstreperous pupil and really *put it across* him.

put ... off (col.) **disturb**

To *put* one *off* balance, or *off* his stride. *Off-putting* is an adjective describing the person or thing that has that effect. It seems just the least bit precious, perhaps jocularly, like other hyphenated adjectives ending in the participial *-ing*, like *shame-making*. It has the special flavor, sometimes, of *appetite-spoiling*, both literally and figuratively; it always connotes enthusiasm-dampening.

315

put one's back into (sl.)   **knock oneself out at**

Expressing the idea of arduous devotion to a task at hand.

put one's feet up (col.)   **relax**

A dinner hostess might say to a tired businessman: "Come earlier and put your feet up." Putting one's feet up connotes easy chairs, possibly a brief nap, freshening up, and in the case of a really kind hostess, even a bloody Mary.

put one's head down (col.)   **get some shuteye**

Also *get one's head down.*

put one's shirt on (col.)   **bet one's bottom dollar on**

put on side (sl.)   **put on the dog**

Sidy is a rare slang adjective which describes the deplorable activity of acting high and mighty. In the north of England *she's got a lot of side to her* means *she puts on airs.*

put paid to (col.)   **finish**

In the sense of *putting an end to.* Thus: "The rain *put paid to* our picnic." Derived from the image of stamping *"paid"* on a bill, thus putting an end to that transaction.

put (somebody's) pot on (sl.)   **squeal on**

To *put* Harry's *pot on* is to *squeal on* Harry.

put the comether on ...   **have ... under one's thumb**

Sometimes it means simply to *cajole;* generally, to *have a strong influence over.* A contraction of *come hither* and suggestion of feminine wiles; therefore usually applied to women.

put the pot, *see* **pot**

put the shutters up (sl.) **fold**

I.e., to *go broke*, and if necessary into bankruptcy.

put the wind up, *see* **get the wind up**

putty, n. (col.) **muddy bottom**

Nautical slang for the kind of stuff you should be careful not to get your keel stuck in.

put up the hare (col.) **get something going**

put-u-up, n. (col.) **convertible sofa**

pylon, n. **high tension tower**

𝕼 | Q

quad, n. (col.) **campus** (app.)

School and university term, short for *quadrangle*. It means the area bounded by college buildings rather than the whole campus. Some American colleges use the term *quad*.

quadrillion, *see under* **billion**

quantity, bill of, *see* **bill of quantity**

quantity surveyor **materials appraiser**

Particularly in the contracting business.

quart, n.

    (1) **1.20095 liquid quarts**
    (2) **1.0320 dry quarts**

See under **gallon.**

quarter, n. (col.)   **quarter of a pound**

One asks for a *quarter* of those chocolates (pointing) at the sweet shop. *Quarter of a pound* would sound ponderous in England. This would apply equally, of course, to mushrooms at the greengrocer's, nails at the ironmonger's, and all that sort of thing.

quarter-day, n.   **due date** (app.)

Quarter-days are the four days in the year when quarterly payments traditionally fall due in England and are the common dates for tenancy terms. They are: Lady Day (March 25); Midsummer Day (June 25); Michaelmas Day (September 29); Christmas Day (December 25).

quartern, n.   **four-pound loaf**

But they don't make them anymore.

quaver, n.   **eighth note**

Musical term. *See under* **breve.**

the Queen (col.)

    (1) **the national anthem**
    (2) **toast to the Queen**

(1) To stay at a dance through *the Queen* is to stay to the very end. It is usual to play *God Save the Queen* to close the proceedings, and *the Queen* in this context is simply short for the title of the national anthem.
(2) *The Queen* is also a complimentary toast drunk at banquets, taking precedence over other toasts. Guests do not smoke until after this toast.

in Queer Street   **hard up**

When the English talk of somebody's being *in Queer Street,* they mean that he is in bad trouble in a bad way, and usually in bad odor as well.

queer the pitch (sl.)   **stymie**

Pitch is a cricket term meaning technically the place between and around the **wickets** (q.v.) but is loosely used to mean the whole *playing field*. To *queer the pitch* for someone, then, is to *mess up* his playing field, not literally, but figuratively, in the sense of *spoiling his chances*. Americans use the verb *queer* in the slang sense of *spoil*, in the expression to *queer the works* for someone; to *ruin his chances*.

quench, v.t. (sl.)   **squelch**

I.e., *shut* somebody *up*.

query, n.   **complaint**

This connotation of *query* is not met with in America. It appears most frequently in the phrase *query department* of an organization.

question in the house   **issue raised in Congress** (app.)

"There'll be a *question in the House*" means "This is going to be brought up in Parliament." The nearest American equivalent would be: "This is going to be *brought up in Congress,* but more likely before a House or Senate committee (God forbid!)."

queue, n., v.i.   **line; line up**

The verb sometimes takes the form *queue up.* Foreigners are often surprised at the self-imposed discipline which leads the British to form queues. Queue-jumping leads to very positive remonstrations.

quid, n. (sl.)   **one pound (£)**

Referring to English money, not weight. No American slang equivalent except *buck* for *dollar*.

quid each way, *see* **have a quid each way**

quieten, v.t.   **quiet down**

Almost never heard in America.

quintillion, *see under* **billion**

quite, adj. (col.)   **up to snuff** (app.)

Quite used as a colloquial adjective—not an adverb modifying an adjective or an adverb—is found in negative expressions only, such as: *"He isn't quite,"* meaning *"He isn't quite acceptable."*

quiz, v.t.   **poke fun at**

Quiz originally meant to *make fun of* and also to *look curiously at,* but because of the popularity of American television quiz programs, the more common meaning of the word in England now is the American one, i.e., to *interrogate*.

quod, n. (sl.)   **poky**

I.e., the *clink*.

R | R

rabbit, n. (col.)   **dub**

In sports, a beginner or a player of little skill; a *duffer*.

race-course, n.   **racetrack**

The English never say *race-track* for *horse racing* but do use the term for auto racing and use *dog-track* for greyhound racing, which is sometimes colloquially shortened to **greycing** (q.v.).

racialist, n., adj.   **racist**

rackety, adj. (sl.)   **harum scarum**

radiogram, n.   **radio-phonograph**

In America a *radiogram* is a *wireless message.*

rag, v.t., v.i., n. (col.)   (1) **fool around; tease**
                                              (2) **stunt; gag**
                                              (3) **coarse stone**

(1) *Rag* is used intransitively to mean *fool around* or *kid around,* in a manner involving a little mild horseplay. Transitively it means to *tease* or *pull someone's leg.*

(2) As a colloquial noun, a *rag* is a *stunt* or *gag* and from this use we get *rag-week,* which is a week at the university during which students put on *stunts* in aid of charity, especially dressing up and riding around on weird and grotesque floats.

(3) *Rag* is also a variety of *hard coarse stone.*

raid, n.   **burglary**

In America *raid* brings up the image of a group assault of one sort or another, particularly military or police. One often reads in English newspapers of a *raid* made last night on a house or shop. All it means is a *burglary* effectuated by one or more naughty persons.

railway, n.   **railroad**

railway, scenic, *see* **scenic railway; switchback**

raise the wind, *see* **get the wind up**

ENGLISH   AMERICAN

rake up (col.)   **dig up**

In the sense of procuring with difficulty. The Americans use *rake up* in the sense of *bringing up* an old sore subject, usually a complaint or a scandal.

rally, v.t.   **kid**

In the sense of pulling someone's leg.

ramp, n. (sl.)   **racket**

A *swindle; ramp* is sometimes used as a transitive or an intransitive verb in a slang sense meaning *swindle*.

rare, adj. (col.)   **great** (app.)

Rare is a colloquial intensive. A *rare* lot of something is a *helluva* lot of it. *Rare* also implies *excellence*. A *rare* something is a *splendid* something. A *rare* time is a *swell* time; a *rare old* time is even sweller. But watch out, because in the expression, have a *rare time of it, rare time* means quite the opposite: a *tough time*.

rather! (col.)   **and how!**

rating, n.   **able seaman**

Lowest form of human marine life.

ratten, v.t.   **molest by stealing or damaging tools**

rattling, adj., adv. (col.)   (1) **brisk**
                                  (2) **damned**

(1) A *rattling* pace is a *brisk* one.
(2) A *rattling* good wine is an *unusually* good one or more likely a *damned good* one.
In the adverbial use, *rattling* has about the same meaning as **ripping** (q.v.).

ravers, *see* **stark ravers**

razzle, n. (sl.)   **spree; binge; toot**

Americans (the lucky ones) go on *a spree;* happy Englishmen
go on *the razzle.* They also go on *the spree* (note the definite
article).

R.D.   **insufficient funds**

These letters are an abbreviation of **Refer to drawer** (q.v.).

R.D.C.   **n.A.e.**

These letters are short for *Rural District Council,* the governing
body of a *rural district,* which is an area comprising a group of
parishes (q.v.).

reach-me-down, adj. (sl.)   **ready-made**

As a plural noun *reach-me-downs* became slang for *ready-made
clothes.* It must have come from the image of a sales person
reaching to get a stock garment *down* off a shelf. It reminds
one of *hand-me-downs,* the American term for clothing *handed
down* to another from the first or subsequent user, but that term
has nothing in common with *reach-me-downs* except its rhythm.
Not heard now: **off-the-peg** (q.v.) is the common term, and
ready-made is creeping in.

read, v.t.   **major in**

One *reads* philosophy at Oxford, for example, or law, or medicine.

reader, n.   **associate professor** (app.)

In a British university, the order of academic hierarchy is assistant lecturer, lecturer, senior lecturer, reader, and professor. The
term *professor* is more exclusive than in America, where it
covers the grades of assistant professor, associate professor, and
professor.

323

ready, n. (col.)   **dough**

Ready is colloquially short for *ready cash.*

ready for off (col.)   **ready to go**

real jam, *see* **jam**

Received Pronunciation   **n.A.e.**

Commonly called RP. This term is described by Barbara M. H. Strang in her book *Modern English Structure* (Edward Arnold Ltd., London, 1962) as ". . . an accent which can be heard from speakers originating in any part of England, but still local in the sense that it is confined virtually to English people and those educated at English public schools." She believes that this accent ". . . can best be called by the name assigned to it by Daniel Jones [author of *Outline of English Phonetics* and *English Pronouncing Dictionary*], Received Pronunciation (RP)." She goes on to quote from David Abercrombie's *Problems and Principles* (Longmans, Green & Co. Ltd., London, 1955) as follows:

RP, as a matter of fact, is an accent which is more than unusual: it is, I believe, of a kind which cannot be found anywhere else. In all other countries, whether English-speaking or not, all educated people have command of the standard form of the language, but when they talk it they have an accent which shows the part of the country from which they come. One of the accents of the country, perhaps, is popularly regarded as the "best" accent, but this is always an accent which belongs to one locality or another. . . . In England, RP is looked on as the "best" accent, but it is not the accent of the capital or of any other part of the country. Every town, and almost every village, contains speakers of RP whose families have lived there for generations. It is significant that the question "Where is the best English spoken?" is never debated by the English. Those who speak RP are set apart from other educated people by the fact that when they talk, one cannot tell where they come from.

See also Introductory Note 19.

reception, n.

(1) **office**
(2) **front desk**

(1) A sign on a place of business reading *Reception* would read *Office* in America.
(2) *Reception* at a hotel would be known as the *desk* or *front desk* in America; and the *reception clerk* at a hotel is he whom Americans know as the *room clerk*.

reception room, n.

room other than bedroom, kitchen, or bath

There is no single American word covering this category. It is used almost exclusively by professionals engaged in real-estate brokerage and in advertisements for the sale or rent of houses. A *reception room* can be a living room (usually *lounge* in England), dining room, library, study, den, and so on.

recordal, n.

recording

The *recording* of a document.

record card

index card

recorded delivery

registered mail

If you want a return receipt, you must arrange for *registered post*, which is the equivalent of American *registered mail*, *R.R.R.*

recorder, n.

criminal court judge

In large English cities and with limited court jurisdiction.

red as a turkey-cock (col.)

red as a beet

redbrick university

non-Ivy-League college (app.)

This term designates an English university other than Oxford and Cambridge; but London, Durham, and certain other universities, though they came later, often qualify as well for ex-

325

clusion from this somewhat pejorative appellation. The name
is derived from the use of red brick in the building of the first
universities established after the original old ones, which were
constructed of gray stone. Now, happily, *redbrick universities*
are built of whatever pleases the architect, including at times
even gray stone. *See also* **Oxbridge.**

red cap   **military policeman**

In America a *redcap* is a uniformed porter (at a railway station).

redemption fee   **prepayment penalty**

A term used in mortgage financing; the fee charged for paying
off before maturity.

red Indian   **Indian**

Meaning *American Indian* (the kind with feathers, tomahawks,
etc.). When an Englishman says *Indian* he invariably means a
native of India. If he has in mind an *American Indian,* he says
red Indian. When an American says *Indian* he usually visualizes
Sitting Bull, Hiawatha, et al., and if he wants to describe a native of India, he has to indulge in a circumlocution.

red rag (col.)   **red flag**

Usually in the phrase "a *red rag* to a bull."

redundant, adj.   **unemployed**

This is a harsh and dreadful word normally used in England to
describe a person who has lost his job because of automation,
reorganization, or deterioration of economic conditions, generally, and not through any fault of his own. *Redundancy* is the
equally oppressive noun for the condition. One would wish that
the English had avoided the unfortunate imagery of superfluous-
ness. *Redundancy pay* is the common term for *severance pay.*

reel, n.   **spool**

Reel of cotton is *spool of thread.*

referee   reference

A *referee* is *one who gives you a reference* when you are applying for a job, admission to a club, etc. The person who gives you
the write-up, as well as the write-up itself, is known as a *reference* in America.

refer to drawer   insufficient funds

Although the English phrase (sometimes abbreviated R.D.) is
much more elegant and discreet, it imparts the same gloomy
news as the American one. *No effects* was the old term in England, but has been in disuse for many years, giving way to the
euphemistic legend *Refer to drawer,* discreetly written in red
on the upper left-hand corner of the face of the check (*cheque*).
This is the customary procedure where the maker's bank doesn't
trust him, and as in America, returns the check to the payee's
bank, which then debits the payee's account. If the maker's
bank trusts its depositor, the legend (still in red ink) is lengthened to: *Refer to drawer; please re-present* (note hy-

Red Indian

phen). This invitation to the payee's bank to try again reflects the bank's willingness to give its depositor a chance to make good, when the payee, notified by his bank, gives the maker the bad news. The payee's bank does not debit his account unless the check comes back again dishonored. A third legend on a deposited check reads: *Effects not cleared*. This means that on the face of it the maker had deposited enough money in check form to cover his own check, but the deposit hasn't cleared yet. The American equivalent of *Effects not cleared* is *Uncollected funds*. In this case, the impression is given that the maker's bank doesn't quite trust him; but again, the payee's account is not debited unless the *uncollected funds* remain uncollected. *See also* **overdraft,** which is quite another matter in England.

refuse tip   **garbage dump**

See also **tip.**

register, v.t.   **check**

The English *register* their *luggage*. The Americans *check* their *baggage*.

registered post, *see* **recorded delivery**

Register Office   **marriage clerk's office**

Often incorrectly called *Registry Office* by the English. A **registry** (q.v.) is something quite different.

registrar, n.   **resident doctor**

Hospital term describing a doctor on call who is an assistant to a specialist.

registry, n.   **domestic help bureau**

Where you go if you still have the money and the courage to seek domestic servants.

regret, v.t.

miss

Regret is a peculiar word among the English, who use it in two diametrically opposite ways meaning (1) *deplore* (as in America) and (2) *deplore the absence of.* One *regrets* the bad things that happened during his unhappy youth; but in the other English sense, one *regrets* his lost youth because it was such a happy one.

relief, n.

deduction; exemption

Income-tax terminology. On your English income tax return you get *relief* for business expenses and *relief* for dependents. The analogous American terms would be *deductions* and *exemptions. Tax relief,* as a general term, would be called *tax benefit* in America.

relief, out- or **outdoor,** *see* **outdoor relief**

remand home, n.

reformatory

Reform school is used in both countries.

Remembrance Day

Veterans Day

November 11, originally called *Armistice Day* in both countries, a holiday honoring the memory of those who fell in World War I (the *Great War* in England). After World War II the concept was enlarged to embrace the additional victims and the names correspondingly modified. It won't have to be called anything at all after World War III.

remembrancer, n.

n.A.e.

Still seen in the official titles *King's* (or *Queen's*) *Remembrancer,* an officer charged with the collection of debts due the monarch, and *City Remembrancer* (usually shortened to *Remembrancer*), who represents the City of London (*see* **city**) before committees of Parliament. With a lower case *r* it has the same meaning in both countries: *reminder, memento.*

removals, n. pl.   **moving**

Thus, on a business sign: J. Smith & Company, *Removals*. On large moving vans it is common to see the phrase *removal specialists*.

remove, n.   (1) **degree removed**
                                          (2) **partial school pro-
                                              motion**
                                          (3) **food course**

(1) This meaning is shared with America, where, however, it is seen much less frequently than in England. The English speak of something which is one *remove* from the dust bin, which means *one step removed* from the garbage can, i.e., just about ready to be thrown out; or something may be based at *several removes* on something else, thus constituting a thinly disguised plagiarism in the arts, for instance.

(2) A *partial promotion* at school, moving the student up a half-grade. It has nothing whatever to do with being removed from school. In some schools a *remove* does not mean the *promotion* but rather the *intermediate grade* itself to which the student is promoted if he is not poor enough to stay back but not good enough to go up a whole grade.

(3) A wholly distinct meaning is that of a *dish* or *course* at a meal, and in this connection it seems to mean any dish except the first one, i.e., any dish which follows a previous course. In this sense *remove*, in the passive voice, is also seen as a verb meaning *follow* or *succeed*. Thus, the Dover sole was *removed* by lamb chops. It is true that if you follow Dover sole by lamb chops the sole is *removed* from that part of your anatomy in which it had previously come to rest, but it does seem a peculiar use. It may also refer merely to the replacement on the table of one dish by another.

repairing lease   **net lease**

Under which the tenant pays all the maintenance expenses, in-

cluding real estate taxes (*rates*) and a net rental to the landlord.

reserve, n.   **surplus**

Term used in corporate finance.

reset, v.t., v.i.   **receive (stolen goods)**

Used by itself intransitively, it means to *act as a fence*.

resident, n.   **person registered at
                                                     a hotel**

Nothing to do with domicile; *see* **nonresident.**

responsions, n. pl.   Oxford entrance
                                                     examination

Originally the first of three examinations for an Oxford B.A. and
colloquially called *smalls*. The name was later applied to the
entrance examination which was abolished in 1960. There are
now two examinations: *moderations* (colloquially called *mods*)
and *final schools* (colloquially called *greats* when the subject is
classics).

restaurant car   **dining car**

Another English name for this luxury, which is beginning to disappear in England, is *buffet car* (*see* **buffet**). The menu in a
buffet car is, however, much more restricted.

return, n.   **round-trip ticket**

In England one might ask for a *return* to London on the train or
bus, meaning a *round-trip ticket*. A *day return* is valid only
that day on certain trains; one can also purchase a *period return*
where the return journey must be completed by a specific date.

return post   **return mail**

reverse-charge call, *see* **transferred charge call**

revision, n.   **review**

A school term meaning going over past work in preparation for
examinations. Also, as a transitive verb, *revise* meaning *review.*
Thus, "We are now *revising* our Latin verbs."

rhino, n. (sl.)   **dough**

I.e., the wherewithal.

ribbon development   **linear suburban expansion**

Building development parallel to a highway, between villages or
towns, containing residences, shops, necessary services, etc., instead of circular expansion, thus (theoretically) tending to preserve more of the green belt.

ride bodkin, *see* **bodkin**

riding, n.   **subdivision of a county**

Not used except with respect to Yorkshire, which is understood
in the expressions the *North Riding,* the *East Riding,* and the
West Riding. The *South Riding,* like *East Dakota* and *West
Carolina,* is nonexistent.

right, adj. (col.)   **real**

Used like **proper** (q.v.), as in "He's a *right* hero," or "She's a
right friend."

right as a bank, *see* **as right as a bank**

ring book   **loose-leaf notebook**

ring road   **circular route**

Which does its best to keep you out of the center of town. Only
roughly circular.

ring the changes (col.)   **change things around**

Like rearranging the furniture. The term is taken from the
complicated terminology of campanology.

ringway, n.   **beltway**

rip, n. (col.)   **hell raiser**

Literally, a *lecher,* a man of lax morals, but more commonly
much less pejorative, with the emphasis on mischief and usually
applied to youngsters.

ripping, adj. (sl.)   **great**

Ripping is also used as an adverb with *good:* one can have a
ripping time or a *ripping good* time. Once in a while one hears
the adverb *rippingly,* as in "Things went *rippingly.*" Used only
by older folks and practically out of the language now.

rise, n.   **raise**

A pay increase.

rise, v.i.   **adjourn**

The House of Commons *rise* for the summer recess or at the end
of a session. Congress *adjourns.*

rising, adv.   **going on**

Used only in expressions of age, as in "she is sixteen, *rising* seventeen."

rising damp, *see* **damp course**

rithe, n.   **brook**

Rarely found.

roach, n.   small carplike fish

Caught for sport only in streams and an occasional moat. Eaten very rarely if at all nowadays, and then only experimentally.

road-sweeper, n.   street cleaner

road up   road under repair

Roadside warning sign.

roadway, n.   pavement

Pavement (q.v.) in England means *sidewalk*.

road works   men working

Roadside warning sign.

Robert (cop), *see* **bobby**

rocket, n. (sl.)   hell

I.e., a *severe reprimand*. To *get a rocket* is to *catch hell*.

rod in pickle for, *see* **have a rod in pickle for**

roger, v.t. (sl.)   lay

Vulgar slang for the act of love.

roll-neck, adj.   turtleneck

A *roll-neck pullover* is a *turtleneck sweater*.

roll-on, n.   girdle

A lady's undergarment.

roly-poly pudding   suet pudding wrapped in
                                                         a cloth and steamed

Also called **spotted dog** (q.v.).

334

roof, n.   **top**

In automobile context, a *roof* in England is a *hard top*. A soft one, i.e., a *convertible top,* is called a *hood* in England. An American *hood* is an English *bonnet.*

roofer, n. (col.)   **bread-and-butter-letter**

Synonymous with a **Collins** (q.v.).

roof-rack, n.   **luggage rack**

roopy, adj.(sl.)   **hoarse**

ropey, adj. (sl.)   **cheesy**

Shabby, coming apart at the seams, like threadbare clothes or a nearly extinct jalopy.

rose, n.   **frog**

In the sense of a *flower holder,* i.e., the article on the bottom of a shallow vase into which you stick the stems. For another variety, *see* **maizie.**

rot, v.t., v.i. (sl.)   **(1) spoil**
                                                              (2) kid

(1) To *rot* a plan is to *spoil* it.
(2) Intransitively, to *rot* is to *kid around,* to *tease.*

rota, n.   **roster**

List of persons acting in turn.

rough, n. (sl.)   **(1) heavy work**
                                                      (2) tough

(1) The *rough* is used to indicate the *heavy work* around the house. Thus, there might be a companion type of servant who did the cooking but somebody else in the household to do the *rough.*
(2) *Street rowdy; tough guy.*

335

round, n.   (1) **sandwich**
                                                       (2) **route**

    (1) The English use the word *sandwich* the way the Americans
        do. After all, it was the Earl of Sandwich who is supposed
        to have invented the sandwich, because he ate meat be-
        tween slices of bread during a twenty-four hour gambling
        bout. But in an English pub you will more often hear the
        customers ask for a *round* of ham or a *round* of beef than
        for a *sandwich*.
    (2) *Round* also means *route,* in the sense of *delivery route*
        (*see* **country round; roundsman**).

roundabout, n.   (1) **traffic circle**
                                                       (2) **merry-go-round**

rounders, n. pl.   **game resembling baseball**

round on (col.)   (1) **turn on**
                                                       (2) **squeal on**

    To *round on* has two distinct meanings:
    (1) To make some kind of unexpected answer to someone, im-
        plying an angry retort; to *let him have it.*
    (2) To *peach* on him.

roundsman, n.   **delivery man**

    With a regular route; thus, the baker's *roundsman,* the milk
    roundsman.

round the bend (sl.)   **nutty**

    Usually in the expression *drive round the bend,* meaning *drive*
    crazy.

Rover ticket   **unlimited travel ticket** (app.)

    A *Rover* or *Rover ticket,* purchased from a transportation com-
    pany, provides unlimited travel for a given period within a
    given area. *Green Rover* tickets, good for a day's unlimited
    travel over chosen routes within a 1,500 mile network, provide

an inexpensive way of touring the countryside. Incidentally, and nothing to do with *Rovers*, ordinary bus travel in the country-side is a good—if not the only—way to get a peek at some of the lovely houses and gardens that hide behind the high hedges that Englishmen maintain to nourish their highly developed sense of privacy (pronounced with a short *i* as in *privy*). Getting back to *Rovers: Red Rovers* do the same thing as *Green Rovers,* except that they work only on the familiar red Central Buses; and *Twin Rovers* include the underground (subway) system and cost more. *Railway Rovers* are good for a week's unlimited travel over rail networks within specified areas. The term has been derived, of course, from the romantic verb *to rove,* but has clearly strayed from its origin in the term *Rover Pass,* meaning a sort of season ticket permitting one to park at a discount as often as one wishes in a particular garage for a specified period —which seems like an especially stationary way to rove.

row-de-dow, n. (col.)   **uproar**

rowlock, n.   **oarlock**

rozzer, n. (sl.)   **cop**

An outmoded term. The English share *fuzz* with the Americans.

RP, *see* **Received Pronunciation**

R.S.M.   **n.A.e.**

The initials stand for *regimental sergeant-major,* which in certain contexts has become a more or less generic bit of symbol-ism of the strict disciplinarian.

rub along (col.)   **get by**

"How do you manage without a maid?" "Oh, we *rub along*."

rubber, n.   **eraser**

rub up (col.)   **rub up on**

To *bone up* on something. "I'll have to *rub up* my Latin irregular verbs." Strangely, in *rub up the wrong way*, the English add *up* to the American idiom; in this one the Americans add *on* to the English idiom.

ruby, n.   agate

Type size. Peculiar that this description of a type size is called by the name of a precious stone in England and by that of a semiprecious stone in America.

ruck, n.   (1) **common herd**
                                                (2) **also-rans**
                                                (3) **rugby scrum**

(1) Usually seen in the phrase *common ruck,* or the phrase *ruck and truck.*
(2) In a more limited sense, it refers to the main body of competition left out of the running.
(3) A specialized meaning; *see* **scrum.**

ruddy (sl.)   damned

Ruddy came into use as a permissible variant of *bloody. Bloody* is a good deal stronger than *ruddy,* bearing about the same relationship as *goddamned* to *damned.*

rude, adj.   (1) **inconsiderate**
                                                (2) **frank**
                                                (3) **indecent**

Apart from its several common meanings, shared with America, this adjective has three uses in England not found in the other country:
(1) *Inconsiderate,* as in: "It is *rude* of me not to be able to let you know my plans sooner."
(2) *Frank, outspoken,* as in: "May I be *rude* and tell you that I don't like your new hat?" Or with a slightly different nuance, "May I be *rude* and ask you how much you paid for that car?"
(3) *Indecent, improper,* as applied, e.g., to a picture or statue. A nanny of the author's acquaintance refused to take her

little charge into an Impressionist show at the Tate Gallery
in London because it was "full of *rude* paintings."

rudery, n. (col.)   **rudeness**

rug, *see* **carpet**

rugger, *see* **football**

rum, adj. (sl.)   **funny (peculiar)**

The usual meaning of *rum* is *funny* in the sense of *peculiar* or
strange. For example: "What a *rum* way to dress!" But in combination with certain nouns, *rum* has other meanings: a *rum* customer is a *dangerous* customer, one not safe to meddle with;
a *rum go* is a *tough break;* a *rum start* is a *funny thing* of the
sort that so often happens on the way to the theater if one can
believe comedians' patter.

rumble, v.t. (sl.)   **see through**

To see the real character of a person; to get to the bottom of a
situation.

rump steak, n.   **sirloin**

Butchers' terms are very confusing. The English use **sirloin**
(q.v.), but there it means what the Americans call *porterhouse.*
See Introductory Note 12.

rumpy, n. (col.)   **Manx cat**

run-away, n.   **drain**

Something to let the water through.

run in   **break in**

What one does to new automobiles. The English *break in* wild
horses but *run in* new cars.

runner beans   **string beans**

Often shortened to *runners.*

running account   **open account**

running shed   **roundhouse**

run out   **put out** (app.)

A term in cricket and *very* approximate. This is not the place to go into the differences between cricket and baseball.

rush, v.t. (sl.)   **soak**

For instance: "How much did they *rush* you for that sherry?" To *rush* is to *charge,* with the distinct implication that the price was too high.

rusticate, v.t.   **expel temporarily from university**

To be *permanently expelled* is, in England, to be *sent down.* *Rustication* occurs in the case of less serious offenses.

rux, n. (sl.)   **tantrum**

School slang. A *fit of temper.*

𝔖 | S

sack, v.t. (col.)   (1) **fire**
                                                 (2) **kick out**

(1) From a job.
(2) From a school. (At university the term for *expel* is *send down.*)

safe storage	**safekeeping**

St. Lubbock's Days, *see* **bank holiday**

St. Luke's Summer	**Indian summer**

Also called *Luke's Little Summer*.

St. Martin's Summer	**Indian summer**

saithe, *see* Introductory Note 12.

Saloon, n.	(1) **sedan**
	(2) **parlor**

(1) A *saloon motorcar*, which can be shortened to *saloon* in proper context, is what Americans call a *sedan*.
(2) The English speak of a hairdressing, billiards, etc., *saloon* where the American term would be *parlor*.

Saloon in America has a definitely pejorative connotation linked with the image of brutish drunkards who let their wives and children starve while they squander their wages on drink. Not so in the mother country.

saloon bar, *see* **pub**

saloon-car	**parlor car**

Also *saloon-carriage*.

salt beef	**corned beef**

Corned beef in England is the name for a canned pressed beef product (normally in a square container) which usually comes from Argentina. Once a staple diet of the British army in the field, its army nickname is *bully beef*.

san ferry an	**it doesn't matter**

British anglicization (World War I) of *cela ne fait rien*.

sap, v.i., n. (sl.)   (1) **cram**
                                                 (2) **grind**

(1) To *sap* is to *cram* (*see also* **mug; swot**).

(2) A *sap* is a *grind,* in the two distinct senses of *zealous stu-dent* and *tough job.* (The American slang meaning *fool* has now spread to England.) One wonders whether that mean-ing, which was originally only exclusively American, grew out of the English slang word and, if so, whether that pro-cess was a reflection of the atmosphere of anti-intellectual-ism which gave rise to the term *egghead. Verbum* sap.

sauce, n. (col.)   **cheek**

In the sense of *impertinence.* Often heard in the phrase *bloody sauce.*

sauce-boat, n.   **gravy boat**

save one's bacon (sl.)   **save one's skin**

savoury, n.   **tidbit**

A *canapé* or sometimes something larger served usually at the end of dinner, after dessert; but the term also covers an *hors d'oeuvre* or *appetizer.* Examples might be a sardine or anchovy on toast, a modest welsh rarebit, and so on.

say boo to a goose   **open one's mouth**

I.e., have the courage to start a conversation. *Boo* is sometimes *bo; say* is sometimes *cry; goose* is sometimes *battledore.* Usually in the negative: "He wouldn't *say boo to a goose,*" meaning "He was afraid to open his mouth" (to say a word).

scarper! (sl.)   **scram!**

scatty, adj. (sl.)   **whacky**

The closest Americans come to *scatty* is *scatterbrained.*

342

scenic railway   **roller coaster**

See also **switchback.**

scent spray   **atomizer**

scheme, n.   **plan**

In England the noun does not always have the American connotation of *slyness* or *sharp practice* (in fact one may talk of government or private *housing schemes*), but the noun *schemer*
and the verb *to scheme* do have that connotation.

schemozzle, *see* **shemozzle**

scholar, n.   **scholarship student**

Learned persons are called *scholars* in both countries, but the
word is not used in America, as it commonly is in England, to
denote a student on a scholarship.

school-leaver, n.   **high-school graduate** (app.)

A student who has completed his or her formal education at a
secondary school level, is not going on to college, and is now
ready to go to work for a living. The term usually comes up in
a discussion of the labor market or youth problems. The shorter
term **leaver** (q.v.) is occasionally used in **prep school** (q.v.) and
public school (q.v.) circles to describe a student about to complete the curriculum there.

school-treat, n.   **school party**

Usually away from school, on private grounds thrown open for
the occasion; but the practice is dying out.

scoff, n., v.t. (sl. and col.)   (1) **good eats**
       (2) **wolf**

(1) A schoolboy term.
(2) To *gobble* or *knock back* food, especially sandwiches.

343

scone, n.   **soda biscuit**

score, n.   **twenty (or twenty-one) lbs.**

If you should happen to be in the English countryside and wanted to buy some pigs, don't think £ 2.99 a *score* is the bargain it seems: *score* doesn't mean *twenty* in this usage. It is a *unit*(?) *of weight,* regional, and applies especially to pig and cattle raising. The flexibility indicated by the definition seems particularly English.

score off, v. (col.)   **get the better of**

In an argument or in repartee.

Scotch egg   **hard-boiled egg in batter**

This is a pub delicacy consisting of a hard-boiled egg, coated with a blanket of pork sausage meat, which is then thickly fried in a batter. Far from ubiquitous; highly recommended.

Scotch woodcock   **scrambled egg dish** (app.)

Specifically, *scrambled eggs* (which the English sometimes call *buttered eggs*) on toast first spread with anchovy paste. This is one of those fanciful food terms, comparable to *Welsh rabbit,* now popularly spelled *rarebit* (a corruption), *Bombay duck* (a fish), and *Cape Cod turkey,* which means *codfish.* The recipe for Scotch woodcock in *Mrs. Beeton's Household Management* follows:

> *Scotch Woodcock (Anchois à l'Ecossaise)*
> Ingredients.—The yolks of two eggs, one gill of cream (or cream and milk in equal parts), anchovy paste, toast, butter, cayenne, salt.
>
> Method.—Cut the toast into two-inch squares, butter well, and spread them with anchovy paste. Season the eggs with a little cayenne and salt; when slightly beaten add them to the hot cream, stir over the fire until they thicken

sufficiently, then pour the preparation over the toast, and serve as hot as possible.

Time.—Ten minutes. Sufficient for six to eight persons.

scout, *see* **gyp**

scraggy, adj.   **scrawny**

scray, n.   **tern**

scree, n.   **mountain slope**

But *scree* (or *screes*) can also mean the pebbles or small stones and rocks that dribble or slide down when people walk up a steep slope covered with loose gravel.

screw, n. (sl.)   (1) **take**
                                                      (2) **nag**
                                                      (3) **twist (bit)**

(1) In the sense of *salary*. It is hard to find an exact American slang equivalent. *Take* may do, but it is broader than *screw* because it would cover the concept of *profit* as well as that of *regular wages*.
(2) An old and shaky horse.
(3) It is occasionally used to indicate a crumpled-up *ball* of paper—the sort thrown into a wastebasket—at other times a *bit* of salt or tobacco or anything of that sort contained in a piece of twisted paper.

scribbling-block, n.   **scratch pad**

Also *scribbling-pad*.

scrimmage, *see* **scrum**

scrimshank, *see* **scrumshank**

345

scrip, n.   **temporary stock certificate**

In England a *scrip* is a *temporary certificate* issued to one entitled eventually to receive a formal stock certificate. In America *scrip* is applied to a formal certificate representing a fraction of a share.

scruffy, adj.   **messy**

scrum, n. (col.)   **melee**

Short for *scrummage,* which is a variant of *scrimmage. Scrimmage* has the general meaning of *confused struggle* or *melee* in both countries. In American football *scrimmage* is used nowadays as a noun to mean *practice session,* and as a verb to mean *practice;* and the *line of scrimmage* is the point where the officials place the ball at the beginning of each play. In English *Rugby* football, the *scrimmage* is the mass of all the forwards surrounding the ball on the ground. As a sports term, the English usually use the shortened form *scrum.* Colloquially, *scrum* is used in England to denote the atmosphere of a group of people working in a state of confusion, whether it be a group of reporters competing for the attention of a celebrity or a confused business conference with everybody working at cross-purposes. An English businessman, pulled out of a smoke-filled conference room by a telephone call from his wife might say, "Sorry, darling, but I have got to sign off now and get back in the *scrum.*" A verbal use of *scrum* is found in the expression *scrum around* (v.i.) meaning *fight your way through,* as in a crowded tea tent (**marquee,** q.v.) at the Henley Regatta, trying to collect tea and goodies for the family.

scrummage, *see* **scrum**

scrumshank, v.i. (sl.)   **goof off**

Military slang meaning to *shirk;* sometimes spelled *scrimshank. See also* **swing it; swing the lead.**

scrutineer, n.   **ballot inspector**

scug, n. (sl.)   **fink**

School slang, and extremely derogatory in the cruel way peculiar to children. It means a person with bad manners, unfriendly,
a bad sport, and generally one to be shunned.

scunner, *see* **take a scunner on**

scupper, v.t. (sl.)   **do . . . in**

Scupper is a noun in both countries, meaning a *hole* in the side
of a ship designed to carry water off a deck. As an English verb,
scupper means *ambush and wipe out.* In nautical circles, to *scupper* is to *sink a ship,* with the implication of finishing off the
crew as well. Colloquially, the American verb *sink,* especially in
the passive voice, means *to do* (somebody) *in.* We're *sunk,* in
America, means we're *done for.* In this sense, the slang English
verb *scupper* would be about equivalent to the slang American
verb *sink.*

scurf, n.   **dandruff**

scutter, v.i.   **scurry**

scuttle, n.   **basket**

A *scuttle* is a coal pail, usually called a *coal scuttle* in both countries. The word, however, has an exclusively English additional
meaning: a *wide shallow basket.*

S.E. , *see* **Standard English**

sea, n.   **beach**

Sea and *seaside* are used in England where Americans would
usually say *beach,* or less commonly, *shore,* to mean a *seaside
resort,* like Brighton in England or Atlantic City in America.
The classical Jack Sprat type of argument between spouses in
America is based on the problem whether to take one's vacation in the mountains or at the *shore.* In England the *shore*
would be the *sea.*

sea front, *see* **front**

season ticket   **commutation ticket**

In America one thinks of a *season ticket* as something entitling one to see all the games at a given ball park. In England it refers to train travel and can be valid for anything from a month to a year. It is occasionally shortened to *season,* as in railroad station signs reading "Please show your *season.*" A *season ticket holder* is a *commuter.*

secateurs, n. pl.   **pruning shears**

second, n.   **magna**

A university term. *Second* is short for *second-class honours* just as *magna* is short for *magna cum laude.* In some universities a second-class degree is further divided into an *upper* and a *lower* second (also referred to as a *2.1* and a *2.2*). *See also* **first.**

second, v.t.   **transfer temporarily**

Accented on the second syllable: *se-cónd.* It describes a temporary transfer of an employee to another department of the company, or of a soldier to another unit in the armed forces. *Secondment* is the noun.

secondary modern, *see* **eleven plus**

secondment, *see* **second, v.t.**

see one far enough   **see one in hell**

"I'll *see him far enough* before I invite him to dinner again." Sometimes to *see one farther.*

see the back of   **see the last of**

Almost always after "I'll be glad to. . . ."

sell, n. (col.)   **let down**

Commonly seen in the expression "What a *sell!*" It is used often
as a reaction to the gap between the promise and the performance.

sell ... a pup (col.)   **stick**

To *sell* someone *a pup* is to *stick* him, i.e., to cheat him, especially by getting a high price for inferior merchandise.

Sellotape, n.   **Scotch tape**

Proprietary name.

sell up (col.)   **sell out**

If an Englishman were to sell his residence and also wanted to
liquidate the furnishings he would speak of *selling up* everything, i.e., *selling out* lock, stock, and barrel. It means *sell out*
also in the sense of *selling out* a debtor's property in a forced
sale.

semibreve, n.   **whole note**

Musical term. *See under* **breve.**

semi-detached, adj.   **two-family**

In America a *two-family house* may be divided horizontally or
vertically. In England a *semi-detached residence* is a one-fam-
ily house joined to another by a common or party wall. The two
halves are often painted different colors. This euphemistic
designation genteelly stresses the detachment rather than the
attachment. When more than two residences are joined together
the building becomes a **terrace** (q.v.).

semiquaver, n.   **sixteenth note**

Musical term. *See under* **breve.**

send down   **expel**

A term from university life. In school the English slang term is *sack*.

send-up, n. (sl.).   **gag**

A *send-up* is a *satire* or a *burlesque*.

send up rotten (sl.)   **pan**

I.e., to deprecate. Lord Snowden designed the large aviary in Regent's Park. In an interview he said the people liked it now but when it was first opened to the public many people *sent it up rotten*.

senhouse hook   **pelican hook**

A nautical term describing a hook on the end of a line or cable for insertion into an eye, to make a firm connection which is nonetheless readily opened by hand. The English call the hook by the name of the inventor; the Americans by the name of the bird whose bill the hook resembles.

septillion, *see under* **billion**

sergeant-major   **top sergeant**

See also **R.S.M.**

servery, n.   **service counter** (app.)

Generally a room from which, rather than in which, meals are served. Thus, at a pub one might find a sign pointing to the *Garden and bar servery*, indicating the room to which one must go in order to obtain food and drink to be consumed in the garden or the bar.

service flat, n.   **hotel apartment**

In the plural, *service flats* is seen in the expression *block of service flats*, which would correspond to an American *apartment hotel* or *residential hotel*.

service lift   **dumbwaiter**

This is rather tricky: A **dumb-waiter** (q.v.) in England is what is
known in America as a *lazy Susan.*

service occupancy, *see* **vacant possession**

serviette, n.   **napkin**

Still used occasionally but *napkin* is taking over.

set, n.   (1) **group** (app.)
                                              (2) **apartment; suite**
                                              (3) **paving block**

(1) A school term; thus the "A" *set,* the "B" *set,* etc., meaning
     group (within a given grade or form) based on the ability
     of the students. In this sense, the word is giving way to a
     newer term, **stream** (q.v.).
(2) In this use, restricted to apartments in such exclusive and
     historic addresses as the residence known as Albany in
     London, with its sixty-nine *sets,* or to groups of rooms at
     the various **Inns of Court** (q.v.), *sets* is short for *sets of
     chambers.*
(3) Variant of *sett.*

set down   **let off**

A term used in transportation: passengers are *set down* in England and *let off* in America.

sett, *see* **set** (3)

set tea   **afternoon tea**

Tea with little sandwiches and cakes, obtainable at hotels and
restaurants.

set the Thames on fire (col.)   **set the world on fire**

Well, to lots of Englishmen the Thames *is* the world.

sewer, n. (sl.)   **jerk**

Derived from the Hindustani word *sua* meaning *pig,* and brought back to England by troops who had served in India. It means a *rotter,* a thoroughly objectionable person. Perhaps a stronger American slang equivalent would be *louse; bastard* might do, too.

sexillion; sextillion, *see under* **billion**

shake down (sl.)   **put up (for the night)**

In England it is very hospitable of you to *shake* somebody *down.* In America it is not only unhospitable, it is a criminal offense, because *shaking* somebody *down* means *extorting money from* him and *shakedown* is a slang American noun meaning *extortion* or *blackmail.* In America, apart from its slang meaning, a *shakedown* is an *improvised bed.* This use is reflected in the English use of *shake down.* None of this, of course, has anything to do with a *shakedown cruise,* which is a phrase used in both countries meaning a new ship's *initial trip* made in order to break in both engine and crew.

shakes, n. pl. (col.)   **seconds**

"I'll be with you in a couple of *shakes*," i.e., *in a jiffy.* A shortening of *shakes of a lamb's* (or *duck's*) *tail.*

shandy, n.   **lemonade-beer**

A drink consisting of beer and lemonade or ginger beer in equal parts, which English children are (not legally) allowed to drink in their early teens in preparation for the eventual **pint** (q.v.).

share pushing   **stock touting**

Not necessarily fraudulent but with the implication of sharp practice.

shave hook   **paint scraper**

352

sheaf, n. (col.)   **bankroll**

Referring to paper money: A *sheaf of notes* would be a *bankroll* or a *wad.*

shell-back, n. (sl.)   **old tar**

In the special sense of a tough sailor who literally and figuratively knows the ropes.

sheltered trade   **domestic monopoly**

Describing a business which gets no competition from abroad, like a railroad.

shemozzle, n. (sl.)   **mix-up; row**

A *mix-up,* a *to-do,* a *mess,* a *confused situation* generally; in a narrower meaning, a *row,* in the sense of *dispute;* a *rhubarb,* a *melee.* The English are Elizabethan in their spelling of this word: variants are *schemozzle, shemozzl, shimozzel, chimozzle, shlemozzl, shlemozzl, schlemozzle, schlemazel,* and goodness knows what else. Its origin is in London racetrack cant. The *"l"* and certainly the spelling *schlemazel,* crept in out of confusion with the totally unrelated Yiddish term *schlemaz(e)l,* meaning *hard-luck guy,* itself a hybrid composed of the German adjective *schlimm (bad)* and the Hebrew noun *mazel (luck).*

shepherd's pie   **hash** (app.)

Not quite: a *shepherd's pie* is usually made of the remains of a roast (which in England is called a *joint*), ground up (*minced*), topped by a layer of mashed potatoes and baked in the oven.

sherbet, *see* **ice**

shilling   **n.A.e.**

See Introductory Note 18.

shilling shocker   **dime novel**

Also known in England as a **penny dreadful** (q.v.) or a *penny blood.*

shindig, n. (sl.)   **brawl**

Quite different from its American meaning of *lively party;* but note that the Americans speak of a real high old time as a *brawl.* **Shindy** (q.v.) means *row* or *brawl* in both countries but is also English slang for *spree.* Apparently the English meaning of *shindig* is related to *shindy* in its standard sense, while the American meaning is derived from its English slang use. It could be that the American usage was influenced by the likelihood that dancing merrymakers might well *dig* into one another's *shins* when the going got rough.

shindy, n.   **racket**

A *hell of a noise;* sometimes used to describe a *street brawl* or similar disturbance. Also slang for *spree.*

shingle, n.   **beach pebbles**

A beach so adorned would be known as a *shingle beach* (as opposed to a *sandy beach*). In America it would be called a *pebble beach* or *pebbly beach.*

shipping order (col.)   **large order**

One of those interminable orders being given by the customer just ahead of you when you're in a mad hurry.

shipshape and Bristol fashion (sl.)   **O.K.** (app.)

Old-fashioned nautical slang, still used occasionally and meaning *very O.K.*

shire, n.   **county**

Now used rarely, except in the plural (the *Shires*) meaning the hunting country. It is found mainly as a suffix in the names of most of the counties, as for example, Hampshire, Yorkshire.

shirty, adj. (sl.)   **huffy**

shoal, n. (col.)   **raft**

I.e., a *multitude*, like a *shoal of correspondence* to attend to.

shocker, n. (col.)   (1) **stinker**
                                                    (2) **cheap novel**

(1) *Shocker* is used to describe a bad case of almost anything;
     a stretch of wretched weather, a new tax, an embarrassing
     utterance by a public figure, a dress in very bad taste,
     overcooked Brussels sprouts, an indescribably boring din-
     ner party. Sometimes it is used in a rather exaggerated
     way, as in: "Isn't letter-writing a *shocker!*"
(2) It can also mean a *sensational novel* as opposed to a *thriller*,
     which is the English name for what Americans know as a
     detective story.

shocking, adj. (col.)   **awful**

"Isn't it *shocking?*" (about the weather, etc.). *Shocking* is used
in much the same way as the first meaning of **shocker** (q.v.).

shoeblack, *see* **boot**

shoe mender   **shoemaker**

See also **mend.**

shooting, n.   **hunting**

An Englishman *hunts* foxes and deer but *shoots* game birds and
rabbits. Americans *hunt* quail, for instance. To *let the shooting*
is to lease the right to hunt birds on your property.

shooting!   **good shot!**

A complimentary observation in certain sports like tennis, basketball, etc.

shooting-box, n.   **hunting-lodge**

355

shooting-brake, n.   station wagon

Also called an *estate waggon* or *estate car* in England.

shoot the moon (sl.)   skip town by night

See also **moonlight flit.**

shop, n.   store

A matter of usage. *Shop* is used in a few English colloquial expressions which one does not hear in America. *"You have come to the wrong shop,"* means *"I can't help you"* (because you are applying to the wrong person). To *sink the shop* is to *keep mum* generally and more specifically to *keep your activities under wraps. All over the shop* means *in wild disorder. A nation of shopkeepers* refers to England itself. *Shop-soiled* is *shop-worn* in America. To *have everything in the shop window* is to *four-flush,* to *play the big shot,* without having anything to back it up.

shop, v.t. (sl.)   (1) **jail**
                                                            (2) **squeal on**

In the English underworld to be *shopped* is to go to *jail,* and by extension, to be *squealed on* by your accomplice so that you wind up in jail (spelled *gaol* in England, but pronounced like *jail*).

shop assistant, *see* **assistant; clerk**

shop-walker, n.   floorwalker

short commons   short rations

Originally a university term meaning the daily fare supplied to students at a fixed charge. The phrase has become somewhat pejorative with the connotation of *subsistence living, meager pickings,* so that the person said to be *on short commons* might also be described as *on his uppers.*

shorthand typist   **stenographer**

This term is now somewhat old fashioned and is being supplanted by *secretary* even if the person involved is not properly speaking a *secretary* but only a *stenographer.* This is an example of the English tendency to pay honor to the dignity of labor—a trend very much in favor at the moment, which explains *shop assistant* for *salesperson, automotive engineer* for *garage mechanic,* etc.

shorthand writer   **court stenographer**

short-sighted, *see under* **long-sighted**

shot, n. (sl.)   **measure of upper cylinder lubricant**

Thus, as you drive up to a gas pump (*petrol station*) in England, you may ask for *two and two shots,* e.g., meaning *two gallons of gas and two shots of lubricant* which is mixed into the gas.

shove halfpenny   **n.A.e.**

An almost ubiquitous pub game. Played by shoving well-polished old half-pennies or token disks with the flat of the hand along a board separated into horizontal sections having numerical values. Difficult to describe; much more fun to play, although possibly the most frustrating game in the world.

show, n. (col.)   (1) **chance**
                                                          (2) **affair**

(1) To say of someone that he had no *show* at all means that he had no *opportunity* of proving or defending himself. One might plead, "At least give him a fair *show!*"
(2) Speaking of his new, up-and-coming partner, the older man might say, "Jones is doing well, but it's still my *show,*" i.e., "I'm still *in charge* around here."
See also **bad show; good show**

357

show a leg (sl.)   shake a leg

show house   model home

show one's colours   stand up and be counted

shrimp, *see* prawn

shunting yard   switchyard

sickener, n. (sl.)   bellyful

After a long unpleasant experience: "I have had a *sickener* of that!"

sicker, n. (sl.)   sick bay

Schoolboy slang for *infirmary*.

sick up (col.)   throw up

A vulgar colloquialism for *vomit*.

side, n.   team

Used in sports, especially cricket. But English rooters yell "School! School!" where Americans would yell "Team! Team!" To *let the side down* is to fail to see something through, to *let* the other party or parties *down*.

sideboards, n. pl. (col.)   sideburns

The English say *sideburns*, too.

side of, *see* at the side of

sidesman, n.   deputy churchwarden

sidy, *see* put on side

signal-box, n.   switch tower

358

sign off   **initial**

In the sense of initialing a document as having read it.

silk, take, *see* **take silk**

silverside, n.   **top round**

Butcher's term.

Silver Streak (col.)   **English Channel**

simnel cake   **Easter cake**

This is a fancy ornamental cake with a thick layer of marzipan
and all kinds of decorations, served at Easter.

simple, adj. (col.)   **not all there**

A term used more by village than city folk meaning something
between *silly* and downright *feebleminded*. *Simpleton* and *sim-
ple-minded* are related; but *simple* used by itself means something a little stronger. One thus afflicted might be said to have a
screw loose, rocks in his head, bats in his belfry, or to be without the benefit of certain of his marbles.

single, n. (col.)   **one-way ticket**

single-track, adj.   **one-lane**

Road term.

sink the shop, *see* **shop**

sirloin, n.   **porterhouse**

What Americans call a *sirloin* the English call a *rump steak*.
There is a legend that King Charles II, while stopping after
hunting at Friday Hall in Chingford, near Epping Forest (outside London), was so impressed by the roast loin of beef that
he exclaimed, "By Sir George it shall have a title," and there-

upon drew his sword and knighted it with the words "Loin we dub thee knight, henceforth be *Sir Loin.*" Incidentally, two sirloins in one roast are called a *baron of beef,* a *Baron* being much bigger stuff than a simple *Sir.* It would be much more fun to believe in this etymological theory than in the prosaic fact that *sirloin* (which was spelled *surloin* hundreds of years ago) came from the Old French *sur longe, sur* meaning *above* and *longe* meaning *loin.* The wit of a king is so much more interesting than the anatomy of a steer.

sister, n.   nurse

The term *sister* is not applied to nurses in America except to nuns who nurse in Catholic hospitals. In England *sister* is the term for the *head nurse of a ward.* There are *day sisters* and *night sisters.* A *theatre sister* has nothing to do with maintaining a first aid post at a place of amusement, the theatre involved being an *operating-theatre,* which is called an *operating room* in America. The *theatre sister* is the kind who hands scalpels to surgeons (called *Mr* and not *Dr* in England). The *head nurse* in a hospital is called a *matron* in England. Used by itself, not in the context of medical practice, *nurse* in England would connote *children's nurse* rather than *hospital nurse.*

sit an examination   take an examination

Also *sit for an examination.*

sit bodkin, *see* bodkin

site, v.t.   locate

Large-scale industry is *sited* in the Midlands. Americans would have said *located* or *situated.*

sitting room, n.   living room

Sitting room sounds old-fashioned in America. *Living room* would be a little peculiar in England unless it described a general family room which included dining space.

situations vacant   **help wanted**

Advertisement page heading. As usual, the English phrase is somewhat grander.

six, n. (col.)   **homer** (app.)

In cricket, a ball hit *beyond the boundary* (which is roughly equivalent to *into the stands* in baseball) scores six runs, and this is the best thing that can happen to the batsman, just as a home run is the supreme achievement of the batter in baseball. To *hit* (sometimes *knock*) a person *for six* is to *knock him for a loop, knock the daylights out of him.*

six of the best (col.)   **a good beating**

Literally six strokes of the cane. The practice has almost died out, as well as the currency of the phrase.

sixpence, n.   **n.A.e.**

See Introductory Note 18.

skew-wiff, adj. (sl.)   **cock-eyed**

In the sense of *all askew*.

skilly, n.   **gruel**

skinful, n. (sl.)   **load on**

An awful lot to drink. To *have got a skinful* or *one's skinful* is to *be stinkin' drunk*.

skinhead, n. (sl.)   **young tough** (app.)

A special breed of hoodlum characterized by very closely cropped hair and **bovver boots** (q.v.).

skint, adj. (sl.)   **broke**

skip, *see* **gyp**

skipping rope   **jump rope**

skirl, n.   **bagpipe sound**

Also an intransitive verb meaning to make the sound.

skirt, n.   **flank**

Butcher's term; a *skirt* of beef.

skirting, n.   **baseboard**

Also *skirting-board*.

skivvy, n. (sl.)   **maid of all work**

A term of derogation of the order of *scullery maid;* the lowest
on the scale (*see also* **slavey**). No American slang equivalent.

skulk, n., v.i.   **shirker; shirk**

As an intransitive verb *skulk* means to *hide* or *slink about* in
both countries. A third meaning, to *shirk,* is exclusively English.
The noun *skulker* could apply to any of those meanings, but
when it is shortened to *skulk* it means a *shirker.*

sky ball   **pop fly** (app.)

A cricket term.

slang, v.t. (col.)   **give . . . hell**

I.e., to *scold severely;* and a *slanging match* is a *helluva row,* in
which everybody washes everybody else's dirty linen but nobody's gets clean.

slang, back, *see* **back slang**

slap, adv. (col.)   **right**

Examples: *slap* through is *right* through; *slap* into is *right* into.
To walk *slap* into someone is to *bump* into him.

362

slap-down, adv. (col.)
one hundred percent

As in: I am *slap-down on his side,* referring to a disagreement between two persons. An American would be likely to say: "I am *one hundred percent* with him."

slap-up, adj. (col.)
bang-up

I.e., *first rate, great, terrific.* The English once used both *slap-up* and *bang-up* commonly; both would be considered old-fashioned there now. A *slap-up do* meant a *bang-up job,* a first-rate piece of work.

slate, v.t. (col.)
pan

To express a harsh criticism. Thus: "The reviewers *slated* the book unmercifully." But (especially in Lancashire) when a girl says, "I am *slated,*" she means something entirely different—that her petticoat is showing. Slate roofs are common in that county; the slabs are affixed in layers, like shingles, and sometimes a slab hangs over the edge when it is not supposed to. Somehow the unintentionally exposed edge of a slip or petticoat reminded local wags of what must have been common errors in roofing technique; hence this picturesque regional colloquialism.

slate club, n.
lodge

In the sense of mutual aid society. The members pay modest weekly dues, called **subscription** (q.v.) in England.

slavey, n. (sl.)
maid of all work

Usually connotes one employed in a rooming house (*see also* skivvy). No American slang equivalent.

sledge, n., v.t.
sled

A *sledge* in America is a heavy vehicle used in pulling loads, usually over snow or ice. Children go *sledging* in England, *sledding,* or more commonly *coasting,* in America. Grownups should, too.

sleeper, n.   **tie**

A railroad term.

sleeping partner   **silent partner**

sleepy sickness   **sleeping sickness**

slice, n.   **bracket**

A term used in connection with English inheritance taxation, which they call *estate duty*. The first *slice* (up to £ 15,000) is exempt; the second *slice* (£ 15,000 to £ 20,000) is taxed at twenty-five percent; and the rates go up as the *slices* go up. American rates follow a similar type of pattern, but the *slices* are known as *brackets*.

sliding keel   **centerboard**

The American term is also used (but it is spelled *centreboard*).

slim, v.i.   **diet**

"I must not have any butter on my toast; I am *slimming*." An American would say: "I am *dieting*," or more commonly, "I am *on a diet*." *See also* **bant.**

slime, v.i. (sl.)   **get away with it**

slip, n.   **extreme side seat**

Theater term. There are *upper slips* and *lower slips* (depending on which gallery), too near the side walls to afford satisfactory vision.

slip-on shoes   **loafers**

slipover, n.   **sleeveless sweater**

slippy, *see* **look slippy!**

slip seat   **jump seat**

slop, n. (sl.)   **cop**

Slop developed as a shortened form of *ecilop,* which is *police* spelled backwards. This is an example of **back slang** (q.v.).

slope off (sl.)   **sneak off**

slops, n. pl. (sl.)   **sloppy clothes**

One wearing *slops* would probably be referred to in America as *dressed like a bum.* Literally, *slops* means clothes and bedding issued to sailors from the *slop-room* or *slop chest* aboard ship, the clothing being largely composed of used items.

slosh, v.t. (sl.)   **smack**

In the sense of *hit.*

sloshed, adj. (sl.)   **smashed**

Tipsy, tight, squiffed, i.e., intoxicated.

slowcoach, n. (col.)   **slowpoke**

slow off the mark (col.)   **slow on the uptake**

slow train   **local**

And *fast* train means the *express.*

slut's wool (col.)   **dust balls**

The stuff that collects under the bed, behind the bureau, and other hard-to-reach places.

sly fox, *see* **Tom Tiddler's ground**

smacker, n. (sl.)   **one-pound note**

Smacker is also old-fashioned American slang for *dollar,* in this sense competing with *simoleon, bone,* and *buck.*

small ad   **classified ad**

small beer (col.)   **small time**

I.e., *insignificant*.

smalls, n. pl.   (1) **undies**
                                                               (2) **first Oxford B.A.**
                                                                   exams

The old-time relationship between panty raids and the campus
has nothing to do with the case. As to the second meaning,
smalls was the colloquial term for **responsions,** an Oxford examination procedure abolished in 1960.

smarmy, adj. (sl.)   **oily**

In the sense of *unctuous*.

smash, n. (sl.)   **smashup**

Traffic accident. The rate keeps rising in both countries.

smashing, adj. (col.)   **terrific**

And a *smasher*, meaning *something terriffic*, usually refers to a
girl, sometimes to a car.

snag, n.   **trouble**

When an Englishman wants to explain what is holding something
up he very often starts the sentence with the phrase, "The *snag*
is . . ." Americans tell you what the *catch* is, or the *hitch*, or the
problem, or the *trouble*.

snapper, n.   **snap**

Fastener used in dressmaking, also called press stud. An American *snapper*, the kind served at children's parties, is a *cracker*
in England.

snick, n. (col.)   n.A.e.

A cricket term meaning a ball not hit squarely but one caught
by the edge of the bat.

366

snicket, n.   **alley**

Synonymous with **twitten** (q.v.).

snob, n. (sl.)   **cobbler**

A shoemaker, for which there appears to be no slang American equivalent.

snog, v.i. (sl.)   **neck**

snookered, adj. (sl.)   **stymied**

The English borrow their adjective describing this unhappy condition from the game of *snooker,* a variety of pocket billiards; the Americans from the game of *golf.*

snorting, adj. (sl.)   **fabulous**

Rarely heard nowadays.

snout, n. (sl.)   **stoolie**

A police informer.

snowboots, n. pl.   **galoshes**

In England *galoshes* are what the Americans call *rubbers. See also* **gumboots.**

snowed up   **snowed in**

snuggery, n. (sl.)   **den**

One's particular hideaway at home.

sock drawer (col.)   **safe place**

To put something into one's *sock drawer* is to secrete it in safe-keeping, like a confidential document, not intended for another's eyes. The closest American colloquialism might be the *cookie jar* where housewives secrete money snitched from the household budget.

sod, n. (sl.) heel

This vulgar term of abuse should really not be used in mixed company (if at all). Technically, it cannot be applied to a woman (any more than **fanny** [q.v.] in England can be applied to a man). The reason is that it is short for *sodomite*. However, English youth of both sexes, unaware of its origin, are now heard to use it of, or hurl it at, persons of either sex. The title of the *Shorter Oxford Dictionary* was at one time changed to *Oxford Shorter Dictionary* solely to avoid the embarrassing initials *S.O.D.* This piece of information was kindly supplied by a former employee of Oxford University Press who became the operating head of the American branch of another English university press. *Sod all* is an intensification of **bugger all** (q.v.), which is, in turn, an intensification of **damn all** (q.v.) and means *not a goddamned thing*. *Sod* means *goddamn* in the expressions: *sod him (her, it, them)*.

soft furnishings curtain material

In an English department store, if you wanted the drapery department, you would ask for *soft furnishings;* if you asked for the *drapery department* you would find yourself looking at dress materials.

soft goods textiles

soldier on (col.) keep at it

To *soldier* (often *soldier on the job*) means to *loaf on the job* in both countries, to *shirk*. To *soldier on*, by itself, means to *persevere doggedly*, to *stay with it*, *keep at it*, *keep plugging*, or whatever else one who resembles John Bull does in the face of hopeless odds.

solicitor, n. lawyer

But it is not that simple; *lawyer* in the sense of *general practitioner*. *See also* **barrister**. In America the use of *solicitor* in the British sense is restricted to the office of solicitor general of the United States and of certain individual states.

solitaire, *see* **patience**

somerset, n.   **padded saddle**

Especially for a one-legged rider like Lord Somerset, who popu-
larized this type of saddle. He died in 1855.

sonic bang   **sonic boom**

soon as say knife, *see* **as soon as say knife**

soppy, adj. (sl.)   **mushy**

sorbet, *see* **ice**

sorbo rubber   **sponge hard rubber**

Used in the manufacture of children's bouncing balls, dog's toy
bones, as well as the interior of cricket balls.

sort out (col.)   **work out**

Very frequently used by the English and in the best tradition
of muddling through. Things are always going to be *sorted out*
later, or will *sort themselves out*. There is a lurking suggestion
of *mañana* in this amiable expression.

souteneur, *see* **ponce**

spanner, n.   **wrench**

A *spanner in the works* is a *monkey wrench in the machinery*.

spare ground   **vacant lot**

sparking plug   **spark plug**

spate, n.   **flood**

speak up!　　　　　　　　　　　　　　　　　　　**louder!**

An exhortation not to courage, not to candor, but simply to audibility.

spectators' terrace　　　　　　　　　　　　**observation deck**

Airport term. *See also* **waving base.**

Speech Day　　　　　　　　　　　　　　　　**awards assembly**

Also *Prize Day.* An aspect of public, state, and prep school life. Prizes are given out, speeches are made, parents mill about, and tea is drunk.

spencer, n.　　　　　　　　　　　　**lady's woolen undershirt**

spend a penny (col.)　　　　　　　　　**go to the bathroom**

This is a term pertaining principally to ladies and derives from the fact that their arrangements, even in the simpler operations, are a little different from men's in that the little cabinets involved are locked and require the insertion of a coin (it used to be a penny) in order to unlock them; just another bit of evidence to prove that it is still a man's world. A lady without a penny might well be a lady in distress. The cost has risen in most places, but the phrase goes on, and will. The term is hardly ever used by men. Their euphemism is *have a wash.* As to pennies generally, see Introductory Note 18.

spinney, n.　　　　　　　　　　　　　　　　　**thicket**

A small bit of woods.

spirits, n. pl.　　　　　　　　　　　　　　**hard liquor**

spiv, n. (col.)　　　　　　　　　　　　**sharp operator**

He lives by his wits, just managing to stay within the law.

split of a hurry (col.)　　　　　　　　　**hell of a hurry**

split on (sl.)**squeal on**

spoil, n.**rubble**

Rare in American, this often-used English term is used to describe the dirt and rubble that comes out of a hole during excavation.

sponge bag**toilet kit**

A small waterproof bag for toilet articles. The old ones were like miniature duffle bags with drawstrings. Nowadays they come with zippers.

sponge finger**ladyfinger**

Sports Day**n.A.e.**

Sports Day is an annual function at most schools. On *Sports Day* the following things happen:

Spend a Penny

371

(1) The parents are invited to watch the students engage in athletic competitions.
(2) Tea is served in a huge **marquee** (q.v.) and platters of goodies are distributed by well-scrubbed little boys.
(3) It rains.

spot, n. (col.)　　　　　　　　　　　　　　　　　　**bit**

E.g., a *spot* of lunch. A *spot of tea* means something more than just a cup of tea. It involves something solid as well, even if minuscule. A *spot to eat* is a *bite*.

spot-on, adv. (col.)　　　　　　　　　　　　　　**on the nose**

I.e., in exactly the right place. The English congratulated Messrs. Neil Armstrong & Co. for landing *spot-on* target.

spots, n. pl.　　　　　　　　　　　　　　　　　　**pimples**

spotted dog (col.)　　　　　　　　　**roly-poly pudding with raisins or currants**

Sometimes called *spotted Dick*. The image is that of a dalmation (*see also* **roly-poly pudding**).

spring-clean, n.　　　　　　　　　　　　　　**spring cleaning**

For once, it's the Americans who add the *-ing;* usually it is the English (*see* Introductory Note 10).

spring greens　　　　　　　　　　　　　　**young cabbage**

With their heads still unformed. Very tender and tasty and never come across by the author in America.

spring onion　　　　　　　　　　　　　　　　**scallion**

squab, n.　　　　　　　　　　　　　　　**back of car seat**

squailer, n.　　　　　　　　　　　　　　**leaded stick**

A not very common country term, meaning a stick with a metal

knob which is used for throwing at small animals like squirrels;
but nothing to do with the game of **squails** (q.v.).

squails, n. pl.   **type of game**

A game played with small wooden disks which are called *squails,*
on a round table called a *squail board;* but a *squailer* is not a

squareface, n. (col.')   **gin**

squarson, n.   **combination of squire
                                          and parson**

A portmanteau word.

squash, n.   **-ade**

A soft drink. A *lemon squash* is a *lemonade,* an *orange squash*
an *orangeade,* and so on. The drink is commonly made from a
concentrate to which water (usually tepid) is added.

Spotted Dog

373

squib, damp, *see* **damp squib**

squiffer, n. (sl.)   **squeeze-box**

Usually refers to a concertina rather than an accordion.

squiffy, adj. (sl.)   **tipsy**

Americans used *squiffed* which, however, indicates a somewhat more advanced stage of the curse of drink than *squiffy.*

squireen, n.   **small landowner**

More commonly used in Ireland than England.

squitters, n. pl. (sl.)   **the runs**

staff, n.   **personnel**

The English use the word *staff* where the Americans would say *servants.* In a business or factory, the English term *staff* would be *employees* or *personnel* in America. *Short-staffed* would be *short-handed* in America. *Staff finder* is occasionally seen as a heading in English newspapers where the American equivalent would be *help wanted. Staff vacancies* is another phrase meaning the same thing.

staggerer, n. (col.)   **blow**

In the sense of a *riposte, retort,* or a *bit of repartee* that knocks the other fellow off balance. Sometimes used to mean an event that knocks the stuffing out of you.

stall, n.   (1) **stand**
                                                  (2) **orchestra seat**

(1) A *stall* generally is an *outdoor counter* or *stand* for the pur-
     veying of goods, particularly food (*see* **coffee-stall**).
(2) A *seat in the orchestra.*

374

stalls, n. pl.   orchestra

The *stalls* are the equivalent of the *orchestra* as a description of that part of a theatre, concert hall, etc., and a *stall* is an *orchestra seat*.

stand, v.i.   run

An Englishman *stands* for office; an American *runs* for it. One might wonder what the sociological implications are in this disparity of usage. The following letter appeared in the London *Times* on June 16, 1970.

STANDING TO SIT
From Mr. Richard Wood

Sir,—Now you've spoiled it—by telling us that David Howell was "running" for election at Guildford. For years I have been telling American friends that, while they run, we stand.

Yours faithfully,
RICHARD WOOD, Standing for Bridlington.
Flat Top House, Bishop Wilton, York.

standard, n.   grade

Still used to indicate the year (first, second, etc.) at school, but rather old-fashioned now and more or less restricted to primary school. **Form** (q.v.) is generally used of secondary and higher schools.

Standard English   nondialectal official English

Commonly abbreviated to S.E. In the words of David Abercrombie (*Problems and Principles*, Longmans, Green & Co. Ltd., London, 1955):

Not only is it different from the dialects linguistically . . . . it differs from them socially and politically also. Unlike the dialects, it is not tied to any particular region or country, but is a *universal* form of English; it is the kind used everywhere by educated people. This, moreover, is the *official* form of English, the only kind which is used for public information and administration. It thus has a quite different standing in the English-speaking world from the dialects. . . . Although it is called "English" it no longer has any necessary connection with England. . . .

standard lamp, n.   **floor lamp**

Other American equivalents are *standing lamp* and *bridge lamp*.

stand in one's light (col.)   **stand in one's way**

stand-off, v.t.   **lay off**

Meaning to discharge employees who have become superfluous or, as they say in England, **redundant** (q.v.).

stank, n., v.t. (col.)   **dam**

This is a Gloucestershire term signifying a *makeshift dam*, e.g., in a little brook to make a drinking pool for cattle. It can be used as a transitive verb meaning to *dam up*, e.g., a brook, temporarily for any purpose. It is also used in the Midlands as a technical canal term, as when a canal has to be *stanked* in order to lay an underground pipe which has to travel under the bed of the canal.

starchy, adj. (col.)   **stuffy**

As in the expression *nothing starchy*.

staring, adj., adv. (col.)   (1) **loud**
                                                  (2) **raving**

(1) Unpleasantly conspicuous, eye-shattering, as a *staring* pink tie or a weird checked vest.
(2) As in *stark staring mad*.

stark ravers (sl.)   **stark raving mad**

starkers (starko), adj. (sl.)   **bare-ass**

start a hare (col.)   **get something going**

Sometimes trouble.

starting handle   **crank**

Automobile term, now rather archaic. However, sometimes quite helpful (*see* **wind**).

star turn, *see* **turn**

state school   **public school**

For the meaning of *public school* as used in England, *see* **public school.**

station calendar   **bulletin board**

On the wall at major railroad stations.

station master   **station agent**

STD   **automatic long-distance dialing**

To be on *STD* means to be hooked into the automatic long-distance dialing system. The letters stand for *Subscriber Trunk Dialing* (*see* **trunk call**).

steading, n.   **farmstead**

A farm with buildings.

stew, n.   **fish tank**

stick, n.   **pole**

Ski terminology.

stick, n. (col.)   **guy**

Particularly in an expression like "He's not a bad old *stick*."

stick, v.t.   **stand**

In the sense of *bear* or *tolerate*, as in: "I can't *stick* it a minute longer!"

stick, get the, *see* **get the stick**

stickjaw, n. (sl.)   **chewy candy**

Like *taffy*, which is called *toffee* in England.

stick no bills!   **post no bills!**

stick out, v.i. (col.)   **stick to one's guns**

stick up, v.t. (sl.)   **puzzle**

English robbers, as well as American, *stick up* their victims. But there is a second English slang meaning which has its approximate American equivalent in the verb to *stick*, meaning to present someone with an unsolvable problem. In this connotation *stuck up*, in England, would mean *completely at a loss*, the American equivalent being *stuck;* but it can also indicate unjustified superiority in England as well as in America. The more usual term for this obnoxious attribute in England is *toffee-nosed*.

sticky finish (col.)   **bad end**

The kind one should do his utmost not to come to.

sticky wicket (col.)   **tough situation**

sting, v.t. (sl.)   **soak**

To *sting* somebody such and such an amount for something is to *soak* him, i.e., *overcharge* him. Thus, in an antique shop, "What do you suppose he will *sting* us for that table?" Its use in America is normally confined to the passive participle (*stung*) in this context.

stock breeder   **cattleman**

ENGLISH   AMERICAN

stockbroker belt   **nouveau-riche suburb**

Stockbroker Tudor is *phony Tudor,* an architectural style in the
manner of Anne Hathaway's Cottage.

stockinged feet   **stocking feet**

The Americans seem to have made the mistake of thinking that
stocking was a present participle.

stockist, n.   **retailer**

A shopkeeper who stocks the article in question.

stodge, n., v.t., v.i. (sl.)   (1) **heavy food**
                                                         (2) **glutton**
                                                         (3) **stuff**

As a verb *stodge* means to *stuff,* i.e., *stuff oneself. Stodging*
makes one dull and lumpish; hence the adjective *stodgy.*

stomach warmer   **hot-water bottle**

Usage is regional and the American term is commonly used.

stone, n.   **14 lbs.**

This is the common meaning of *stone* as a measure of weight.
English bathroom scales, as well as those in railroad stations and
similar public places, are calibrated in *stones, half-stones,* and
pounds, but Americans find it rather difficult to translate *stones*
into *pounds* because 14 is a hard number to handle in mental
arithmetic. To make things worse, a *stone* of meat or fish is 8
pounds, a stone of cheese is 16 pounds, etc., etc. Eight 14-lb.
stones make a hundredweight, which is 112 pounds in England
(more logically, 100 pounds in America). Perhaps a table of
terms used in the trade would help, showing the meaning of
stone applied to various commodities. (*Man* will be omitted, as
not being in the nature of a commodity, except to the military
mind.)

379

Commodity	Weight in lbs.
hemp	32
cheese	16
potatoes	14
iron	14
wool	14*
meat	8
fish	8
glass	5

All of this will become a thing of the past with the complete adoption of the metric system.

*Caution! 14 lbs. in sales to outsiders, but 15 lbs. in the case of sales to other growers or dealers.

stone the crows! (col.)   **good heavens!**

A gentle expletive, now going out of fashion.

stonewall, v.i. (col.)   **stall**

The unsportsmanlike practice of playing for time in cricket. The trick is for the **batsman** (q.v.) merely to defend his **wicket** (q.v.) rather than attempt to score runs, so that time will run out. Like *keeping possession* in American football and taking plenty of time to go into and out of the huddle with your eye on the clock, or *freezing the ball* in basketball. As with many cricket terms, it has been taken into the general language to describe *stalling for time.*

stood out   **postponed**

Procedural term, in law.

stop, v.i.   **stay**

Thus: "He *stops* in bed till noon," or, "Why don't you *stop* at my house instead of the inn?" To *stop away* is to *stay away.* Also, "I'm happy and I want to *stop* like this"; but this usage is fading out. A good pal will *stop up* with you all night when you're in trouble.

stop, v.t.   **fill**

Dental terminology. Cavities are *stopped* or *filled* in England, and a *stopping* is a *filling.*

store, n.   **warehouse**

It is also used to mean a *shop,* usually a large one. *Stores* (n. pl.) means *supplies,* like food provisions at home, or *stock* in the sense of the inventory of a business. *In store* means *in storage,* but also has the same figurative meaning as the American usage: "What has the future *in store* for me?"

stove up, v.t. (sl.)   **delouse**

To disinfect generally, as to *stove up* clothing in a flop house. *Stove-up* is the noun describing the procedure.

straightaway, adv.   **right away**

straightforward, adj.   **cut-and-dried**

This word means *frank* and *honest* in both countries. A common additional English meaning is *simple,* in the sense of *presenting no complications.* Someone is presented with a contract to sign and after reading it through says that it seems perfectly *straightforward;* or a garage mechanic looks at some engine trouble and answers that the problem is perfectly *straightforward.*

straight on, adv.   **straight ahead**

stream, n.   **(1) lane**
        (2) student classification

(1) Traffic usually flows in *streams* in England rather than in *lanes* as in America. It is customary in England to speak of the left *stream,* the right *stream,* and the wrong *stream.*

(2) For school usage, *see* **eleven plus.** *Stream* is also used as a verb in this connection meaning *classify according to ability* and then divide into groups.

street, n. (col.)   (1) **class**
                                                                 (2) **alley**

(1) "She's not in the same *street* as her sister" means that
      "She's not in the same *class.*" And to be *streets ahead* of
      someone is to *outclass him.*
(2) If something's *up your street,* it's *up your alley.*

street rough (sl.)   **toughie**

'strewth! (sl.)   **good God!**

Somewhat old-fashioned, but still heard. It is a contraction of
God's truth.

strike off   (1) **disbar**
                                                                 (2) **drop**

(1) Short for *strike off the rolls,* applying to lawyers.
(2) Short for *strike off the register,* applying to doctors. But
      strangely, a doctor who is *struck off* in England may con-
      tinue to practice, being deprived only of the right to pre-
      scribe dangerous drugs or sign a death certificate.

strip lighting   **tubular lighting**

strip-wash, n.   **sponge bath**

strong, adv.   **numbering**

The English sometimes speak of a *four-strong family,* i.e., a family consisting of four persons. Americans would normally refer
to a *family of four.* The phrase *one-strong family* is also seen,
i.e., a *family of one* or a person living *solo.* Americans use
strong this way, too, but generally in the case of larger groups
such as military forces, and the noun precedes the number, followed by *strong:* a detachment 200 *strong;* a working party
150 *strong.*

stroppy, adj. (sl.)   **touchy**

struck on (col.)   **stuck on**

I.e., *nuts about.*

strung up (col.)   **het up**

I.e., *on edge;* nothing to do with lynching. *Strung* is seen in the American expression *high-strung* (*highly strung* in England), but that describes a type of person, while *strung up* describes the condition of the moment.

stuck up, *see* **stick up**

studentship, n.   **scholarship**

In the sense of an award of financial aid. *Scholarship* is the common term in both countries, but *studentship* is used at some English colleges.

stuff, v.t. (sl.)   **lay**

A particularly unattractive word for the sexual act.

stumer, n. (sl.)   **bum check**

By extension, a *counterfeit bill* or a *slug* (*counterfeit coin*); and by further extension, *anything phoney.*

stump, n.   **butt**

Cigar *stump* (also *stub*); cigarette *end.*

stumps, *see* **up stumps; wicket**

stump up (sl.)   **come across**

I.e., *pay up.*

sub, n., v.i. (col.)   **touch** (app.)

As a noun, a *sub* is an *advance* on future earnings or expectations. Thus: "He had to take a ten-shilling *sub* on next week's

screw" (q.v.). One *takes* (or *gets*) a *sub;* one *makes* a *touch.* *Touch,* however, evokes the image of a reluctant victim who doesn't know how to say no. As a verb it means to *make a touch,* and with *on* can take as its object the future earnings or the lender involved. Thus, one can *sub on* next month's dividends, and one can *sub on* one's pal or daddy. It is always followed by *on* and must be an abbreviation of *subsidy.*

sub-editor, n.   **copy reader**

A newspaper term.

subfusc, adj.   (1) **dull**
                                                     (2) **dusky**

(1) Its common meaning is figurative: *dull, characterless.*
(2) It also has the literal meaning of *dusky* in both countries. *Subfusc* clothes are not necessarily *drab;* in this sense the word may mean merely *quiet* or *modest.*
It is rarely used in America in either sense.

subject, n.   **citizen**

A British *subject;* an American *citizen.* There is still enough loyalty to the British monarch to permit the use of a word which might be offensive to the American sense of independence, at least since the Yorktown surrender. When an Englishman speaks of himself as a *citizen,* it is usually of a town or city. He would seldom be a *citizen* of Great Britain.

subscription, n.   **dues**

An Englishman pays his *subscription* to his club or other organization; never *dues. Subscription* is an American euphemism for *price of admission* to a dance, political dinner, charitable affair, etc., in which use the English settle for *ticket.*

subscription library   **lending library**

subway, n.   **pedestrian underpass**

In America a *subway* is an underground railroad, which is called *underground* or *tube* in England. *Subways* in England are for getting to the other side of the street without peril to life and limb. They have them in Moscow and other civilized places, too.

sucks to you! (sl.)   **so there!**

suffer an assessment for   **be taxed on**

How descriptive!

sultana, n.   **white raisin**

In England a *sultana* is a *small seedless raisin,* light yellow in color. *Sultanas* are used in puddings, cakes, buns, etc. (*see* **bath bun**). In America *sultanas* are a variety of grape, pale yellow in color, which when dried become what Americans call *white raisins.* They are also used as a source of white wine. With an upper-case *s, Sultana,* in America, is a trademark for a particular brand of seedless raisin, whether dark or white.

summer time   **daylight saving time**

Nothing to do with Porgy and Bess. The American term is also used in England; it is now permanent and referred to as *British Standard Time* (as distinct from Greenwich Mean Time).

sump, n.   **crankcase**

Automobile term.

sunny intervals, *see* **bright periods**

super, adj. (col.)   **terrific**

Also used as an expletive: *Super!* (pronounced *soo-pa*). Americans say *terrific!* or *great!* or *marvelous!* but never *super!*

ENGLISH   AMERICAN

super-elevated, adj.   **banked**

Of roads and highways.

supplementary benefits   **welfare payments**

A special usage.

supremo, n.   **governor; overseer**

An official installed by an outside authority.

surgery, n.   **doctor's office**

Or *dentist's office*. It has another use: "Doctor has a very large
surgery today," said by a nurse through whom one is trying to
make an appointment, means that doc has lot of patients, is
having a busy day, has got an office full. *Surgery* also means
(as it does in America) the act of cutting people open. Incidentally, doctors are called *Dr.* but surgeons are called *Mr.*; so
are dentists.

Surgery

surgical spirit   **rubbing alcohol**

This has nothing to do with zealous surgery.

surveyor, n.   **building inspector** (app.)

The general meaning is the same in both countries, but a *chartered surveyor* is a *licensed architect* and is usually engaged by a careful English prospective purchaser to look over the building before the contract is signed. If things go wrong later, the purchaser can sue the surveyor, who has received a fee for his written report. In this sense *surveyor* describes a privately engaged expert building inspector.

suspenders, n. pl.   **garters**

Vertical ones, whether ladies' or men's; not the round kind like those worn by Knights of the Garter. *Suspenders* is the American term for the apparatus which holds up trousers, called **braces** (q.v.) in England.

swab, n. (sl.)   **oaf**

swagger, adj. (col.)   **swell**

In the sense of *smart*, but with the pejorative implication of ostentation.

swan, n., v.i. (sl.)   **junket**

A trip of one sort or another whose ostensible purpose is official business, but whose primary motivation is pleasure. To *go swanning* is to take such a trip.

swan-upping   **n.A.e.**

An annual function that goes back centuries: the taking up and marking of the swans which inhabit the Thames. There is an official swan-upping pennant which royal swan-uppers affix to their boats when they go out to take inventory of the sovereign's cygnets on the Thames from London to Windsor.

swat, *see* **swot**

swede, n.   yellow turnip

sweet, n.   dessert

Or *sweet course*. In American *dessert* is broad enough to include anything served as the last course. In England **dessert** (q.v.) is generally a fruit course served at the end of dinner. There is a good deal of Anglo-American confusion about this and a certain amount of internal British confusion. It is impossible to resist setting forth in extenso the following barrage of angry letters to *The Times* (please note the headings), all of which appeared between September 3 and September 9, 1971:

The Dessert
From Mr John Russell
Sir, When will Katie Stewart—and other writers of cookery recipes who appear to be American—learn that there is no such course as *desserts* in an English meal? What the Americans call *desserts* is what we English call *the sweet*.

There is, however, the *dessert* (singular) course in an English meal. It is the last course of all in a full course dinner, and consists of fruit, nuts and trifling sweetmeats, and it is at this stage of the meal that the port appears. It is a course which, for the ordinary household, has now disappeared except for special occasions.
Yours, etc,
JOHN RUSSELL
Bures, Suffolk.
September 1.

The pudding
From Mr Robin McDouall
Sir, "What the Americans call *desserts* is what we English call *the sweet*" writes Mr John Russell of Bures (September 3). Let him speak for himself: others call it *pudding*.
I am, Sir, your obedient servant,
ROBIN McDOUALL,
2 Formosa Street, W9.

The pudding

From Brigadier R. B. Rathbone
Sir, Well done indeed, both Mr Russell (September 3) and Mr McDouall (September 6). "Pudding" certainly, but what is far more important is to kill (though alas I fear it is too late) the gross misuse of the word "dessert." It appears in its American sense not only in recipes but in restaurants and in ordinary conversation, sometimes by those who should know better.

Why, oh why, do we quietly absorb, instead of resisting, these unnecessary (and in this case misleading) transatlantic importations which, far from enriching, nearly always degrade our beautiful language?
I am, Sir, your obedient servant,
R. B. RATHBONE
Arreton, Blockley, Gloucestershire.
September 6.

From Mrs G. R. R. Treasure
Sir, As an American, I should like to correct Mr John Russell (September 3) on the subject of desserts. We call it dessert, period!—as in "Whadya gonna have for dessert?"
Yours faithfully,
MELISA TREASURE
3 The High Street, Harrow on the Hill,
Middlesex.
September 6.

From Major-General R. H. Allen
Sir, Mr Russell may call it "The Sweet," Mr. McDouall may call it "Pudding," but a considerable experience of driving for "Meals on Wheels" has taught me that the recipients invariably called it "afters."
Yours faithfully,
R. H. Allen
The Pound House, 70 High Street,
Chinnor, Oxford.

switchback, n.   **roller coaster**

Now more commonly called *scenic railway.* But a *switchback railway* is a term describing zigzag railways for climbing hills.

swizz, n. (sl.)   **swindle**

swop, v.t. (col.)   **swat**

swop, n., v.t., v.i.   **scythe**

A country term. The scythe in question is a small one also known in the country as a *bagging-hook.*

swot, n., v.t., v.i. (sl.)   **cram**

Swot (also *swat*) means *cram.* A *swot* is a *grind,* synonymous with **sap** (q.v.). To *swot up* is to *cram* or *bone up* and is synonymous with *mug up* (*see* **mug**).

T

ta (sl.)   **thanks**

To be avoided, but still heard here and there. The Americans appear not to have developed any slang corresponding to this bit of fluff.

table, v.t.   **submit for discussion**

This term means exactly the opposite of what it means in America, where to *table* an item is to *shelve* it or to postpone discussion of it, perhaps hoping it will never come up again.

tack, n. (sl.)

chow

Good tack is *good eating.*

tail-coat, n.

cutaway

take a brace, *see* **duck** (1)

take a decision

make a decision

take all one's time (col.)

be all one can do

"It *takes me all my time* to pay for the food" means "It's *all I can do* to pay for the food." Thus, "He's so fat it *takes him all his time* to get up the stairs."

take a rise out of

get a rise out of

take a scunner on (col.)

take a dislike to

take away

take out

Referring to food which is prepared for consumption off the premises: "Sandwiches made up to *take away.*" Incidentally, the *made up* would be *put up* in America.

take down

take

Sometimes used by the English in addressing their secretaries: "Miss Jones, will you please *take down* a few letters?"

take in charge

to arrest

See also **charge-sheet.**

take it in turns to

take turns in (at)

The English form is followed by the infinitive of the verb, the American form by a gerund. Thus in England two good friends of a sick man would *take it in turns to* sit by his bedside, while in America they would *take turns in* or *at* sitting there.

takeover, n.   **acquisition**

Where one company buys all the shares of another, or enough
to obtain control of the company *taken over.*

take silk   **become a K.C. (or Q.C.)**

K.C. stands for *King's Counsel* (and *Q.C.* for *Queen's Counsel*),
a specially recognized **barrister** (q.v.).

take the mickey out of (sl.)   **poke fun at**

take the shilling (col.)   **enlist**

From the days when the Recruiting Sergeant gave the new re-
cruit a *shilling*, known as the *King's* (or *Queen's*) *shilling.*

take your finger out (sl.)   **get going**

Delicacy forbids any comment on the literal meaning of the expression.

taking, n. (col.)   **fit**

To be in a *taking* is to be *upset,* to be having a *fit* of anger or
nerves. An old-fashioned idiom.

tally plan   **installment plan**

A *tally plan* or *tally system* was the method by which a *tally
shop,* owned or serviced by a *tallyman* or *tallywoman,* operated
a retail business accommodating needy customers who could not
pay cash, the accounts being recorded in a pair of matching
books, one for each party, and usually paid weekly without bill-
ing. Except perhaps in quite depressed areas the practice has
pretty well died out, giving way to regular installment buying, called **hire-purchase** (q.v.), or more popularly the **never-
never** (q.v.) in England.

talk the hind leg off a donkey (col.)   **talk a blue streak**

talk through (out of) the back of one's neck (col.)	**talk through one's hat**

I.e., to babble nonsense.

tallboy, n.	**highboy**

tanner, n. (sl.)	**sixpence**

Not to be confused with a **tenner** (q.v.). See Introductory Note 18.

tantalus, n.	**locked container of visible bottles of wine or liquor**

From the old legend. The term is not used in America.

tap, n.	**faucet**

Tap (as a noun) is rarely heard in America, *faucet* almost never in England, but Americans speak of *tap*-water, never *faucet*-water.

taradiddle, tarradiddle, n. (col.)	**fib**

tardy, adj.	**sluggish**

Also has the American meaning of *late*.

tarmac, n.	(1) **tar road** (2) **airfield**

(1) As a transitive verb, *tarmac* means to *tar* a road. In America *tarmac* refers to the bituminous binder used in the making of tar roads. *Tarmac* started out as a trademark for a binder for road surfaces, but now generally refers to any bituminous road surface binder. It is a shortening of *tar macadam,* which in America means a pavement built by pressing a tar binder over crushed stone, and in England a prepared tar concrete poured and shaped on a roadway to construct a hard surface. *See also* **macadam.**

(2) *Tarmac* has now acquired the specialized meaning of *airfield*, especially the part made of this material.

tart, n.   **pie**

Pie in England is the equivalent of an American *deep-dish pie*. Simple *apple pie* or *cherry pie* would be *apple tart* or *cherry tart* in England.

tart up (sl.)   **doll up**

tatt, n. (sl.)   **frills**

Thus: "The décor of the apartment was lovely and without *tatt*."

tea, n.   **supper** (app.)

In England you can drink your *tea* or eat your *tea*. When you eat it you are having a *light supper*. *Tea* meaning *supper* is heard more among the working classes and children. It is really short for **high tea** (q.v.). *See also* **cream tea; set tea.**

teach (one's) grandmother   **bring up father** (app.)
   to suck eggs (col.)

To give advice to your elders or to anybody more experienced than yourself. Rebel college students might be a good example.

tea-lady, n.   **tea-maker**

A woman who comes to the office twice a day to make the tea which is handed around at 11 A.M. and 4 P.M.

tea towel   **dish towel**

Also referred to as a *washing-up cloth*.

team-ups, n. pl.   **separates**

tear a strip off (sl.)   **bawl out**

The *strip* is a noncommissioned officer's stripe. The expression literally means demotion for a misdemeanor.

tearaway, n.   **hellraiser**

The term does not necessarily connote a bad character. A *tear-away* is a wild youngster who is probably going to straighten out in time.

teat, n.   (1) **nipple**
                                                      (2) **bulb**

(1) On a baby bottle. In this case the British, reversing the form, appear to overstate.
(2) The *rubber bulb* of a medicine dropper.

teetotalist, *see* **TT**

telephonist, n.   **switchboard operator**

telly, n. (col.)   **TV**

temporary guest   **transient**

Hotel term.

tenner, n. (col.)   **ten**

A ten-pound bill (*note*). Not to be confused with a **tanner** (q.v.).

term, n.   **semester** (app.)

Semester is *very* approximate. On all educational levels the English divide the year into three *terms,* separated by long vacations, while the Americans prefer two terms, which are called *semesters,* separated by a very long summer vacation. In other words, *term* and *semester* are the respective English and American designations for a fixed part of a school year. To complicate matters (as usual) *terms* often have quite different names at different institutions. As only one example, the three eight-week terms at Oxford are called Michaelmas, Hilary, and Trinity. At Cambridge they are Michaelmas, Lent, and Easter. *Half-*

sweet Fanny Adams (sl.)   **not a damn thing**

Fanny Adams was a real live girl who was killed at just about the time of Napoleon's Moscow fiasco. Her unpleasant murderer cut her into little pieces and threw them into a river. The legend of that obscene crime led to the coining of the name *Fanny Adams* as military slang for *tinned mutton*. This seems to have nothing whatever to do with *sweet Fanny Adams* meaning *nothing at all*. Sometimes abbreviated to *Sweet F.A.*

sweets, n. pl.   **candy**

Boiled sweets are *hard candy*.

sweet-shop, n.   **candy store**

swept-out, adj.   **streamlined**

swimming-bath, n.   **swimming pool**

swimming costume   **bathing suit**

Or *bathing costume*.

swing door   **swinging door**

swing it (sl.)   **goof off**

To *swing it* is American slang for something entirely different —it means to bring something about, to *cinch* something, usually with the implication of successfully getting together the financial wherewithal to accomplish an objective.

swing the lead (sl.)   **goof off**

Synonymous with **swing it** (q.v.) and **scrumshank** (q.v.).

swipes, n. pl. (sl.)   **lousy beer**

Inferior beer or "dishwater."

Swiss roll   **jelly roll**

term is a brief vacation occurring about midway through the
term in most English schools.

terminus, n.   **terminal**

A railroad or bus term. The English, however, use *terminal* to
refer to the city center where one picks up the bus to the airport.

terrace, n.   **row of joined houses**

A specialized English use of the word.

terracing, n.   **standing room**

Used only of a sports arena.

terylene, n.   **Dacron**

Test Match   **international match**

This is principally a cricket term, now also applied to rugger. A
Test Match, e.g., between England and Australia, has about the
same importance in England as the *World Series* in America.
The English team is always referred to as the *England side*,
never the *English side;* but the Australians are always referred
to as the *Australian side*, the South Africans as the *South African side*, etc. *Test Match* is oftened shortened to *Test:* thus,
"What happened in the Melbourne *Test?*" To help Americans
more clearly to understand what cricket is all about the following
explanation of a Test Match, offered by a small English boy to
a group of visiting Americans, is offered herewith:
It's quite simple; you have two sides, one out in the field,
one in. Each man on the side that's in goes out, and when
he's out he comes in and the next man goes in until he's out.
When they're all out, the side that's been out in the field
comes in, and the side that's been in goes out and tries to
get out those coming in. If the side that's in declares, you
get men still in not out. Then when both sides have been in
and out including not outs, twice, that's the end of the
match. Now do you see?

tetchy, adj.   **peevish**

Sometimes spelled *techy* and not a corruption of *touchy.*

that's torn it   **that's the end**

Said in exasperation when things have just gone too far.

theatre, n.   **operating room**

Short for *operating-theatre;* and a *theatre sister* is an *operating-room nurse.*

theological college   **divinity school; seminary**

there's a . . .   **that's a . . .**

As in *"There's a* good boy."

thermic lance   **blowtorch**

thick ear (sl.)   **cauliflower ear**

thimblerig, n.   **shell game**

The English use thimble-shaped cups instead of walnut shells but it's the same old swindle.

third, n.   **cum laude**

University term. *See* **first.**

third party insurance   **liability insurance**

thriller, n.   **detective story**

Throgmorton Street (col.)   **the market** (app.);
                                        Wall Street (app.)

A street in **the City** (q.v.) of London whose name is used as a nickname for the London Stock Exchange, and the securities fraternity and their activities generally, just as nearby *Mincing*

Lane is used for the wholesale tea trade. For the financial community generally, Englishmen are prone to use the term *the City*.

through, adj.   **connected**

This meaning is restricted to telephone operator usage. Thus, "You're *through!*" means "Your party is *on the line!*" or "You're *connected!*" When an English telephone operator says "You're *through!*" it sounds about as grim to an American as, "Your *time is up!*" must sound to an Englishman. In either case it is as though the Grim Reaper were calling. In England the operator does not tell you when your time is up; instead there are three short beeps on a long distance call or a series of rapid pips on a local call from a pay station.

throw out   **add on; build**

Referring to adding an extension to a structure: to *throw out* a wing, thus enlarging a building or a room. The English also talk of *throwing out* a pier, i.e., building one out into the water.

thumping, adv. (col.)   **enormously**

Rarely used by itself to mean *enormous;* usually in combination with *great* or *big:* a *thumping great* feast. *Thumping good* means the same thing: a *thumping good* victory is an *overwhelming* one.

thundering, adv. (col.)   **mighty**

In the sense of *extremely*—a *thundering* good actor; a *thundering* good piece of mutton.

tick, v.t., v.i.   **check**

"Please *tick* where appropriate," seen in instructions for filling out a form or on an advertisement coupon. A *tick list* is a *check list.*

399

ticket-of-leave, n.   **parole**

A *ticket-of-leave* man is a *parolled* convict.

tick, half a, *see* **half a tick**

tick off (sl.)   (1) **check off**
                                                       (2) **tell off**

tick, on, *see* **on tick**

tick over   **turn over**

Referring to a car or other engine. Extended metaphorically, for example, to office or business routine: "When he's away on holiday, things just *tick over*" (the activity slows down to a trickle).

ticket pocket   **change pocket**

Tailor's term.

ticketyboo, adj. (sl.)   **hunky-dory**

Also spelled *tiggerty-boo*. Still heard but outdated.

tickler, n. (col.)   **poser**

A delicate situation; a tricky problem.

tiddler, n.   **minnow**

tied, adj.   **affiliated** (app.)

The word has different meanings in England depending on the noun it modifies. Thus a *tied cottage* is one which a farm worker occupies incidentally to his job. When the job is over he loses the cottage. In a television interview, Prince Philip was asked about his living accommodations and he answered, "Buckingham Palace? A *tied cottage*. It goes with the job." A sterling example of understatement. A *tied garage* is one which serves one company exclusively. A *tied house* is a **pub** (q.v.) affiliated with a particular brewery and serving only that brewery's brand of beer and ale. It is the opposite of **free house** (q.v.).

tiepin, n.   **stickpin**

Synonymous with *breast-pin*.

tig, n. (sl.)   **tizzy**

But a **tizzy** (q.v.) in England is a *sixpence*.

tiggerty-boo, *see* **ticketyboo**

tights, n. pl.   **pantyhose**

A term borrowed from the ballet world. An English salesgirl (*shop assistant*) would understand *panythose* but she and the customer would normally say *tights*.

timber, n.   **lumber**

In America *timber* means *standing trees,* but the English use the term the way Americans use *lumber*. However, **lumber** (q.v.) in England does not mean what it does in America, but rather superfluous household junk that you don't know what to do with.

time!   **closing time!**

The full phrase is: "*Time,* gentlemen, please!" *See* **during hours.**

time-limit, n.   **deadline**

timetable, n.   **schedule**

In English schools the list of periods and subjects is called a *timetable*. The Americans refer to it as the *schedule*.

tin, n.   **can**

A food container; and naturally the English say *tin-opener*.

tinker's cuss (col.)   **tinker's damn**

The *cuss* is slang for *curse*, of which *damn* is only one example. The English use *damn*, and sometimes even *curse*, in this connection.

tinpot, adj. (col.)   **crummy**

tin tack   **carpet tack**

tip, n., v.t., v.i.   **dump**

The English *tip* their *refuse* into a *refuse tip.* Americans *dump* their *garbage* into a *garbage dump.* A *tip-truck* is a *dump truck.* An American might well be mystified at the sight of a sign out in the open country reading *"No tipping."*

tip-up seat   **folding seat**

tit-bits, n. pl.   **tidbits**

titchy bit (col.)   **just a drop**

A *tiny bit* of anything.

tizzy, n. (sl.)   **sixpence**

Tizzy is a corruption of *teston* (also *testoon*), a term now obsolete and of interest only to numismatists, meaning certain European coins one side of which was decorated with a head. *Teston* was derived from *testone*, an Italian word augmentative of the Italian word *testa*, meaning *head.* The term *teston* was specifically applied to a Henry VIII shilling which suffered from inflation and fell in value to sixpence.

toad-in-the-hole, n.   **sausage in batter**

tobacconist's shop   **cigar store**

Toc H, *see* as dim as a Toc H lamp

toco, n. (sl.)   **belting**

In the sense of *thrashing;* also spelled *toko.*

tod, *see* **on one's tod**

toff, n. (sl.)   **swell**

More indicative of a way of life than wealth. It is the way of life that's gone.

toffee, n.   **taffy**

toffee-nosed, adj. (sl.)   **stuck-up**

to hand   **within reach**

A shop will have certain merchandise *to hand,* or *ready to hand,* i.e., available. "Your letter *to hand,*" used in old-fashioned correspondence, means "your letter *received.*"

toke, n. (sl.)   **grub**

Food generally, but it has the special meaning of *dry bread.*

toko, *see* **toco**

tollol, adj. (sl.)   **so-so**

Fair-to-middling. Apparently a corruption of *tolerable.*

tolly, n. (sl.)   **candle**

From *tallow* (?).

tommy, n. (col.)   **GI**

Short for Tommy Atkins, derived from the initials T.A. (Territorial Army), and of World War I origin.

Tom Tiddler's ground   red light

A children's game: one stands in front, all the rest some distance behind him in a line. The ones in back try to sneak forward. The one in front can turn around whenever he chooses and if he sees anyone moving, he sends that one back to the starting line. Also known as *sly fox* or *peep-behind-the-curtain* in some parts of England.

ton, n.   **2,240 lbs.**

An American ton contains 2,000 lbs. Note that an English hundredweight contains 112 lbs. (not 100) so that 20 of them make up an English ton.

ton, n. (sl.)   **100**

The expression "the *ton*" means *100 m.p.h.* Thus the proud owner of a motorcycle says, "It can do the *ton.*" *Ton-up,* as a slang adjective (e.g., the *ton-up boys*) is a somewhat derogatory term referring to the motorcycle set, the type that do 100 and scare you to death. (When you get to know them, they can be charming.) In the English game of darts, a *ton* means a score of 100 attained with the 3 darts which make up a single round. This can be done by hitting the treble 20 with one dart and a single 20 with each of the other 2, or hitting the single 20 with 1 dart and the double 20 with each of the other 2. It is an extremely rare achievement. In cricket, a ton is 100 runs by one **batsman** (q.v.), also known as a **century** (q.v.).

tonk, v.t. (sl.)   **clobber**

too good to miss (col.)   **too good to pass up**

top, n.   **head (beginning)**

As, for instance, in the expression *top of the street. See also* **bottom.**

top gear   **high gear**

top-hole, adj. (sl.)   **great**

Anything the speaker regards as *first rate*. Now going out of fashion.

topliner, n.   **headliner**

top of one's bent   **heart's content**

See *Hamlet*, Act 3, Scene 2.

top of the bill (col.)   **headliner**

top of the tree (sl.)   **top banana**

The *top of the tree* is *head man;* one who has *arrived*.

topping, adj. (col.)   **great**

Simply terrific. A British synonym is **super** (q.v.). Rather old-fashioned.

Ton

topside, n.   **top-round**

Butcher's term.

top up, v.t.   **fill**

E.g., the gas tank, the crankcase, the battery. Also used of salary. Fringe benefits or supplementary payments will *top up* a salary.

torch, n.   **flashlight**

to the wide (col.)   **utterly**

Done to the wide means *done in* or *dead drunk,* depending on the context, so be careful. To distinguish: Use *whacked to the wide* when you mean *done in* (*out on one's feet*) and *dead to the wide* or *sloshed to the wide* to describe the shameful condition of extreme intoxication.

totting-up procedure   **point system**

Whereby, on a cumulative basis, one's driving demerits reach a total sufficient to result in the suspension of one's license for a given period.

touch, (sl.)   **thing**

In the sense of a particular *sort of thing:* "I don't go for the sports car *touch.*"

tour of ops, *see* **ops room**

tout, n., v.i.   **scout race horses**

Americans and British are both familiar with the racetrack *tout* who tells you how to bet. A special English meaning of the word as an intransitive verb is to *spy* on race horses in training to gain advance knowledge.

town, n. (col.)   **London**

In the **Home Counties** (q.v.) *town* means *London,* even though it is not a town but a city. One has spent the day *in town;* tomorrow one is going *to town* or *up to town* and the *town* in question is always *London.*

town and gown   **townspeople and students**

I.e., non-university and university groups, respectively, at Oxford and Cambridge especially. *Town,* in this phrase, means those persons in the town who are not connected with the university as students, fellows, etc. *Gown* means the university people. The phrase *town and gown,* with the same connotations, is not unknown in America and is used occasionally in some American college towns and cities. In England, a *townee* (pronounced *town-eé*) is university slang for one of those persons who collectively constitute *town.* In American college towns, *townie* (pronounced *town-ie*) means the same thing, but unlike *townee,* is pejorative. The English use *gownsman* in contradistinction to *townee,* where one might have expected the apparently nonexistent form *gownee.* At Harvard College there are *townies* and *Harvies,* and the students at the affiliated women's college, Radcliffe, are *Cliffies;* at Yale there are *Yalies;* and this practice is undoubtedly widespread in America.

town boundaries   **city limits**

trade, n.   **business**

Trade is often used in England where Americans would say *business:* "He is in the necktie *trade.*" The expression *in trade* means simply *in business.* A *roaring trade* is a *rushing business.* *Trader* is often used where Americans would say *storekeeper.* A *trading state* is a business area, and sometimes more particularly a shopping center.

trade(s) directory book   **yellow pages**

The American term is now beginning to be used in England as well.

traffic block   **traffic jam**

tram, n.   **streetcar**

Short for *tramway*, which is never heard and never seen anymore either.

transferred charge call   **collect call**

This is the correct technical term for this operation in England.
Reverse-charge call is a popular variant. In America one uses
the verb *reverse* in the phrase *reverse the charge* but calls the
transaction a *collect call*.

transport café   **truck drivers' all-night
diner**

In England this might also be called a *lorry drivers' all-night
pull-up*. Since the word *café* (pronounced *caffay*) implies a
more prestigious establishment, many Englishmen will deliberately and jocularly mispronounce it as *kaif*.

transport system   **transit system**

trapezium, n.   **trapezoid**

In America a *trapezium* is a quadrilateral having no sides parallel. In England it describes a quadrilateral having two sides
parallel, which in America is always called a *trapezoid*. (The
English sometimes use *trapezoid* as synonymous with their *trapezium*.)

traps, n. pl. (col.)   **gear**

Traps mean *personal belongings*, especially *luggage*. An Englishman might ask a porter to get his *traps* into a taxi; Americans would say "my *things*" or "my *stuff*."

traveller, *see* **commercial traveller**

treacle, n.   **molasses**

a treat (col.)　　　　　　　　　　　**terrifically**

An old-fashioned Englishman might say to the lady: "You dance *a treat*," or he might say: "My wife is *taking on a treat* about the lack of service, i.e., *making a terrific fuss* about it.

treble, *see under* **double**

trews, n. pl.　　　　　　　　　　　**tartan trousers**

But loosely used, occasionally, to mean any kind of trousers. Either short and worn (alas!) under the Scotsman's kilt or long and worn as part of a military uniform.

trick cyclist (sl.)　　　　　　　　　**head shrinker**

The English slang results from an attempt to approximate the difficult word *psychiatrist*. The American equivalent started as a joke, and the term is now often shortened to *shrink*. But we had better leave it to the profession itself to verify these derivations—maybe it's all because you hate your mother.

trifle, n.　　　　　　　　　　　　　**n.A.e.**

A dessert. The base is sponge cake (or ladyfingers, called **sponge fingers** in England) soaked in liqueur, wine, sherry or rum, to which custard and jam and fruit and rich milk or cream are added. Very sweet and very fattening.

trilby, n.　　　　　　　　　　　　　**felt hat**

trillion, *see under* **billion**

tripos, n.　　　　　　　　**honors examination at**
　　　　　　　　　　　　　　Cambridge University

The term is derived from the three-legged stool (*tripos*) on which the Bachelor of Arts sat to deliver his satirical speech in Latin on commencement day.

ENGLISH   AMERICAN

tripper, n. (col.)   **holiday-maker** (app.)

A pejorative term for those who are having a day out at the shore, in the country, visiting stately homes, etc. The trip can last longer than a day, perhaps as long as a week or even two.

trolley, n.   **pushcart**

Trolley in England means also a *hand-lever operated small truck* that carries railroad workers along the rails; but a *trolley-table* (sometimes shortened to *trolley*) is a *tea wagon. See also* **barrow.**

truck, n.   **gondola car**

A railroad term. In railroad parlance what the Americans call a *truck* is a *bogie* in England. The American road *truck* is a *lorry* in England.

truckle bed   **trundle bed**

trug, n.   **flattish garden basket**

Originally known as *Sussex trug.* A convenient flattish garden basket coming in many sizes, made of thin woven slats.

trumpery, adj.   **cheap**

In the sense of *tawdry* or *gaudy.* Sometimes also used as a noun meaning something that fits the description.

truncheon, n.   **billy**

Also known in America as a *nightstick* whether brandished by night or by day.

trunk call   **long-distance call**

trunk enquiries   **long-distance information**

England is a small country and when you want to ascertain an out of town telephone number, it is usually sufficient to ask the

operator for *Enquiries* or *Directory Enquiries,* but some people
take the precaution of asking for *Trunk Enquiries.*

trunk road, *see* **arterial road**

try it on (col.)   **try it out**

With the strong implication that one is taking a shot at something in the hope of getting away with it.

TT, n., adj. (col.)   **teetotaler; teetotal**

And the English occasionally say *teetotalist* instead of *teetotaler,*
but it all comes to the same degree of rectitude.

tube, n.   **subway**

Synonymous with **underground** (q.v.).

tub-thumper, n. (col.)   **soapbox orator**

tuck, n. (sl.)   **eats**

Indicating a big meal, particularly of the gourmet variety. Variants are *tuck-in* and, less commonly, *tuck-out. Tuck-in* is also a
verb meaning to *put on the feedbag,* i.e., *eat hearty.* A *tuck-
shop* is a *pastry shop* and a *tuck-box* is one for the safeguard-
ing of goodies and is generally school jargon. To *tuck into* something in the food line is to *dig into* it.

Tunbridge box   **ornamental marquetry
veneered box** (app.)

Tunbridge Wells is a pretty, thriving town of about 40,000 souls
in the county of Kent, 34¼ miles south by southeast of London.
It is 5¼ miles south by southeast of another pretty, somewhat
smaller Kentish town called Tonbridge. Both towns are on the
main railroad line out of Charing Cross Station, London, to
Hastings and other southeast coastal towns. Weekend guests
unacquainted with the region coming down from London by
rail, advised by their hosts to get off at Tunbridge Wells and

look around for the green Daimler or the red Wolseley, quite often alight hastily and prematurely at Tonbridge, having spotted the station sign through the train window and assumed that the spelling difference was simply another case of English orthographical flexibility lingering from Elizabethan times. In fact, even despite explicit warnings issued simultaneously with the invitation, considerate hosts sometimes dispatch emissaries to both stations. Tunbridge Wells is located in the borough of Royal Tunbridge Wells, which derives its name from the fact that it was once a favorite watering place of the English court, under the aegis of Beau Nash. Tunbridge Wells is famous for its ancient mineral wells, technically known as chalybeate springs, rediscovered in 1606 by Dudley, 3d Baron North. They still produce an allegedly health-giving drink which you can buy from an attendant for a pittance. The town is also famous for *Tunbridgeware,* a name given to small examples of the cabinetmaker's art, decorated with a kind of wood mosaic forming pictorial patterns; the most common category of this ware is the *Tunbridge box.* These boxes were first made in Tunbridge Wells around 1830 and were a thriving business until the middle of the nineteenth century. The boxes vary in size from two inches by three inches to two feet by three feet, and the veneer consists of extremely narrow rectangular pieces of multicolored wood, some of them as narrow as toothpicks. The art was imitated in many other English towns but wherever they were made the boxes were called *Tunbridge boxes.* Not all *Tunbridge boxes* are antiques: it is rumored that they are still being made today. *Tunbridge boxes* are used for a variety of purposes: the little ones usually for jewels; the big ones as hope chests; and the middle ones for the secreting of illicit love letters by English lady characters in detective stories written by other English ladies.

tuppenny one (sl.)   **sock on the jaw**

Twopence and *twopenny* are pronounced *tuppence* and *tuppenny,* and are sometimes slangily spelled that way. One also hears of a *fourpenny one,* which apparently means the same thing as a *tuppenny one,* not necessarily twice as devastating.

tuppet, v.i. (sl.)   **clickity-click**

A bit of onomatopoeia applied to ladies in spiked heels.

turf accountant   **bookmaker**

A preposterous euphemism for *bookie*. *Commission agent* is an equally euphemistic synonym.

turf out (sl.)   **throw out**

Usually applied to rubbish, whether a pile of old magazines or undesirable people; or even nice people after pub-closing time.

turn, n.   **(1) act (vaudeville)**
                           (2) attention getter
                           (3) dizzy spell

(1) This is a vaudeville term (remember vaudeville?). *Turn* in this sense is short for *variety turn* or *music hall turn* and by extension can mean the performer as well.

(2) A *star turn* is one who attracts attention because of an idiosyncrasy: "That Jones is a *star turn;* all he has to do is walk into a room and trouble starts!"

(3) Turn can mean *shock* ("It gave me quite a *turn*") in both countries. Less educated Englishmen also talk of having a *turn* to indicate the experiencing of a *dizzy spell*.

turnabout, adj.   **reversible**

Applied to overcoats.

turncock, n.   **water main attendant**

turning, n.   **turn**

The first *turning* on the right means the first right *turn*. The English say, "Take the first *turning* on the right" and the Americans (when they are willing to bother), "Take your first right."

turn out, v.t.   **clean up**

In England one *turns out* a room or a closet by moving everything out of it, cleaning it up, and then moving everything back.

turn-up, n.   **trouser cuff**

The term *cuff* in England is confined to sleeves.

turn up trumps (col.)   **come through nobly**

To *rise to the occasion;* to show yourself a real pal in a crisis.

twee, adj. (sl.)   **arty**

Or *terribly refeened.* Usually seen in the phrase *fearfully twee.*
Implies archness, affected daintiness, quaintness-for-quaintness'
sake, and so on.

tweeny, n. (col.)   **assistant maid**

A maidservant, one who assists both cook and chambermaid,
and whose position is thus "between" downstairs and upstairs.

twicer *see under* **oncer**

twice running   **twice in a row**

twig, v.t. (sl.)   **catch on to**

In the sense of *understanding. Dig* is a common synonym in
America, sometimes also heard in England.

twin-bedded, *see* **double-bedded**

twin with ...   **n.A.e.**

Seen on roadside town signs to indicate a special friendly relationship with a foreign town.

twister, n. (sl.)   **sharpie**

twitten, n.   **alley**

An enclosed type of narrow walk in a village or town, as opposed to open country, where it would be called a *footpath.*
Mainly Sussex.

414

twizzle, v.t. (sl.)   **spin**

No American slang equivalent. To *twizzle* somebody or something *around* is to *twist* or *spin* him (it) *around,* e.g., to examine from all angles.

twopence coloured (col.)   **gaudy**

Spectacular with a slightly pejorative tinge. Said, for example, of Churchill's career by C. P. Snow. In common speech, the phrase usually comes out *twopenny* (pronounced *tup-penny*) *coloured;* its opposite is **penny plain** (q.v.).

twopenny-halfpenny, adj. (col.)   **junky**

Pronounced *tup'pny-hay'pny.* It can mean worthless, negligible, nothing to worry about, or even contemptible, depending on the context.

two-seater, n.   **roadster**

Does anybody under fifty still say *roadster?* Maybe *sports car* is closer in feeling, if not so accurate.

𝔘 | U

ulcer, n.   **canker sore**

Not used that way in America.

unbelt, v.t. (sl.)   **shell out**

undercut, n.

(1) **tenderloin**
(2) **uppercut**

(1) Butcher's term. The English use *fillet* for the same cut, adding an "l" to *filet*, accenting the first syllable and pronouncing the "t."
(2) Boxing term.

underdone, adj.

rare

Referring to meat.

underground, n.

subway

Also called the *tube*. A *subway* in England is an *underground pedestrian passage*.

Underground

under offer

for sale

Sign seen on buildings, vacant lots, etc.

under the harrow (col.)

in hot water

unit trust · **mutual fund**

university man · **college graduate**

The English make more of a fuss about one's having graduated from college. This is, of course, because college educations, which are beginning to be taken for granted in America, are still comparatively rare in England, although the trend is very much on the increase. The English are notoriously prone to putting lots of initials after people's names, particularly on business letterheads. These initials may refer to **Birthday Honours** (q.v.), membership in a trade or professional association (anything from architects to veterinarian surgeons), or just plain college degrees. On an ordinary business letterhead it would not be uncommon to see listed *John Jones, B.A. (Oxon.), George Smith, B.Sc. (Cantab.)*, etc. (*Oxon. and Cantab.* are abbreviations reflecting the Latin spellings of Oxford and Cambridge). Such ornamentation in America would be deemed boastful.

unmade road, *see under* **metalled road**

unmetalled road, *see under* **metalled road**

unseen, n. · **sight translation**

In an examination or classroom recitation: "He did well in his Latin *unseens*."

up, adv. · **to London**

See also **down; down train.**

up a gum tree (sl.) · **up a creek**

In a pickle; in a fix.

upper ten (col.) · **upper crust**

The upper classes; short for the *upper ten thousand,* a phrase that originated in America.

uppish, adj. (col.)   **uppity**

upsides, *see* **get upsides with**

up sticks (col.)   **pack up and go**

This can describe moving one's entire ménage or simply clearing up after a picnic.

up stumps (col.)   **pull up stakes**

I.e., to *clear out and leave.* One of the many terms derived from cricket. Not to be confused with **stump up** (q.v.).

up the wall, *see* **drive . . . up the wall**

up to the knocker (col.)   **in great shape**

up train, *see* **down train**

Up a Gum Tree

𝔙 | V

v.   **very**

Common abbreviation in informal correspondence.

vac., n. (col.)   **college vacation**

Less commonly, a school vacation. Simply a shortening. *See also*
come down; holiday.

vacant possession   **immediate occupancy**

One sees in most real-estate advertisements the expression *"vacant possession* on completion," meaning *immediate occupancy*
on closing title. This is sometimes qualified by the addition of
the phrase "subject to service occupancy" or less commonly,
"service occupations," meaning subject to the occupancy of part
(rarely all) of the premises by persons living there and render-
ing services in payment of rent. The purchaser can get them
out by legal means, but it is an arduous process. It almost always applies to agricultural properties.

vacuum flask   **thermos bottle**

vains I!, *see* **fains I!**

valve, n.   **tube**

Radio term. Transistors are making them obsolete, whatever
they are called.

van, n.   **(1) small truck**
                                                 (2) closed baggage car

(1) A road vehicle. In America the word means a *large covered
    truck.*
(2) Railroad term. In this sense it means a *closed baggage car.*

419

van, removals, *see* pantechnicon; removals

variety, n.   vaudeville

See also music hall.

variety turn, *see* turn

verge, n.   grass shoulder

Verges vary in width and are favorite spots for picnicking **trip-pers** (q.v.). This is an English phenomenon. Americans are amazed to see the equipment employed in this happy activity: Folding tables and chairs, ornate tablecloths, electric kettles, elaborate picnic baskets, deck chairs, too; everything but the kitchen sink.

vest, n.   undershirt

For what Americans mean by *vest*, the English say *waistcoat*.

Vest

vet, v.t. (col.)   **check up on**

With particular reference to candidates for a job.

vice-chancellor, n.   **president**

A university term meaning the active head of the institution.
The *vice-* is used because the chancellor is an honorary officer,
always a prominent person, sometimes even royalty.

view, v.t.   **inspect**

In connection with selecting a residence. *See* **order to view.**

view-point, n.   **lookout point**

A special English meaning in addition to meaning *point of view,*
as in America.

village, n.   **town** (app.)

Village in England is more a description of a way of life than a
label applied to a particular political subdivision. An article by
Paul Jennings in the November 14, 1970, issue of *The Illustrated
London News* bears the title "What is a Village?" and says,
"Everyone knows what a village is . . . [but] there is no legal
or official definition of a village in Britain." The usual demo-
graphic distinction between *village* and *town* in England is
based simply on population, and the break comes somewhere
around 3,000. Hawkhurst, in Kent (pop. 3,400) is said to be the
largest village in England. For an American analogy, *small town*
is about the best we can do. For excellent evocations of the
image of an English village, see *"A Day in the Life of Mediam,"*
by Paul Jennings in the same issue of *The Illustrated London
News,* and Ronald Blythe's *Akenfield* (Pantheon Books, New
York, 1969). While we're on the subject, an English *city* is a
town created by charter. The popular legend is that the presence
of a cathedral creates the distinction, but, as you might expect,
there are English cities without cathedrals and English towns
with cathedrals.

ENGLISH	AMERICAN
visiting card	calling card
viva, n. (col.)	oral examination

Short for *viva voce,* Latin for *aloud.*

𝔚 | W

w. (col.)   **with**

A common abbreviation in informal correspondence.

Waac, n. (col.)   **Wac**

A member of the Women's Auxiliary Army Corps (WAAC) in World War I. This became A.T.S. in World War II and is now WRAC, for Women's Royal Army Corps. The female branches of the air force and navy are, respectively the WAAF and the WRNS (*see also* **Wren**).

waffle, n., v.i. (sl.)
       (1) **twaddle**
       (2) **pad**
       (3) **gabble**
       (4) **yelp**

(1) As a noun *waffle* means anything *silly* or *useless.*
(2) To *waffle* in writing a paper at school is to fill up space, i.e., to *pad.*
(3) To *waffle* conversationally is to engage in silly chatter: to *gabble, prate.*
(4) To *waffle* a cry of pleasure is to *yelp* it. Rarely *woffle.*
Reflecting uses (2) and (3), a British parliamentarian, writing on the art of *waffle,* describes it as the art of that which is superficially profound.

ENGLISH	AMERICAN
wage-snatch, n.	**payroll holdup**
wages sheet	**payroll**
waggon, n.	**car**

Railroad term, especially *goods-waggon,* meaning *freight car.*

waistcoat, n.	**vest**

An English *vest* is an American *undershirt.*

wait, n.	**Christmas caroler**

walking stick, *see* **cane**

walk out, v.i. (col.)	**go steady**

A courtship term.

walk slap into, *see* **slap**

want, v.t. (col.)	(1) **take** (**require**)
	(2) **need** (**lack**)

These usages are not elegant but rather somewhere between colloquial and incorrect.
(1) Example: "It *wants* a bit of courage to sail the Atlantic alone."
(2) Example: "All the wheels *want* is a drop of oil." In this connection a special use is found in expressions of time: "It *wants* ten minutes to twelve," meaning that it *is* ten minutes to twelve.
Richard II, in the great abdication speech (*Richard II,* Act 3, Scene 3), says:
  Down, down, I come: like glistering Phaethon,
  Wanting the manage of unruly jades.
Phaethon (son of Helios, sun god of the Greeks) was permitted to drive the paternal chariot across the heavens for one day. He *wanted* (lacked), the *manage* (management, i.e., control)

423

of the *unruly* (uncontrollable) *jades* (vicious horses) and was struck down by a Jovian thunderbolt lest he crash to earth and set it afire.

want jam on it, *see* **have jam on it**

warder, n.   **prison guard**

See also **keeper.**

Wardour Street (col.)   **movie business**

A street in London which is the center of the *film industry* and used colloquially to mean that business, the way Americans use *Hollywood.*

ware wheat! (col.)   **look out for my corn!**

"Ware. . . !" (a shortening of *beware*) means *"Look out for. . . !"*; and *wheat* is a jocular substitution for *corn*. All this is very old-fashioned stuff.

warm air   **hot air**

As a description of a heating system.

warned list   **ready calendar**

Procedural term, in law.

wash, n. (col.)   **use of the bathroom**

When your host asks whether you would *like a wash* he is offering you the use of *all* his bathroom facilities.

wash, v.i. (col.)   **stand up**

Always used in the negative: "It (that story, that excuse) won't *wash."*

wash-cloth, n.   dishcloth

For what Americans mean by *washcloth* (*facecloth*), the English say **flannel** (q.v.).

washing-book, n. (sl.)   account book

An informal *account book,* for instance as between friends on a trip where one pays all the expenses and there is a settlement at the end. It can also mean a *running score,* as during a social weekend of bridge. No American slang equivalent. Undoubtedly, this is derived from the concept of entries washing one another out.

washing-up bowl   dishpan

How do the English advertise hand lotions?

washing-up cloth   dish towel

Sometimes called a *tea towel.*

washing things   toilet articles

wash leather   chamois

Often shortened to *leather.*

wash up   do the dishes

Do the dishes would confuse an Englishman no end because of the restricted meaning of **dish** (q.v.) in his country: *platter* or *serving-dish.* Logically, he calls his dishwasher (if he has one; they are far from ubiquitous) a *washing-up machine.* To him a *dish-washer* is a *water wagtail,* a small bird (it comes in a variety of colors) equipped with a long tail that it keeps wagging constantly, as though it were washing a platter.

waste bin   wastebasket

watch-glass, n.   **crystal**

The American equivalent is used in England by jewelers but not by the general public.

watching brief, n.   **amicus curiae brief** (app.)

A law brief for a client indirectly involved or concerned in a matter to which he is not a party. Its technical meaning refers to the situation of a lawyer charged with the duty of attending litigation in which the client is not directly involved, where, however, a point of law affecting the client generally may be involved. To have (or hold) a *watching brief*, broadly speaking, is to *keep aware* of a situation which may ultimately involve your interests. Thus, an Englishman asks, "Are you in the picture?" meaning "Are you au courant?" "Are you up to date?" "Do you know what's going on?" And an Englishman might answer, "I have a *watching brief*," i.e., "I'm *keeping tabs*" on the situation.

water, n.   **river; pond; lake**

One sees occasional river, brook, pond, or lake names in which *Water* (with an upper case *W*, as befits part of a proper noun) is used where *River, Brook, Pond,* or *Lake* would be used in America. Thus, *Aften Water* and *Eden Water* (rivers), *Derwent Water* (a lake).

water-cart, n.   **sprinkling wagon**

waving base   **observation deck**

At an airport. The English expression implies much livelier activity than just looking. At Scottish airports they call it by the rather stuffy term *spectators' terrace.*

waxy, adj. (sl.)   **jumpy**

way, n. (col.)   **dither**

To be *in a way* or *in a great way* is to be *in a dither* or *in a tizzy.*

wayleave, n.   **easement**

way out   **exit**

Ubiquitous sign in public places and nothing to do with the hippies. *"Exit"* signs seem to be confined to theaters.

way, permanent, *see* **permanent way**

wayzgoose, n.   **printing company's annual picnic**

w.c.   **lavatory**

Stands for *water closet.* One of many euphemisms.

w/e   **weekend**

Common abbreviation in informal correspondence for *weekend* (*week-end* in England). Not merely a designation of a part of the week, rather more the name of a social practice among the idle rich, as hinted at in the definition in the *Concise Oxford Dictionary:* "Sunday and parts of Saturday and Monday (occas. from Friday to Tuesday) as time for holiday or visit."

Weald, n.   **n.A.e.**

The *Weald* is a district in southern England including parts of the counties of Kent, Surrey, Hampshire, and Sussex, having a certain geological makeup. It is commonly heard in the phrase the *Weald of Kent. Wealden,* rarely seen, is the adjective.

wear, v.t. (col.)   **stand for**

As in "Oh no, he won't *wear* that!" said, for instance, by a lawyer to a client who suggests an outrageous proposal to be made to the other side.

weather-board, n.   **clapboard**

The *weather-boarded house* is a *clapboard house,* and *weather-boarding* is the *clapboard* itself.

Webb, n.   **iceberg** (**lettuce;** app.)

. . . week   **a week from . . .**

The English say *today week* or *a week today* where the Americans say *a week from today; Tuesday week* where the Americans say a *week from Tuesday,* and so on; *last Sunday week* where Americans say *a week ago last Sunday,* and so on; and the same difference in usage applies to **fortnight** (q.v.).

weigh up (col.)   **weigh**

The English *weigh up* a situation. The Americans drop the *up.*

weir, n.   **sluice**

An opening in a river or canal bank, off at an angle and sloping downward, for the purpose of spilling part of the water into a pool or reservoir.

well cooked   **well done**

A description of how you would like your meat. The English use *well done* also. It may be imagined that they would prefer *well cooked* in circumstances where it was important to avoid giving the waiter the impression that he was being complimented (*see* **well done!**).

well done!   **nice going!**

Attaboy! is not often heard in England.

Wellingtons, n. pl.   **rubber boots**

See also **boot.**

the West End (col.)   **Broadway** (app.)

I.e., in reference to the *theatre.* The term also implies the way of life characterized by theaters, restaurants, and parties.

wet, adj. (sl.)   **wet behind the ears**

Both countries use the scornful term *drip*. What is the connection between stupidity and dampness? Is it a reference to a just slicked-up country bumpkin?

wet fish   **fresh fish**

Sign in a fish-and-chips luncheon place which also functions as a fish store: "Open for *Wet Fish* 9 A.M. to 1:30 P.M. only."

whack, n. (sl.)   (1) **gob**
                                                   (2) **stretch**
                                                   (3) **share**

(1) A big *whack* of something is a *gob* of it, i.e., a *large hunk*.
(2) Prison term.
(3) To *pay your whack* is to *chip in*, as when the class buys the teacher a Christmas gift.

whacked to the wide (col.)   **done in**

To be *whacked to the wide* is to be *beat, pooped*, etc. *See also* **to the wide.**

whale, n. (sl.)   **shark**

An American who is expert in a given field is said to be a *shark* at it. An Englishman so skilled might be called a *whale* on it. There is an echo of the English usage in the expression a *whale of a*. . . . Thus Jones is a *shark at math* in America, a *whale on maths* in England, and a *whale of a mathematician* anywhere.

wharf, n.   **dock**

A *dock*, in England, is the basin of water between what the Americans call *docks*.

what?   **no?**

At the end of a sentence expecting the answer "yes," like *nonne* in Latin, where Americans would say "*Isn't he (she, it,* etc.)?*"

429

Example: "He's a clumsy chap, *what?*" Now outdated. The sort of expression that might be used to caricature a relatively unintelligent member of the upper classes.

what a sell!, *see* **sell**

what's the drill? (col.)   **what do we do now?**

Drill is a military term meaning *dress* or *uniform.* Therefore the question originally meant, "What dress or uniform is to be worn on this particular occasion?" From this it acquired the more general meaning of "What happens next?" Synonymous with "What's the form?"

wheeled chair   **wheelchair**

However, usually called a **bath chair** (q.v.) in England.

wheeze, n. (sl.)   **hunch**

When-I, n. (col.)   **n.A.e.**

Many, many Englishmen, now retired, have spent much of their lives in far-flung places, usually in what used to be the Empire and is now what is left of the Commonwealth. They like to reminisce, and these oral memoirs almost invariably start, "When I was in Singapore . . . ," "When I was in Bombay . . . ," "When I was in Hong Kong . . . ," etc. A number of these retired gentlemen live in tax-haven parts of the United Kingdom, like the Channel Islands, which include the Isle of Mann, where the term *When-I* is in current use to describe members of this group fortunate enough to find an audience.

whilst, conj.   **while**

Now used less frequently than *while* in England; never used in America.

whinger, n.   **dirk**

whip, v.t. (sl.)   **snitch**

whip-round, n. (sl.)   passing the hat

whipsy, n. (sl.)   milk shake

white feather (sl.)   cowardice

In World War I, "patriotic" ladies presented *white feathers* to young men not in uniform. The taunt of cowardice was expected to shame them into enlisting.

white fish   n.A.e.

Generic term for all sea fish other than herring, salmon, and sea trout. In America it refers to any one of several distinct freshwater species.

Whitehall, n. (col.)   the government

So-called because so many government offices are located on *Whitehall*, a London street between Trafalgar Square and the Houses of Parliament. Perhaps a close colloquial equivalent would be *Washington* in the American scene.

white spirit   alcohol

Methylated or denatured, for nonimbibing uses.

white wax   paraffin

In England *paraffin* is what the Americans call *kerosene*.

wicket, n. (col.)   situation

In cricket, *wicket* has two distinct technical meanings:
(1) A set of three vertical stumps on which rest two horizontal bails which the batsman defends against the bowler.
(2) The space between the two sets of stumps and bails over which the batsmen run to score points.
The physical condition of the *wicket*, in this sense, greatly affects the game and the strategy of play. Since cricket is the English national sport, it is understandable that many colloquialisms, having nothing to do with the game itself, have been taken

into the language, as in the case of baseball in America. Thus, derived from the second meaning given above, to be on a *sticky wicket* is to be in a *bum situation* or *tough situation;* to be on a *good wicket* with someone is to be *in favor* with him. In this colloquial sense *wicket* means *situation* generally; an article in the London *Times* spoke of "the American military *wicket* in Vietnam."

wick, get on someone's, *see* **get on someone's wick**

widdershins, *see* **withershins**

wide boy(sl.)   **sharpie**
Shady character.

wide, to the, *see* **to the wide; whacked to the wide**

Wigan, n. (col.)   **beautiful downtown Burbank** (app.)

A small manufacturing town in South Lancashire, population about 80,000; used figuratively in music hall patter as a prototype of small city architectural horror and cultural provinciality. To *come from Wigan* is to be a small town hick, like one's aunt in Dubuque, for whom the editors of *The New Yorker* declared at its inception that that sophisticated periodical was not intended. (By now things have undoubtedly changed in Dubuque, too.) America is so vast that every part of the country must have its *Wigan* and the names of a number of places occur to the writer, but fear of regionally restricted significance (to say nothing of retribution from local Chambers of Commerce) prevent their identification. However, network television being the unifying force it is, *beautiful downtown Burbank* can now be boldly identified as the American national symbol closest in meaning to the figurative use of *Wigan*. The town has a pier although it is not on the seaside. Recommended reading is George Orwell's *The Road to Wigan Pier,* in which he writes, without sentimentality or snobbery, about the culture of the working classes.

wigging, n. (col.)   **call down**

To give somebody a *wigging* is to give him *hell*. *Wig* is a transitive verb in both countries and means *rebuke*. Its use as a verb is rare and it is usually found in the substantive form *wigging*.

wimpy, n. (sl.)   **hamburger**

A *wimpy bar* is a *hamburger joint*. From *Wimpy*, the character in the *Popeye* comic strip, who could eat an infinite number of them.

win, v.i. (col.)   **gain**

In the sense of *making progress, getting there*. A gardener engaged in an unequal combat with weeds might say (if lucky), "We're *winning*."

wincey, n.   **type of cloth**

Consisting of a mixture of cotton and wool, or wool alone. *Winceyette* is a more finely woven version used for shirts, nightgowns, and so on.

wind, v.t.   **crank**

Despite the near-universality of the self-starter, once in a while an Englishman still has to *wind* his car. *See also* **starting handle.**

wind, *see* **get the wind up; have the wind up; put the wind up; raise the wind**

windcheater, n.   **windbreaker**

winding point   **turning-around place**

This is a canal term and means the place in a canal wide enough to permit the boat to turn around. The first *i* in *winding* is short, as in *windlass*.

window-gazing, n.	window shopping

The American term is now coming into general use in England.

windscreen, n.	windshield
windy, adj. (sl.)	jumpy
wine merchant	liquor store
wing, n.	fender

Automobile term but **fender** (q.v.) in England is *bumper* in America. *See* Introductory Note 26.

winkle, n.	periwinkle

Or any edible sea snail.

winkle out, v.t. (sl.)	squeeze out

In both senses: for instance, to *winkle out* information by pumping a weak character previously sworn to secrecy; and to *winkle out* a rival by outmaneuvering him. To *winkle* one's way *out* of something is to *wriggle out* of it, and conversely to *winkle* one's way *in* is to *worm* one's way *in*.

win one's cap, *see* **blue** (n.); **cap**

wireless, n.	radio

Going out of fashion now in favor of the American term.

witch, *see* Introductory Note 12.

withershins, widdershins, adv.	counterclockwise

It is said to be bad luck to walk around a church *withershins.*

within the sound of Bow Bells, *see* **Bow Bells**

with knobs on! (sl.)	and how!

with respect   **with all due respect**

In the sense of "Excuse me, but. . . ."

witness-box, n.   **witness stand**

In America one *takes the stand* or is *on the witness stand*. In England one *enters the witness-box* and is *in* it rather than *on* it.

wizard!, adj. (sl.)   **terrific!**

Synonymous with *super* and *smashing*. World War II slang in the RAF, usually applied to a successful mission.

wodge, n. (col.)   **chunk**

wog (sl.)   **n.A.e.**

A *wog* originally meant an *Arab*. Now it has been extended to include Mediterranean types and other dark-skinned foreigners. Disregard the false etymology: *w*estern *O*riental *g*entleman. It is short for *golliwog* and unpleasantly racist.

wonky, adj. (sl.)   **wobbly**

won't go   **won't work out**

Example: "Putting Jones in charge of that department *won't go*."

wooden house   **frame house**

wood wool   **excelsior**

The English name has nothing to do with sheep and the American name has nothing to do with banners bearing strange devices. Simply *wood shavings* by another name.

woolly, n. (col.)   **sweater**

Americans do not speak of a *woolly* but do use *woollies* to mean *heavy underwear*. No equivalent American colloquialism.

work-day, n.   **weekday**

Interchangeable in England with *weekday*. Where an American would use the expression *workday*, the English would say *working-day*.

workhouse, n.   **poorhouse**

But the term has given way to *old people's home.* It is unfortunate, but not a blot on one's character, to go into a workhouse in England. In America a *workhouse* is a *jail*, particularly for petty criminals.

working party   **committee** (app.)

A *working party* is one of those *committees* to which the prime minister, a cabinet minister or Parliament refers a question for study and report. It is equivalent to a *committee* appointed by the President or other governmental entity in this country. *Working parties*, like *committees*, are often devices created to give a decent burial to nagging questions.

work in hand, *see* **in hand**

works, n. pl.   **factory**

A tractor *works* is a tractor *factory*. But the roadside sign *Road Works* means *Men Working;* sewage *works* means a sewage *system;* and a **spanner** (q.v.) in the *works* is a monkey wrench in the *machinery*.

worth a good deal of anybody's time (col.)   **a good sort**

A highly complimentary description of a person. *See also* **have time for.**

work to rule   **work by the book**

Describing what a union does when it takes advantage of the rule book technicalities to cause a slowdown. A form of protest short of a strike. Like a *job action*, short of a strike.

436

work to time (col.)   **watch the clock**

wotcher! (sl.)   **howdy!**

wowser, n.   **fanatic puritan**

A real Watch-and-Ward-Society type, intent on improving the
"morals" of the community. Also called a *Mrs. Grundy,* from
which is derived the word *Grundyism,* synonymous with prud-
ery (from "What will Mrs. Grundy [a neighbor] say?" in
Thomas Morton's *Speed the Plough*).

wrangler, n.   **mathematics honor graduate**

Formerly, at Cambridge University, the Senior Wrangler was the
top man. From an obsolete sense of *wrangler:* to argue publicly
on a thesis. Worlds apart from a western U.S. *wrangler,* a *horse-
handler,* and loosely used for *cowboy.*

wrap up!   **shut up!**

Wren, n. (col.)   **Wave**

A member of the Women's Royal Naval Service (WRNS). In
praise of these patriotic ladies: "Up with the lark and to bed
with a wren."

𝔜 | Y

year dot (col.)   **year one**

Usually seen in the phrase *"Since the year dot,"* meaning *for
ages.*

years, donkey's, *see* **donkey's years**

yeoman, n.   (1) small landowner
                                        (2) volunteer cavalryman
                                        (3) beefeater

This word has several historical significances in England including:
(1) *Small landowner.*
(2) Member of the *yeomanry,* a volunteer cavalry force.
(3) It is also short for *yeoman of the guard* (*see* **beefeater**).
A *yeoman* in America is a *petty naval officer* having clerical
duties. *Yeoman's service* or *yeoman service* is used figuratively
in both countries meaning *loyal assistance, help in need.*

yob, n. (sl.)   **lout**

   Back slang (q.v.).

$$Z \mid \mathrm{Z}$$

z-car, n.   **police car**

   Pronounced, of course, *zed-car.*

zed, n.   (letter) z